ART MARKETING HANDBOOK

By

CALVIN J. GOODMAN
Management Consultant in the Arts

FLORENCE J. GOODMAN
Editor

gee tee bee
11901 Sunset Boulevard, 102, Los Angeles, California 90049

Printed in the
United States of America
ISBN: 0–917232–04–6

Table Of Contents

Facility Planning

Varieties Of Sales Activities

Promotion

Promotional Sales Aids

Marketing Planning

Financial Planning, Accounting, & Budgeting

Finding & Training Salespersons

Introduction

1. Adam Smith and the Contemporary Art Market

In 1776, Adam Smith, a brilliant Scotsman who is gen—erally considered the founder of the systematic study of economics, published his great treatise on *The Wealth of Nations*. Smith advocated free trade between nations; he vigorously opposed government regulation of trade and declared that monopolistic business practices of any sort were a danger to society. He insisted that customers must be free to choose between competitive products and services. Finally, prefiguring the views of Thomas Jefferson, he held that great wealth was the result of great liberty.

Although Smith's point of view was extremely influential for many decades and did indeed form the basis of many advanced societies, his *laissez faire* concepts gradually found themselves under attack on all sides. In our times, the world's business affairs – – for better or worse – – are primarily conducted by vast monopolistic corporations or by state – owned agencies. Operators of small businesses, those modest enterprises of the kind Smith and Jefferson so warmly admired, have found it increasingly hard to survive in almost every field of economic endeavor. The family – owned ethnic restaurant may serve more interesting, even less expensive food, but it is hardly a competitor against such fast food giants as MacDonalds and Kentucky Fried Chicken. Independent grocers have virtually disappeared in most communities, having been gobbled up or squeezed out of business by the major food chains. Studebaker, Packard, and the other independent automobile manufacturers disappeared decades ago.

In short, monopoly and state control rule – – except for the art market. There are no IBM's or General Motors, no Duponts or Standard Oils in the art market. On the contrary, it is difficult to find a visual artist who grosses as much annually as many middle management executives in major corporations, and an art dealer who sells art in excess of the annual volume of a single supermarket store is virtually unheard of.

Almost alone among the many different subdivisions of economic activity of modern society, artists and art dealers of the Western world are free of the domination of monopolistic enterprises. In fact, as will be seen, the efforts of giant merchandizing firms to enter this arena have been rather spectacular failures. Further, where customers are often faced with a non-choice between tweedle-dum and tweedle-dee in other fields (a good example would be the miniscule differences between a Ford and a Chevrolet) in the field of art, clients may choose from a vast array of images, works of a bewildering variety of media, sizes, shapes, and prices.

Further, with the exception of a few works which are protected in certain countries as national treasures, art moves freely and without duty accross national boundaries. The enterprise of making art no longer requires membership in a guild or academy and the enterprise of selling art re—quires relatively little capital — — the sort of funding which is accessible to many individuals and families. All of these characteristics are more typical of Smith's notions of free enterprise than of modern monopoly capitalism or socialism. The art market is truly a game in which any number can play.

Even on the issue of government support for the arts, where a great deal of public attention has been focused since President Kennedy first proposed the use of tax funds to assist artists and arts organizations, such assistance is intimately tied to a system of tax incentives for voluntary contributions by individuals and corporations to specific cultural activities rather than to blanket support for artists and their endeavors. We tend to view outright subsidies of the arts with great suspicion, and our artists worry a good deal about interference with freedom of expression. In fact, some of the most unfortunate arts enterprises in recent years are those which owe their very existence to some form of state subsidy.

Adam Smith

Art in America and in most of the Western world is a refreshing example of the basic concepts of free enterprise as Adam Smith set them down in the eighteenth century. And the great freedom of artists in our society, in sharp contrast to the severe restrictions on artistic expression in totalitarian countries such as Russia, China, and Cuba, has led to a vast flowering of art. I believe that future generations will look back on the present era not in terms of its petty corruption or even in terms of its wars, which are not all that different from the corruption and war of other eras; but in terms of the art of our society which is inventive, expressive, free, and extremely varied. Adam Smith might not have understood it all, but I feel certain he would have approved.

This *Handbook* is dedicated to the proposition that freedom of artistic expression is not simply desirable. It is necessary to our well—being as a viable culture of free people. It is the foundation on which our individuality rests. It is one of the primary differences between a conformist society of blue ants and a creative society of free agents.

Alternate Routes
How Art Works Reach Their Market

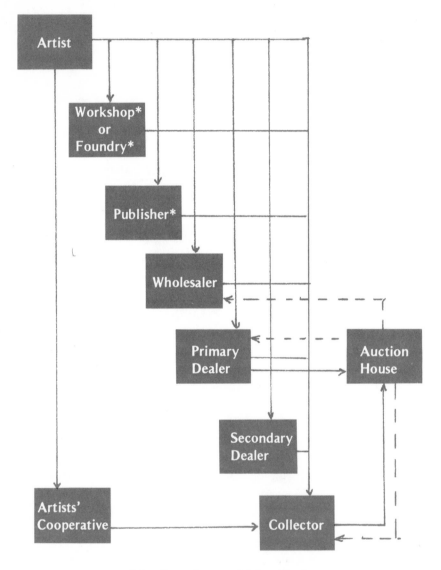

Applies only to multiple originals.

How Art Works Reach Their Market In The United States

2. Channels for Distributing Art

The art market in the United States was shaped in the European model, where individual artists historically have been represented by a single firm which acts as both a general sales agent and as a local retailer. In some cases a dealer like Wildenstein, firmly established in the Parisian market, found it useful to open a gallery in New York as he did in the early 1900's. This ubiquitous art dealer and his heirs were also responsible for producing special projects, managing major commissions, and a host of promotional, framing, publishing, and financial tasks for their artists. One of the key features of this exceedingly simple system of distribution is that most collectors made their acquisition decisions in a single metropolis or two. In the period prior to World War I, art was bought and sold almost entirely in a few major cities: Paris, London, New York, Berlin.

In those days, most of the art works acquired by our American collectors were, in fact, purchased in one of these centers. To be sure, American artists like Winslow Homer and Albert Bierstadt exhibited their works to interested international audiences in the latter days of the nineteenth century. But one did not expect to find the works of major artists or major art dealers in communities like Chicago or San Francisco. A Philadelphian such as Dr. Barnes might indeed prowl through the lesser known galleries of Paris looking for a Soutine, but he would never have looked for art in Rittenhouse Square, let alone near his own home in Lower Merion or in nearby Bala Cynwyd, which houses several fine galleries today.

With the end of the war and the advent of a series of radical changes within the art world and within the American population, this centralization became meaningless. Serious collectors may now be found in every section of this country. These clients travel more widely and more often, and they buy works while away from home, but they also patronize their local art dealers. Today, an artist whose work is shown and sold in a single metropolitan center of the United States or in a single gallery is almost necessarily under–represented.

Even within a particular market area, an artist may easily be under–represented. If a collector can find excellent orig–inal graphics in Scarsdale or unusual sculptures in Soho, what is the inducement to travel to Madison Avenue? The collec–tor may well wish to see what is new and different in "the art world." But this might necessitate a trip to Venice, California or Venice, Italy to see works which are virtually unavailable in the once more fashionable East Coast galleries. Only a few contemporary artists are well–represented in most of the major centers which constitute their potential markets.

I recently worked with a sculptor who is internationally respected and whose work is in many major museums. For years, he has been well represented in both New York and London; but in recent times he has begun to sell extremely well in Scottsdale and San Francisco. Curiously, he was not yet represented in Chicago, Los Angeles, Boston, Philadel–phia, Dallas, or Houston when I started working with him. The problem is that while the art market's distribution apparatus has been growing vigorously, it is still fundamen–tally immature, relying on an ill–defined network of independent dealers who are often under–capitalized and inexperienced, who lack broad sources of supply, and who operate in a marginal realm where failure is easy and success is often measured in rather modest terms. I am happy to report that more mature entrepreneurs, men and women who are experienced, properly capitalized, and capable of selling art with greater consistency, are now becoming more common. And the channels through which they work are better developed.

During the sixties, the first few wholesalers appeared in the art market, and several of the newly-organized publishers of multiple editions of original art work developed certain interesting and very effective systems of distribution. Today, a number of wholesalers travel widely in the major market areas, offering original graphics and other art works by world-famous European and American artists to independent art retailers at established trade discounts. So, too, a few major art dealers have established chains of galleries in several key cities or have created what amounts to franchise relationships for the exclusive distribution of the works of their artists by selected independent art dealers in other market areas. This is discussed more fully in the section on Wholesaling.

In one way or another, it has become possible, particularly for certain of those artists who produce original prints, sculpture editions, craft works, and other multiple originals, to find representation in more than their own local communities. In some cases, this method of multiple outlet distribution has spread to include watercolors, drawings, and pastels. But it seldom involves unique oils and acrylics or unique sculpture unless the artist is prolific enough to supply several markets at once.

Another channel of distribution has been established by those workshops and publishers who have developed private subscription organizations, such as print clubs, through which individual and institutional collectors may acquire works, often on a prepublication basis, and generally at some discount from the established retail prices.

Through this approach, it is possible for an *atelier* or a publisher to commission a group of works and then distribute them not entirely though the retail art dealers; but, in part, directly to collectors. Gemini, G.E.L. Ltd. which publishes artists such as Johns and Rauschenberg has done well with this business format.

Still another distribution channel has developed through the major auction houses. These institutions specialize in distributing art works which have already been purchased by a collector or an institution which wishes to dispose of specific works or liquidate an entire collection. The auction houses, too (e.g. Southeby Parke Bernet and Christies) have found it necessary in recent years to reach a wider market by operating in other metropolitan areas of the United States, in addition to their New York locations.

Such new and more ubiquitous practices in distributing art have not developed without difficulties and problems. First, a few of the wholesalers, publishers, and auctioneers, have engaged in practices which proved to be at least partially unethical and which certainly have been shortsighted. Collectors have, in some cases, acquired works which were not quite as "original" as the sales representation suggested.

Some "original" lithographs have turned out to be signed posters. Some "original" serigraphs turned out to be machine–made photo–mechanical reproductions. As often happens, a number of unscrupulous promoters, who thought they had a scheme to get rich quickly, ended their careers in dire financial straits instead, while their competitors, who were not as greedy and whose reputation for integrity was impeccable, have prospered. More on this question of art business ethics, later.

In spite of these important problems, the outlines of change in the area of art distribution are clear. We shall undoubtedly find a continued trend in the art market toward multi–city galleries, retail franchise activities of several kinds, and a variety of regional and nation–wide art collectors' "club" programs, all aimed at broadening and diversifying the channels through which art works move from artist to collector.

One major market outlet which many had expected to unfold in the sixties has, in fact, not developed to any substantial degree. In 1965, when Sears, Roebuck announced plans for a grandiose system of art galleries in " at least a hundred" of their stores, I predicted that the department store chains would not be able to gain a significant foothold in the art market. Both the prestigious department stores and the discount chains have experimented with selling art, on the theory that their customers would enjoy buying original works under the multi–purpose umbrella of a large, well–located store.

It was claimed that the advertising pull of such stores, their credit facilities, their reputation for integrity and fair–pricing practices, as well as their access to higher–income clients made them natural beneficiaries of the bourgeoning art market. In addition to Sears, dozens of multi–purpose chain retail stores opened art departments and galleries to sell art during the sixties. The effort has been a notable failure. Sears abandoned the enterprise years ago. Most of the others have dropped out as well. These abortive efforts should be studied carefully by every student of the art market. The lesson is highly instructive.

Where the department stores have succeeded, as in the J. L. Hudson gallery in Detroit, they have carefully followed the mode of operation of the traditional art gallery. They have avoided the "mass marketing" approach which characterizes the department store techniques used in selling household appliances or ready–to–wear garments. I shall come back to this issue many times since it is a central thesis of this book: *Art marketing is unlike mass marketing in many ways.* The reason is quite simple.

Regardless of our other motives, we buy art works to differentiate ourselves as individuals from the stereotyped mob, to express and develop our own individuality. This motivation is not dissimilar from the motivation of the artist. We all need a means of expressing our individuality. The merchant who tries to press art into the rubric of mass merchandise effectively forestalls the experience of discovery and the sense of "self" which an art collector at least sub—consciously needs, seeks, and deserves. Although there are fashions and even fads in buying art, the acquisition of an original work of art is not so much part of a "herding" instinct as it is an effort at the rejection of much that is "ticky—tacky," machine—made, and readily distributed to everybody.

Any retailer who recognizes this principle and applies it with conviction, taste, and good planning should succeed in marketing art. Few managers of discount and department stores seem to be able to do so. They mistakenly believe that *any* product or service can be promoted and sold "automa—tically." On the other hand, the great art dealers of this era and of earlier ages, have all exhibited a singular capacity for developing the sensibilities and tastes of their individual clients, often in strange, new pathways. The art marketing problem is not one of "bringing art to the masses" but rather one of bringing out the individual in the process of selling art.

In short, the art market provides distribution for works in a rather chaotic manner, through a variety of outlets. Some are as simple as direct artist—collector sales. Others are very complex, involving workshops or foundries, pub—lishers, wholesalers, and retailers in many cities. However, the giant merchandizers have no significant role in the enterprise.

The Special Role
Of Artists In The
Contemporary Market For Art

3. When Should Artists Market Their Own Art Works?

Of course, a fair amount of art has always moved directly from the artist to the collector, with *no* intermediaries or dealers. Some artists enjoy the contact with collectors too much to ever abandon such direct relationships. Others are forced by the nature of their specialization to do a good deal of direct selling. This is characteristically true of artists who work on special project commissions for architects and de—signers. It is also quite common for portrait artists. Further, there are many artists who are faced with the alternative of making no sales at all unless they establish their own markets because for one reason or another they have no dealer. On the other hand, a few artists — — like James Peter Cost in Carmel and Ted DeGrazia in Tucson — — who have developed extremely successful double careers as artist—dealers.

Even those I know who "hate" business generally agree that artists need both the income and the gratification which derives from the sale of their works. Although an artist may consider the business scene distasteful, even distressing, a negative attitude towards commerce can make it exceedingly difficult for artists to function effectively in their chosen profession. Regardless of their intention, artists who make art primarily at their own expense, without finding a market for it, are fundamentally and objectively hobbyists. Unless they have other income sources, they must find a way to sell their works to collectors to support their chosen modes of expression.

Art critics like Harold Rosenberg might prefer to call such non—selling artists "amateurs." Mr. Rosenberg has often indicated that he feels that art is not a truly profes— sional activity like medicine or law and should not be aimed at commerce. While I detest the commercialization of art, this position has long troubled me, since it leads directly to dilettantism for the artist and a form of collector abuse which borders on anti—social behavior. I have quite a dif— ferent position, *viz*: the artist in our society is, perforce, a professional business person — — a member, if you please, of the *petit bourgeoisie*. We shall return to this argument.

Of course, well—established artists, those with a sub— stantial following of collectors, will have relatively little difficulty enlisting the services of art dealers to sell their works for them. A significant number of artists manage to place their works with a number of dealers, thus achieving broad distribution in several different market areas. Since dealers are specialists in marketing art work, they are gen— erally more capable of finding collectors and selling works than most artists can expect to become. Furthermore, they may experience less constraint in praising the artist's work or in encouraging a collector to buy.

Nevertheless, relatively—unknown artists and artists with good reputations but naturally small markets must find their own collectors. A market is "naturally small" if the artist's image is rather private in its symbolic language or if the imagery appeals only to a handful of special people. Some— times this rather private kind of art can achieve a fairly wide audience over a period, as in the constructions of Cornell who became very widely known after his death. It may seem an onerous and even an embarrassing task, but there is seldom any other way for an artist to develop a significant number of collectors who are devoted to the artist's work.

First, there simply are not enough qualified art dealers oper—
ating today to handle all the salable works which our better
artists produce. I believe that the United States could pro—
fitably support twice as many first—rate galleries as currently
exist. But they are not forming fast enough.

Further, most art dealers prefer to represent artists who
have already achieved broad critical recognition and who
already have a substantial number of clients. It is a risky
business — — introducing "untried" artists — — and the costs
are high compared to prospective returns. This leaves many
excellent but lesser—known artists to their own devices.
They soon discover that they must sell their own work if
they are ever to achieve any recognition, reputation, or com—
pensation for their labors.

The encouraging truth is that selling art works is not as
complex as it may seem. Indeed, as indicated above, a few
artists I know have mastered the craft of marketing so well,
that they prefer to continue selling their own works directly
to collectors, even after they are so well established that
dealers are anxious to handle their works for them.

Some of these artists believe that they can earn more
money by selling their own works, retaining the dealer's
share of the price. It is unlikely that this is true. No artist's
sales efforts are entirely without some cost, and in most
cases, the effort required to cultivate collectors and sell
works of art significantly reduces the energy needed to create
new works.

Few artists are so inexhaustible in their resources that
they can continue for a long period to do a wholly satis—
factory job of creating a substantial output of works of
art while simultaneously selling them at a good rate. As
a general rule, artists should sell their works only until more

efficient and effective distribution channels become acces— sible. They should then find the best art dealers available and turn over most of the marketing tasks to these specialists.

Artists should recognize, however, that there is a social aspect of selling their own work which is rather important, aside from the monetary significance of the effort. Every artist is, in some sense, a communicator. Often, for the visual artists, this function involves *non—verbal* communi— cations — — an effort to reach directly to the viewer's viscera or to impinge somehow upon the viewer's sensibilities, with— out extensive recourse to written or oral language.

When artists take the trouble to study the way people respond to their work, to listen to their reactions, they can learn a great deal about how their effort is succeeding. They may, if they are astute and open—minded, even discover aspects of a particular work which were not in their own consciousness when they were creating it.

Thus, showing, discussing, selling art works can be useful to the artist in more than a financial sense. It can improve the artist's understanding of what these works are really achieving. I do not believe, however, that the artist can ever benefit from "explaining" a work to others. Collectors may sometimes need a little clarification, guidance, or encourage— ment, but pat explanations cannot substitute for the collec— tor's personal esthetic experiences and discoveries.

As indicated elsewhere in this *Handbook*, artists often band together to show and sell their works cooperatively and collectively. This approach can be spectacularly successful. More often, the effort to combine forces and resources re— sults in loss of focus, amateurism, and very poor sales results. I have come to believe that such enterprises can only succeed when the participating artists have a great deal in common, esthetically and are also willing to share their time and funds in a true partnership. Even then, results will be poor unless the group's efforts and funds are expended in a highly pro— fessional way.

4. Establishing a Reputation as an Artist

Except for the case of highly decorative art images which are generally sold for their color or their subject matter, before an artist can expect to sell more than a handful of art works, some energy must be devoted to the establishment of a professional reputation. Credentials are important in all professions, particularly for that large class of clients who place their trust in the judgment of others. In earlier times, membership in an academy provided the professional credentials as membership in the medical society legitimatizes the physician. To acquire such credentials today, a capable artist generally must exhibit widely under appropriate auspices.

Artists may enter works in established group exhibitions, especially shows which are juried by well—respected artists, curators and critics. The annual open competition of the American Watercolor Society is a good example of such a show. They may also enter any of the numerous local and regional competitions which are advertised and available to relatively unknown artists. The trade magazines, *Art News* and *American Artist,* regularly list such competions, well in advance of deadlines. Many of the newer regional art publications such as *Art Week* in Oakland and *New Art Examiner* in Chicago also list competitions. Freight companies which specialize in crating and transporting art works also publish lists of exhibitions which are open to artists. The names of such companies can generally be found in any large city's *Yellow Pages* and in the advertising section of the major art magazines.

Successfully entering competitive exhibitions will accomplish two ends. First, it will lend prestige and authority to the artist's implied claims that these works are unusual, interesting, or noteworthy. Second, it will bring the work and the artist's name to the attention of many people in the art world, including critics, dealers, and collectors, many of whom visit these exhibitions to view the works which are displayed.

I know artists who feel that submitting their work to a jury or a committee in some way acts as a brake upon their creative freedom. This may be true in certain instances. But artists who are not well known and who are unwilling to participate in juried shows and competitions, must find recognition in other ways. They might avail themselves of the assistance of friends who are already established in the art world or they might seek advice from other artists and from collectors. But they should understand that even connoisseurs are often unsure of their own judgment. Many collectors rely upon the testimonials and recognition of juries, prize committees, well known critics, and other artists. Even very advanced collectors often seek assurances from others to reinforce or validate their own views and experiences.

While it is important that artists enter shows and com—petitions, doing so is not inexpensive. Usually, a two dimensional work must be matted and/or framed before it may be submitted. In many cases, an entry fee is required, which is not returned if the work is rejected. Some insti—tutions also require the payment of membership fees as a condition of exhibition. Also, the awards and purchase prizes are not necessarily commensurate with the market value of the works so "honored."

Suppose an artist spends five or ten dollars on an entry fee, thirty—five to fifty on a frame, twenty—five or more crating and shipping, and then is "fortunate" enough to receive a two hundred and fifty dollar check for a work which has a fair market value of five hundred dollars. The artist should realize that an operating loss was incurred on the transaction. This loss may or may not be offset by the increased prestige and collector interest which the award arouses in the artist's other works.

To further complicate matters, many art institutions, including some very well—known museums and art centers, have made a practice of using fees from juried exhibitions to finance their own operations. It is not unusual to find a competition which is widely advertised so that entry fees amount to tens of thousands while prizes and exhibition costs are only a small fraction of the sum received. The Artists Equity Association has long campaigned against such malpractices, holding that refused artists should not have to subsidize arts organizations. They have recently enlisted the support of the National Endowment for the Arts which will withhold funding from exhibition programs which are plainly designed to enrich the sponsors.

For these and related reasons, many well established artists avoid competitions entirely. They must feel that the economic disadvantages are not adequately counter—balanced by an improvement in their reputations or any increased exposure to collectors. On the other hand, juried exhibitions often offer really attractive rewards, including legitimate prizes. Some of the best of these prizes are not purchase awards, but simply honoraria, good catalogs, pres—tigious openings, and widely read critical notices. Certain juried shows even provide legitimate sales opportunities for the artist's works.

A client with whom I work has had many excellent experiences as a result of her systematic and very carefully considered participation in such competitive juried shows as she feels are appropriate to her works. She has found new clients, received favorable critical attention, and even been invited to give solo exhibitions in museums as a result of this activity.

The Shape And Structure Of The Market For Art Works

5. The Mission of the Artist and the Mission of the Art Dealer

For many years, I have made it a practice to ask artists why they make art. Their answers tend to fall into two familiar categories. Either they make art because they feel "compelled to discover (or develop) themselves" more fully or because they seek "to discover (or understand) the universe" in which they live. Occasionally, an artist will indicate a deep–seated need to explore both interior and exterior spaces.

To do these things, the artist – – regardless of medium or esthetic bias – – must select, rearrange, abstract, eliminate, simplify, focus, and – – most important of all – – communi–cate. While the making of art can (often should) be intensely personal and private, its function is basically social. To succeed, an artist's work must, somehow impinge upon the conscious or unconscious experience of others in a meaningful or interesting way. However, whereas the artist is often most deeply involved in some sort of activity or process, the viewer is often most deeply involved with an object which results at the conclusion of that process.

The mission of the artist is, then, generally associated with generating processes and objects which can foster the artist's discovery of self and universe and which others (viewers, and collectors) can share. To achieve this mission, artists must not only make, but also find ways to exhibit and sell their work. In our culture selling works is really an integral part of the artist's creative process. When this works, the sale of an art work performs a socially useful function.

For the art dealer, the mission is easier to define. Dealers are truly entrepreneurs − − acting as go—betweens, with the artist and the collector at opposite ends of their activity. Artists function as their prime source of supply and collectors are their prime source of income. For all this apparent func—tional simplicity, an art dealer who wishes to perform a unique or critically significant function is faced with a bewildering variety of collector types, artists, art media, modes of business operation, and methods of financing these operations, to name just a few of the many variables. No single approach exists which would be appropriate for every dealer. But the complexity of the problem can be reduced to manageable proportions by analyzing the shape and structure of the art market and the options which are available to dealers.

Thus, artists may be sub—divided in terms of their reputation, and galleries may be sub—divided in terms of the intensity of their representation of artists. Artists may also be usefully divided in terms of their particular esthetic interests and in terms of their styles.

Collectors of art may be divided into sub—groups in terms of their prior activity and current performance as collectors. Primary collector motivations can also be identified. Art works offered for sale may be divided in terms of media employed. So, too, galleries differ in the sources of the works they show. In no case should these categories be considered judgmental. An inexpensive, original print by a relatively unknown abstract artist is not necessarily "inferior" to a higher priced representational oil by a famous artist. The sub— divisions discussed here are useful from the point of view of helping a dealer to define available options. They suggest little about the intrinsic merit of the works to be offered for sale.

Obviously, no dealer can attempt to serve every facet of the art market. Each gallery owner should develop an indi— vidualistic set of specifications by selecting elements or categories pertinent to that dealer's location, resources, and opportunities. The dealer's activities should be based on an understanding of the biases, limits, and refinements within which operations are to proceed. Otherwise, a tendency will arise for the gallery to project a diffuse and confusing image.

Paramount in this discussion is the issue of why the art dealer has decided to enter the art market in the first place. It is not the easiest or surest way to make money. I can think of many fields of endeavor where the risk is less and the potential financial reward is greater. There are usually other factors urging themselves on the would—be dealer.

Some dealers are frustrated artists or art historians who simply want to be active in the art world, if not as creative or critical forces, then as mediating and useful contributors. Others want to help an artist or a group of artists whom they admire to find public recognition. Still others are really collectors who want to put their own passion for art on a sound financial foundation. Some hope to move from the ranks of dealers to those of curators. More than a few view the field as a pleasant diversion which may not earn much money, but can be at least partially written off against other taxable income. In any case, each art dealer must carefully select an appropriate role which is unique and meaningful. The options and alternatives are many, and their relative merits vary significantly.

6. Artist's Reputation/Depth of Representation

Art dealers are regularly differentiated in terms of the reputation of the artists they represent and in terms of the depth in which these artists are represented. Thus, some dealers only show works of art of a particular region or school while others feature works by internationally famous artists. On a handy, but somewhat misleading scale, we might start by identifying relatively unknown artists, recent art school graduates, and part—time artists. This group contains many inventive and original creative personalities who have somehow not yet achieved significant public stature.

A former client of mine who operates a major gallery in the East has made a practice for many years of including one or two relatively unknown artists in each year's exhibition program. On one occasion, she included an all—but—forgotten German expatriate. On another occasion, she showed a very promising recent art school graduate. In still another in—stance, she chose an outstanding industrial designer who paints primarily as an avocation. More than once, the effort has succeeded and a significant clientele has been developed for such artists. I find that her practice, however laudable, is not too widely followed by well established dealers. The art dealers of San Francisco have undertaken an annual "new faces" program to introduce artists who have otherwise not been exhibited too widely. Unfortunately, however, relatively unknown artists are found, when they are seen at all, only in the newer or smaller galleries.

The next step on the "ladder" of artists' reputations contains that group of artists who have a following in a particular community or region. Since the distribution of artists' works is still relatively immature, excellent artists in St. Louis or Detroit may be totally unknown outside their areas of residence. One major metorpolitan dealer, with whom I have worked, has carefully researched this issue and often arranges shows in his own gallery for artists who are well established elsewhere. He finds that this method is more certain to succeed than more random methods of selection. Interestingly enough, his collection has a certain homogeneity and cohesion despite the fact that his artists seldom know each other. This common esthetic outlook has been constructed on the basis of the dealer's own bias, and it gives his clients a fairly consistent variety of art works from which to select. Some highly specialized art dealers follow a similar pattern in importing art works from overseas. Thus, the artists found in M. M. Shinno's gallery near the Los Angeles County Museum of Art generally enjoy good reputations in Japan and Taiwan, but are not too well known in this country.

Next, there is a group of well established, nationally reknowned artists − − men and women who are well known in many art circles and whose art work may be found in important public and private collections. Such artists are usually listed in *Who's Who in American Art*. They generally have had significant museum exposure, and they may have exhibited outside our own country as well. Many art dealers steadfastly refuse to represent any artists who have not already achieved major critical attention and significant followings. A New York dealer once told me that he simply cannot "afford" to offer for sale any art works priced under a thou−sand dollars; therefore, he consistently will refuse to handle artists without national or international reputations. This position is not entirely logical, but it is fairly common.

Finally, there are the super−stars − − internationally famous artists − − who, for one of a number of reasons, are the center of attention of the art world at any given moment or who have enjoyed their star status for a longer period. Membership in this group may change radically from year to year. Since these artists are exposed to wide public scrutiny, their work is under constant discussion. If their image stays the same too long, fails to show innovtion, ceases to impress a powerful party in the art establishment, the "star" may fade. When artists are really inventive and their works find broad favor, they may maintain this super—star status for an indefinite period.

Of course, such artists generally have their pick of dealers and market areas. I regularly run into novice dealers like the lady from Louisville who, with no prior experience or special qualifications in the art world, insisted that she wanted to represent only very famous artists, presumably because she felt that their work would be easier to sell. What she wound up with was a collection of faded stars of yesteryear who were in enough trouble economically that they were willing to take a chance with her untried gallery. The enterprise failed after two troubled years. She would, in my opinion, have had a better chance if she had tried to develop a good clientele for lesser known, but more viable artists.

With each of these categories of artist's reputation, an art dealer may have any of several working relationships. The dealer may represent an artist with a few works held on consignment, or the artist may be represented with signifi— cant, personally selected art works representing many of the artist's primary moods, interests, and historical periods. Alternatively, the artist may be represented exclusively in a specific market area or even internationally by a single dealer. There is a rather significant difference between an art dealer who owns a few art works by several internationally famous artists and one who represents intensively and exclusively an artist whose reputation is regional but very well established.

Of course, many art dealers can operate at several levels simultaneously. They may have several well established artists whom they represent intensively and exclusively.

In addition, they may occasionally acquire a few works by several "super—stars," and they may also hold certain works on consignment which have been created by relatively un— known artists. This will give them an interesting mixture of artists' works in terms of reputation, ranging from occasional unknowns to intensive well—knowns.

I generally encourage my art dealer clients to begin their careers by finding artists whose work they understand and wish to support, whose need for encouragement and market development is still fairly substantial. I would rather see a new dealer do a first rate job of intensively representing a few rising artists. Other art works by other kinds of artists can be added along the way. This approach is slower than the more commonly used, high—risk method where the dealer begins by purchasing a sizeable inventory of art works by relatively famous artists. The case of a former dealer I know is very instructive on this point. When she first came to see me, she had spent more than a hundred thousand dollars on remod— eling a store in Western Canada. She had little money left for promotion, and she was discouraged and convinced that her friends were philistines because they had not been snapping up her high—priced offerings of art works which had been in the market for some time before she acquired them. Now, a more modest approach with less famous artists would have been slower but surer.

7. Purchasing Motivations — — Why Do People Buy Art?

To better understand the structure of the market for art, it will be useful to consider some of the underlying motiva— tions for a collector's purchasing decisions. Almost every art purchase results from a number of interactions between the client and an artist's work. However, a few primary forces characterize collector motivations most significantly, and they can be readily identified. Satisfying certain of these interests in a particular fashion can be an important characteristic of an artist's or dealer's method of operation.

Some art is collected for its decorative qualities. In the experience of the relatively uncultivated personality, it is easy to confuse art with decoration. For many collectors, including a significant number who are hardly novices, the primary motivation for acquiring art works may be stated in terms of decorative values. At its worst, this can represent a quest for art which makes no demands, which pleases and titillates at the most superficial level. At its best, this can mean a healthy interest in enhancing an otherwise sordid or plain environment by making it a more colorful and inter-esting place to live and work.

Our culture is deeply involved with color, texture, and form. Artists of many persuasions work with images which have a significant decorative content. However, many leading designers and architects are cautious about employing art in a context which is too strictly decorative lest this dull our sensibilities. Ideally, the decorative aspect of an art work is only the surface veneer. Other values of more lasting and significant merit can be found in the works of most esta-blished artists.

The works of some of the best kinetic artists are a good example of these multiple layers. Thus, Agam will produce a technically very meticulous work which contains, among other things, an elegant color spectrum. Since the human eye finds rainbows of any kind generally rather lovely, such works function in a highly decorative manner. And yet, for Agam, the rainbow is also a significant and almost universal symbol of God's promise to Noah of hope and life, and this makes it more than a simply decorative image.

Another motivating factor which can encourage the acquistion of art works is the need for social status which dominates the activity of many in our culture. Just as the young society matron contributes effort and money to a worthy charity to earn recognition from her peers as a "good person," so, too, the aspiring investment banker or dental surgeon may acquire contemporary art works to enhance a reputation as a sophisticate among peers and clients.

Not too long ago, it was almost obligatory for the Holly—wood starlet to acquire a Rolls Royce, a full—length mink, and a French Impressionist painting as symbols of status in a society where achievement can be hard to measure. Today, the make of car and the color or styling of the coat may have changed. So, too, the impressionist painting may have given way to a more contemporary, but still expensive, art style. But the primary motivation is still the same − − improved social recognition.

Recently, a newly—arrived Hollywood producer retained the services of a Los Angeles art dealer to help him assemble a "major" collection. She put together a half million dollar collection of art in less than six months, concentrating on California artists who had achieved some level of critical attention in the late sixties and early seventies. Whether these works have lasting esthetic value may well be arguable, but they represent a distinct collector bias and, more important, they amount, in their size and specialization, to a very visible collection. Since the client seems to have been mainly con—cerned with the issue of social visibility, his expenditures may very well have achieved their primary objective.

Other collectors buy art works primarily to demonstrate their affluence, as a special form of *ego—satisfaction.* Like Thorstein Veblen's conspicuous consumers, they derive great satisfaction from watching others who envy their possessions and their financial prowess. Such collectors often seem to be crass and exhibitionistic. Their art works tend to function as personal adornments. The self—gratification motivating these collectors is obvious, easily identified, even occasionally unpleasant.

− 27 −

Such people do not usually build collections of uniform quality since their narcissism discourages those cautious, more esthetic pleasures that the true collector enjoys. When they buy, they demand works by widely recognized artists, often in the highest price ranges. The high price they pay for an art work seems important to their own self—esteem.

A more constructive kind of egoist collector enjoys locat— ing and supporting artists who are just beginning to attain recognition. Here the satisfaction derives from the collector's early recognition of "rising stars." In each case, the primary purchase motivation is a curious view of art as an extension of the collector's ego. Still, it takes a certain knowledge, taste, and courage to endorse an unknown. Thus, this kind of egoist is sometimes more supportive to artists and more palatable to dealers than the type previously described. Obviously, such a collector will want quite different art works than will appeal to his crasser counterpart.

Even in the most altruistic personality, a fair measure of egoism is often present, and it is generally satisfied to some degree when an art work is acquired. Egoism is healthiest when art is acquired as a means of expanding, enriching, and cultivating the collector's personality. Just as artists are often seeking to discover their own personalities in their work, so the best collectors discover and develop themselves through their collections.

There are, of course, collectors who look upon their acquisitions primarily as investments that will increase in value and become the basis of some variety of substantial capital gain. The history of art in the twentieth century is studded with success stories about astute or lucky collectors who acquired works at low prices and held them until they had grown prodigiously in value. Since art works have an economic as well as an esthetic value, this emphasis is not surprising.

The extensively publicized collection of Mr. and Mrs. Robert Scull is an excellent example of works which enjoyed rapid economic appreciation over a relatively short period of time. To be sure, there is a good deal of drama in the story of art works which cost only a few dollars in the first place and which rise in value to many thousands. The question remains, however, regarding cause and effect. Were these works intrinsically underpriced in the first place or did they achieve economic appreciation primarily as the result of clever promotion?

Of course, there are many examples of less successful selections which should serve as a caution to the investment—oriented collector.* A collector who is successful financially with his collection usually has been well advised esthetically and has exercised good taste and judgment in assembling that collection. Most of the notable losses in the art market have been accompanied by a remarkable lack of sensitivity re—garding esthetic values on the part of the collector—investor.

On the other hand, the most successful of these specula—tors are precisely those whose esthetic judgment was sound. Art works only appreciate over the long—term if they are excellent. But, even when they are successful, only a few collectors actually find that they can readily and inexpen—sively liquidate their investments in art works which have appreciated significantly. Nevertheless, this motivation for acquiring art has become common. In some art galleries, investment appreciation potential has become a primary sales argument, often when it has little validity.

* *Richard H. Rush in his comprehensive work, Art as an Investment, Prentice—Hall (Elizabeth, N. Y., 1961), has established a strong case both for the validity of such an approach to collecting and the pitfalls that may attend the unwary speculator.*

The most valid reason for acquiring any art work is the life enhancement it generates for the collector. To this class of collector, the esthetic significance of any work is all that really matters. Artistic merit cannot properly be measured by the approval of others or even by the promise of capital gains. Often, only a few collectors will recognize the value of an artist's work for a long period of time before the in—vestment—oriented, ego—oriented, or society—oriented art collector takes note. For the sensitive eyes of a connoisseur, using the yardstick of esthetics alone, an art work has value whether or not it is widely acclaimed by others, whether or not it increases in economic value.

I find it comforting to note that ego satisfaction, social approval, and investment appreciation are only available in the long run to art collectors who are able to find some valid esthetic justifications for their decisions. Only esthetics is intrinsic to the works. Psychology, sociology, and economics are necessarily extrinsic or secondary considerations for art collectors. If the work is not fundamentally "good" it will fail in the last analysis.

Just as there are a wide variety of individual personalities in the healthy adult community, so there are many shadings and varieties of esthetic responses. To some art collectors, color, surface, and form are most significant. Others relate esthetic qualities to contextual issues, such as subject matter or historical reference. Still others are concerned with the intellectual or emotional impact of the work. Because these factors are the key to developing clients, they will be dis—cussed more fully in the section on selling. Regardless of other motivating factors, every collector's esthetic bias and development will influence purchasing inclinations. The art works already collected will, in turn, influence the collector's artistic interests and personality.

8. Different Levels of Collector Development

Every artist and art dealer should expect to encounter many kinds of prospective clients. Some are very knowl—edgeable; others know relatively little about art. Some have developed a highly refined, perceptive acuity for particular images, esthetic qualities, or technical considerations; others are just beginning to develop their interests; still others have none. Artists and dealers must be sensitive to these different levels of development.

It is the proper function of an artist or a dealer to assist collectors in moving from one plane to another in collecting works which will bring interest and satisfaction over a long period. If art has anything to do with the cultivation and focus of the individual, then the seller should play the roles of mid—wife, nurse, tutor, and colleague in the progressive development of the collector's perception and personality. The stages are discernable but uneven.

The non—collector generally has little conscious under—standing or appreciation of art. However, the members of this large group are not without artistic needs and interests. Few humans can live entirely without some art. Turning non—collectors into regular clients of a particular gallery or followers of a particular artist is not easy, but it is a very rewarding endeavor, financially and phychologically.

Non—collectors seldom become collectors unless their interests are deliberately cultivated by an artist, by a dealer, or by some other social force — — a curator, an editor, a teacher, or a friend. In our rapidly changing culture, men and women who have not previously been actively concerned with art still represent the largest, perhaps the most impor—tant, potential market for art. They constitute an immense reservoir for the future of the art market. A substantial segment of these non—collectors is already at least partially predisposed to buy art works, providing that their interests are properly developed. Available media and appropriate agencies have not given sufficient attention to this task over the past few decades. How this attention can be focused more effectively is discussed elsewhere in this *Handbook.*

The sophisticated student of marketing will recognize at once that the art market is by no means "saturated." That is, most of those who need, want, and can afford original art are not yet collectors at any level. Unlike the automotive market or the men's shoe market, where just about everyone who needs cars or shoes has them, art is still an underdevel—oped aspect for most potential clients' lives. As a result, the annual rate of growth of the U.S. art market far exceeds the average rate of growth of our economy. I estimate that a good deal less than thirty percent of the art market's poten—tial clientele is actually buying original art these days on any sort of regular basis. As a result, we have a remarkable, but not unusual, situation where a new gallery opens in a com—munity that already possesses several excellent galleries and proceeds to find a substantial market over a period of years without taking any significant amount of business away from its "competitors." The point is that they have found and developed clients who are new to art collecting — — usually by offering a kind of art which was not previously available in that community. Many of these new clients are novices and were previously non—collectors.

Not long ago, a highly cultivated art collector told me that she has a scheme for "transforming" the lives of certain friends and relatives who have never expressed an active interest in art. She selects modest but fine works in various media as gifts. In several cases, the recipients subsequently found it necessary to dispose of the cheap reproductions and wall decorations which had been hanging on their walls because they had to bring their home environment up to a higher standard once this start had been made for them on an art collection.

Unlike the non—collector, the novice already is aware of art and may even number a few more advanced art collectors among friends and associates. Novices might be young pro—fessionals or students eager to learn more about the art and artists of our culture, or they may be older persons whose interests have bloomed later in life for a number of reasons. When a novice buys an art work, it is usually for display on a wall at home or in an office although occasionally novices also buy art as gifts for others.

The artist and art dealer should not assume that the novice is interested only in low—priced works. One well—established art dealer made this error not long ago when he directed an otherwise excellent catalog to the "needs and interests of young collectors who are in search of original prints which are both of high quality and of a price range amicable to limited budgets." The thrust of such an appeal is unintentionally rather negative, suggesting that just because one is new to collecting, one is also young and/or short of funds. Actually, most new collectors are at least verging to—wards thirty. Many are much older and are relatively secure financially when they begin collecting. Their early works represent considered best judgments regarding appropriate disposal of a portion of their discretionary income.

A novice collector usually has a fair amount of such income, and often spends money on " things that show" — — a medium or even a high priced car and home, fashionable clothes, extensive recreational and cultural activities, good furniture, etc. The novice institutional collector may also be a small business proprietor or a professional who wants to improve and individualize the image projected to the public through office or store. Most often, novices can be moving upward economically and socially. They will often begin collecting art as a means of visibly registering their current level of advancement.

Novices may remain novices all their lives, or they may move on to more sophisticated tastes and interests. A great deal usually depends on how the artist or dealer who first involved them in collecting follows up on their early acquisions. It is clear, however, that collectors seldom stop buying art after they have made their first acquisitions, despite the fact that their tastes and interests may change enormously.

An intermediate collector has already acquired a small collection of art works, but is not an expert in the field. This is probably the largest and fastestgrowing category of collectors in the art market today. The intermediate collector often owns art works in more than one medium. This kind of collector also generally owns more than one work by the same artist.

The intermediate collector may know something about the technology of art − − the rudiments of painting, sculpture, and printmaking. The intermediate may have studied art or art history in college, may subscribe to one or more art publications, attend gallery and museum exhibitions. On occasion, this person is also an amateur artist. Some amateur artists collect art works by professionals, only rarely. Others enjoy such art and collect assiduously.

Often the intermediate collector knows a fair amount about the work of a few artists and has developed some regular sources for acquiring works − − that is, this type of collector may be a regular client of one or more artists and art dealers. As the intermediate collection outgrows available wall space, part of the growing collection may be stored. The intermediate regularly becomes an advanced collector.

Intermediates may encourage their non−collector friends and associates to become collectors. They will bring such people with them to exhibition openings and other functions.

They give art works as gifts and they encourage artists and art dealers to contact their friends. One art dealer — client with whom I work has regularized his business relationship with several of his clients who are well—connected intermediates. He keeps careful referral records and credits them with ten percent of the amount of any sales they stimulate as an offset against work which these clients may wish to purchase in the future.

Institutional intermediates, like their individual counter—parts, occasionally lend art works for public exhibition by museums and colleges and may even make donations from time to time to benefit public collections. The primary dif—ferences between a novice and an intermediate often relate to matters of self—conciousness regarding art and collecting. Novices seldom think of themselves as collectors.

Advanced collectors frequently specialize in particular kinds of art works, in schools, or in periods. The advanced collector is apt to know the facts regarding various specific states of an original print, the history of a particular painting, and the methods and problems associated with a medium. Advanced collectors are deeply interested in the careers of the artists in their collections, and take pride in their own appreciation of these works. They work hard to get others to recognize the merit of their collections. Partly as a result, their artists are often rather well known.

There is a general assumption that advanced collectors only acquire works by well established artists. Such is not always the case. Thus, Dr. Barnes was the first serious col—lector of the works of Soutine, and he devoted a fair amount of time and money to the issue of getting that artist's works better known in this country. In more recent times, Joseph Hirschhorn acquired a great deal of art by artists who were quite unknown at the time he expressed an interest in their work. Some went on to become well established. Others did not.

Such connoisseurs have been collecting art for some time, occasionally for more than one generation, and have devel— oped sizeable collections. They may be distinguished from the intermediate collector by the length of time they have devoted to collecting, by their well developed sources for works, and by their appreciation of their works. Advanced collectors often participate in important auctions, buying and selling works on an international scale, and are usually well known to the major dealers in their fields of special interest.

It would be naive to assume that advanced collectors consistently buy excellent works while intermediates and novices do not exercise comparable good judgment or good taste. Unfortunately, some of the world's leading art collec— tors have made monumental blunders in their selections, even buying clever forgeries and cheap imitations. Meantime, many really important art works have been acquired by collectors who were novices when they made their earliest purchase decisions.

Even more often, well known advanced collectors have bought authentic works by established artists, but have made selections which were not distinguished examples of the work of these artists. Anyone can err in judgment, even after years of collecting. It is particularly easy when one's expertise is not equal to one's reputation or when one is seeking famous autographs rather than outstanding esthetic values. Further, every collector, whether novice, intermediate, or advanced, may err by buying works which follow fads and fashionable trends rather than because of their intrinsic merits. These pitfalls are discussed further in terms of buyer motivations. They can apply to all kinds of collectors, veterans as well as newcomers.

Professional collectors constitute one more category of customer for art. They include museum curators, art school administrators, art dealers and wholesalers, as well as design— ers, architects, and contract art buyers. While the ultimate interests of the individual members of this group may differ greatly, they are alike in that they are not usually assembling a collection for themselves, but rather for others. On occa— sion, such professional collectors may even supress their own interests in deference to the specifications of the employers or clients in whose behalf they are engaged. These kinds of collectors can be extremely important in the development of the careers of artists since their active support can add significant visibility and market value to the output of an artist.

The professional collector sometimes advises and acts for the advanced collector, both private and institutional. Major collectors often employ several experts on a full or a part— time basis. Professionals often seek works on behalf of other professionals. They may also place commissions with artists and assemble exhibitions for clients. I recently had occasion to watch the working methods of an interior designer who commissioned several complete editions of multiple originals for use in the guest rooms of a major luxury hotel. This professional worked closely with the two artists and their dealer to make sure that his client got precisely what he thought was needed. In the last analysis, his client's collec— tion of art proved to be outstanding and contributed mightily to the distinct and very unusual character of the hotel.

9. Business Formats

While most of the artists and art dealers in the United States have organized their businesses as retail proprietor—ships, a number of significant variations have arisen in recent years which are worthy of examination. The proprietorship is an intensely personal business format, in many ways well—suited to the need for personal identification which seems to motivate most artists and art dealers. This simple structure has advantages for certain art dealers, just as it offers advan—tages as a business format to many artists.

If a business is expected to operate at a loss, especially in its formative years, and if the operator of that business has a significant amount of taxable revenue from other sources, a proprietorship may be particularly useful during the start—up period, in that it permits an offset of business losses against other personal income tax liabilities. That is, the proprietor's art gallery business losses may be employed to reduce payments which would otherwise be due on non—art income. So too, the artist's income as a teacher or the artist's spouse's income is generally subject to income tax which may be recaptured during the formative years of an artist's business.

This singular tax advantage is available, for example, to a doctor or lawyer whose spouse elects to beome a fine art dealer. Although the advantages are not as apparent to many couples, it is equally available as a taxable income offset to the spouse of an artist. In either case, the cost of starting a small business is absorbed partly by the federal and state tax agencies. If this sounds like a "loophole" in the tax law, it is an honorable one in that it is a useful way to reduce the cost of starting a business.

I have often been told that a certain accountant had advised an artist and a spouse that the Internal Revenue Service will "disallow" tax deduction claims if an artist fails to report a profit within three consecutive years. The tax courts have ruled otherwise. If you are actually engaged in seeking new clients and otherwise conducting your affairs in a business—like way, (if you are not a hobbyist) the fact that you report losses is not a problem since many excellent businesses have difficulty getting started.

Similar tax advantages can be obtained if the business is organized as a partnership of two or more unrelated individ— uals. Here, of course, the losses or profits are shared for tax purposes by the individuals comprising the partnership, in direct proportion to their investment interest in the studio or gallery. The partnership format has the further advantage of permitting more than one individual to share in the oper— ating and investment responsibilities for such an enterprise. Partnerships are inexpensively organized and easy to form, but they can present certain problems of their own. Unless special legal precautions are taken, a partner is free to under— take financial and other obligations which must be honored by the other partners out of their own personal resources. Further, any partnership may be terminated and dissolved rather easily as a result of the death or disaffection of a single partner without the approval of the other partners.

I do not like to see partnerships formed without a written partnership agreement. Although the laws of the various states may not require such an agreement, the common law governing partnerships provides tax liabilities, partnership dissolution, and other provisions which are generally quite unacceptable to the participants in an on—going business. I prefer an agreement which can limit the tax liability of the partners, provides for the orderly survival of the business in the case of the retirement, death, or incapacity of a partner, and also establishes some form of governance for the bus—iness. Such provisions are fundamental to the welfare and survival of the business institution itself.

Comparable advantages, without certain of the same difficulties, can be achieved through a business format called a Sub—Chapter "S" Corporation. This is a closely—held corporation consisting of ten or fewer stockholders which enjoys many of the tax benefits of a partnership but fewer of its limitations and dangers by virtue of the special regulations governing such firms. Several wholesale art distributors have organized along these lines in recent years. There is no real reason why artists banding together to share studio space and sales activities could not use this format as well.

However, most small business operators who have elected to abandon their status as sole proprietors switch to ordinary incorporation as "close" corporations, so—called because the stock ownership is closely held by an individual or a small group. This is a particularly useful business format for the art dealer or artist whose busines is both profitable and ex—panding. Since corporations are taxed at lower rates than individuals, this format permits the retention in the business of a larger portion of earnings than would otherwise seem possible. The close corporation is a favorite business format for performing artists as well as for visual artists who use it as an investment vehicle. It has come into wide use among art dealers as well during the past few decades.

In a few cases, art dealers, particularly those who operate in several cities, have elected to organize publicly—held corporations, selling stock to the investment community as a means of financing their operations. Usually, these firms were already in operation when their stock was made avail—able for public ownership. In other cases, art dealers have merged their businesses into corporations which are already publicly–held. Thus Ferdinand Roten, the large Baltimore–based wholesaler of original graphics, has been acquired by Crowell–Collier–MacMillan, making the financial resources of one of the largest book publishing and distributing firms in the world available to this firm, which has now become a publisher as well as a wholesale distributor of fine original graphics. Roten has also opened a chain of mini–galleries in a number of Brentano bookshops. These shops are also owned by the parent company.

In other instances, publicly–held firms have ventured into the field of original art from a base which was allied to the arts. For example, the Harry Abrams firm, long active in the publication of art books, and now a subsidiary of the Times–Mirror Corporation, in recent years launched a publishing and distribution venture for original multiples in a variety of media. So, too, the Franklin Mint, which originally dealt primarily in limited edition medals and coins, has now entered the field of original porcelains and has been exploring other art projects as well.

In these and similar cases, vast financial, promotional, and distribution resources are available. Thus far, such organizations have confined themselves almost entirely to the production and distribution of original multiples, leaving the distribution of unique works for the smaller and more conventional art dealers. Further, the top management of such large enterprises seem to be easily discouraged by the slow turnover rate and high risk of art publishing ventures. During the seventies, most of these enterprises have been abandoned about as quickly as they were formed.

Another business format which has started to appear regularly on the art scene is the joint venture. Technically, a joint venture is a partnership, although it may be a partnership in which one or more corporations can participate.

In the art world, it is usually formed between an artist and a dealer, between a dealer and a print workshop, or between several dealers to develop and exploit some specific enterprise which has a limited scope and a limited life expectancy.

Thus, two or three dealers might form a joint venture to publish and distribute an artist's suite of original prints. Also, a joint venture might be formed by an artist, a dealer, and several investors to finance a large—scale sculpture for subsequent display and sale. Joint ventures generally entail all of the benefits and liabilities of most ordinary long—term partnerships, unless specific steps are undertaken to forestall certain of the liabilities by limiting the obligations of specific parties to the venture.

A well known East Coast accountant, Ruben Gurewitz, is credited (some might say discredited) with a most unusual "new" twist on the idea of the joint venture. He has organ—ized a series of "tax shelter" ventures, designed to connect high—risk venture capital with the activities of artists and original print publishers. This plan involves treatment of the plates or stones from which the prints are made as capital investments on which investment credits and depreciation may be claimed by the investor. Such claims can function as tax shelters providing the tax people decide to go along with the plan.

Characteristically, the promoters in such enterprises get their fees at the start of the venture, so they cannot lose. However, as the Art Dealer's Association and several news letters such as the *Art Letter* and the *Print Collectors News—letter* have been prompt in pointing out, no one else has any guarantees − − not the investors, nor the workshop, nor the artist. Such plans generally presuppose a rapid and con—tinuing appreciation in the worth of the art works which are at their basis. While some art works do, in fact, increase

in value over a period of time, others do not. Some publish—
ing ventures do not attract collectors. And many publishing
ventures are more slow moving than their sponsors had
anticipated. I generally treat schemes of this variety as I
would a proposal for a perpetual motion machine, with a
good deal of skepticism. We will return to this issue in the
section on Business Ethics.

Finally, art may be distributed through any of a number
of tax—exempt institutional formats. The most common of
these is the artist's cooperative, which is often eligible for
designation as a tax—free institution by the Internal Revenue
Service. Briefly, the IRS is empowered under the Federal
Tax Laws to exempt certain institutions from paying income
taxes by virtue of their educational, religious, and philan—
thropic functions. Most states also have special sections in
their corporate codes providing for the incorporation of
cooperative societies of producers (farmers, artists, utitlity
companies, etc.) who wish to market their products or ser—
vices cooperatively. Such firms enjoy many advantages over
ordinary business organizations.

Of course, the artists who participate in a cooperative
are expected to report and pay personal income tax on any
income which they may receive personally through such an
institution. Artists' cooperatives are often rather ineffective
because they are under—financed and not operated by pro—
fessional managers and sales people. In those cases where
management and financing are adequate, results are more
impressive.

Art museums and art departments of colleges, which
sometimes offer art works for sale or for rent, may also be
generally tax—exempt institutions by virtue of their status
as educational organizations. During the early 70's, a group
of Detroit art dealers objected rather vociferously to the
role being played by the Detroit Art Institute in selling

works of art, on grounds that they were competing unfairly with legitimate, tax—paying businessess. Federal agencies and tax reform laws have become increasingly sensitive to this problem in recent years, but the regulatory agencies and the courts have not yet resolved the problem of the role of tax—exempt institutions in income—producing situations. Meantime, organizations as prestigious as the Metropolitan Museum have entered the field of selling art reproductions, based largely on their collections, with in—creased commitment. Such projects contribute mightily to supporting these tax—free institutions.

10. Methods of Financing Operations

Although many approaches have been employed to finance the activities involved in distributing art, the nine—teenth and twentieth century in the United States may well be characterized, with notable exceptions, artist—financed, cash—and—carry retail business. That is, artists traditionally make art works at their own expense. They store them. They find someone to exhibit them, generally on a consign—ment basis. When an exhibitor finds a collector, the work is delivered and paid for, and the proceeds are subsequently divided between the seller and the artist. In this historical pattern, the dealer invests little or nothing in inventory and acts as a sales agent in the artist's behalf. Fundamentally, "agents" sell that which they do not own, while "merchants" sell their merchandise, which they previously acquired.

A variant of this procedure puts the art collector in the status of the financially responsible party. In such cases, the client "commissions" a work and makes advance payments covering the cost of designing, fabricating, and installing it. The art dealer here, too, may act as an agent, making a minimum financial investment and never actually acquiring the work which is to be sold. Instead, the dealer arranges the transaction, helps along the way, collects, and distributes the funds.

In either case, the seller invests little or no money in inventory. Such arrangements are seldom encountered in other retail businesses. They are not altogether desirable, since they give rise to the curious situation of people entering the art market who may be financially rather irresponsible. Without any financial stake in the work, dealers may feel justified in offering unwarranted discounts and improper credit terms. They may also treat works carelessly and even "forget" to pay the artist when works are sold. In my own work with artists and dealers, hardly a week passes that does not bring a new instance of art dealers who "forget" that the credit and the funds involved in art sales may not be entirely theirs to dispose of as they wish.

It is not surprising, therefore, to note that some well—known artists whose works are in great demand refuse to support their dealers by financing dealer inventories. On the other hand, most artists have little choice. They must either consign work or undertake to do their own selling. This issue is examined more thoroughly elsewhere in the *Handbook*.

I find it gratifying to report that in recent years, the financial folkways of the art world in the United States have begun to shift significantly. First, many art dealers have dis—covered that they cannot survive on the modest margin which they might earn acting solely as sales agents. Second, the producers of multiple originals by major artists have, in many instances, been unwilling and unable to finance their dealer's inventories. Where the art dealers have wanted to acquire these desirable multiple originals, they have simply had to invest their own capital. In the process, they have improved their own opportunity to survive because they have often acquired good works at lower prices than would have been otherwise possible.

As a result, we now have four common sources of funds to support the functions of the art market: *viz.* artists' investments, collectors' advances, dealers' investments and publishers' (or wholesalers') investments. Because the wholesalers and publishers prefer to sell their work outright, they are forcing dealers to make fairly substantial invest— ments in inventory. With some regularity, these publishers and wholesalers have also brought about a shift in traditional advertising practices, since their promotional budgets are typically a good deal larger than those of the retail dealers. This, in turn, has radically changed the apparent focus of the art press.

A fifth source of funds has been developing over the past few years. This is the funding which becomes available when the collector leases the works instead of buying them out— right. In this case, the leasing company provides the funds. Many who are unfamiliar with leasing confuse such programs with more familiar art—rental programs, in which many arts organizations are engaged.

In traditional art—rental programs, the initial investment is made by the artist or the art dealer, and works are placed in a collector's hands on the basis of a certain periodic fee, generally on a month—to—month basis. Thus, a museum's art rental gallery usually spends no more on acquiring an inventory than does any ordinary art gallery. However, in a lease—financing program, an outside party, often a bank or a specialized leasing agency, acquires title to the work by buying it from the new owner, promising, in writing, to make regular payments until the full cost of the work, plus a charge for the use of the funds, has been paid. This is generally a three—to—five year base period.

At the end of this time, the collector may continue to pay a periodic leasing fee, but the amount is vastly reduced. Where the collector never takes title to the work, there may be significant tax and balance sheet advantages, since neither the obligation nor the asset is ever "booked." If the collector is a corporate institution, its directors may be attracted to the advantages of not carrying a non—depreciable asset* on the balance sheet, while they may claim all lease payments as fully—deductible "operating" expenses. Of course, if the lease agreement turns out to be really a conditional sales agreement in slightly disguised form, most public accountants would insist on treating the transaction as an outright (time—payment) purchase. The lease—financing method of acquiring art works is being employed by a number of institutional art collectors.

Still another financing method, of particular interest to artists and dealers who engage in costly projects, is the above—mentioned joint venture, in which a number of inter—ested individuals or organizations combine their financial strength on a partnership basis, sharing in the costs, the risks, and the profits on some sort of pro—rata basis. These plans may amount to a simple (or a limited) partnership in which interests, funds, and responsibilities are pooled and distribu—ted along equitable lines or there may be more sophisticated arrangements, designed to accomplish rather different ends for investors, workshop operators, promoters, and artists and involving the distribution of art works and tax benefits as well as income to the participants.

* *Art, like land, cannot be depreciated by a business to offset tax liablilities.*

11. Artists and their Media

Just as artists have many divergent feelings and views regarding the nature of artistic expression, so too artists work with a wide variety of materials and methods to transform their perceptions, emotions, and interests into objects which may subsequently find some kind of meaningful response from others. Some of these materials will lend themselves to the development of unique works, while others are capable of employment to generate editions of multiple originals.

There has been a great deal of confusion in the art market surrounding the issue of uniqueness. Some otherwise rather astute commentators have mistakenly suggested that a work of art is necessarily less valuable if it is not the only one of its kind in existence, ignoring the fact that many unique art works have little real value for reasons which have nothing to do with this issue.

Certainly, rarity is a factor of some significance in deter—mining the appropriate worth of an art work. But esthetic values are not necessarily diminished when an original art work is part of an edition. For example, foundry processes do not impede an artist, an art dealer, or a publisher from casting an edition of bronze works, which are all fundamen—tally identical in their interest and appeal. The total cost of making each work may be reduced in this way, while the intrinsic merits of such works are not essentially affected. So, too, an impression of an edition of original lithographs is not necessarily inferior just because other impressions are identical to it. Indeed, for some images, the technologies of the multiple original may permit esthetic values which are attainable in no other way. Rembrandt seemed very con—scious of the esthetic virtue of his intaglio prints. Rodin was very interested in the issue of multiple bronzes.

Of course, there can be significant limitations which the experienced artist will usually place on the production of multiple editions. These limits are dictated first by the tech—nology of the medium itself. Certain delicate washes will not hold up for large lithographic editions. Certain intaglio and engraving techniques wear down rapidly, making very large editions quite impossible. Also, limits may be placed on the investment which a publisher is willing to make in a multiple original art venture. Finally, there are limitations which are imposed intentionally in an effort to limit the availability of a particular work for economic reasons.

Many artists who work in multiples prefer to make a variety of different works in relatively small editions, rather than fewer works, each produced in larger quantities. The economic implications of this preference should be obvious, but it also has an artistic significance since over—exposure of any image may produce *ennui*. Interestingly enough, some of the most significant successes in the field of the multiple original have been rather small editions, while a few of the larger—sized editions have been relatively spectacular failures. I generally recommend original print editions in a range of fifty to two hundred impressions, depending upon the mar—ket potential for the image. I like to see small to medium—size sculptural editions in the range of six to forty castings per edition.

Although photographers have, from the very beginning in the mid—nineteenth century, insisted that theirs is an art medium, the art collecting public has been slow to recognize this. Only in recent years have dealers, auction houses, and art museums devoted any significant attention to the photo medium. A limiting factor has, of course, been the extensive promotion of photography as an amateur and as a commer—cial material. I think that the failure of many photographers to concern themselves with issues of longevity and edition documentation and control has also impeded the growth of the medium as an art form.

Turning to the media which are used primarily for unique works, the most commonly studied, most widely employed material for making art is oil paint — — a substance which combines the versatility of colored pigments with a relatively slow—drying vehicle to permit color mixing, underpainting, overpainting, and many varieties of intentional and accidental combination. For several hundred years, the oil painting has been the primary art object of Western culture, varying in scale from tiny miniatures to works of heroic proportions. While oil paints are occasionally produced on particle board, wood, and even paper, they are more often applied to spec—ially prepared canvasses.

In this century, many artists have turned from oils to *acrylic paints,* a switch which creates a whole new variety of problems and opportunities. Some artists find acrylic materials more vivid and more challenging. Others enjoy the flatness and special textures offered by this material. Whether employing oils, acrylics or other pigmented vehicles such as tempera or bee's wax, most artists seem to employ painting to approach their esthetic interests because the medium is fairly easily mastered, controlled, and corrected. It is also relatively inexpensive, and seldom requires the help of collaborating craftsmen. In this respect, it seems to suit the rather iconoclastic temperament of many modern artists, as well.

In recent decades, a number of artists have experimented with *shaped canvas,* sometimes deviating from the familiar rectilinear form and sometimes departing from the old two—dimensional aspect which conventionally characterizes works on canvas. But the primary function of all such art works is still that of occupying wall space in a private or public place, the better to call attention to the artist's perceptions.

In addition to oils, acrylics, encaustics, and tempera paintings on canvas, a large number of artists work in water color on rag paper. Although this medium is less amenable to underpainting, correction, and color blending, many artists are attracted by the immediacy of the imagery and the wide range of transparent and translucent colors available to water media users. Such works are generally made on fine papers although rag board is also coming into use as it becomes more readily available.

Another medium which is beginning to find favor, and which also generally employs fine paper, is the monotype. Although many fine artists have made these unique works which usually involve a combination of printmaking and painting techniques for centuries, the art collecting com— munity has only begun to prize and appreciate monotypes in recent years. I believe that this medium will become even more important in the eighties.

One artist of my acquaintance now works exclusively in watercolors. Her watercolors are so exciting and original that her exhibitions regularly sell out completely. Another artist with whom I have been associated works only in oils and pastels. His pastels consistently outsell his oils, partially be— cause his collectors find the subject matter and the rendering more pertinent and more exciting in this medium.

Other things being equal, unique works on paper tend to bring higher prices than multiple original prints by the same artist. This again is more a matter of rarity than of intrinsic merit. Of course, the artist whose career is growing in several market areas, may encounter an output problem which can only be resolved by creating a sufficient number of good mutiple originals.

While unsigned unique works on canvas and on paper can be photographically copied and mechanically reproduced by a variety of techniques, the original is clearly more interest— ing, more vivid, and more valuable than the reproduction. Efforts to replace original paintings by using less expensive reproductions seem destined never to satisfy the esthetic needs of any significant segment of the public. Recently a rather elaborate program was developed which employed an extremely costly, new space—age technology to imitate the textures and colors of original oil paintings. It failed to attract adequate customer support despite large—scale pro— motional efforts by the now defunct firm which sponsored the project. The product was not technically bad, but the works were not appreciated, partially because they were not originals.

During the first half of the seventies, several large firms and a number of artists, particularly those specializing in wildlife imagery, inaugurated what seemed to them a very profitable series of enterprises. They produced large color reproductions — — usually by the four color photo offset printing process, sometimes on good quality papers. These were often comparable in scale and quality to the reproduc— tions which have long been available from such firms as the New York Graphic Society at nominal prices. However, the newer firms asked their artists to sign and number their reproductions and sold the works as "fine art prints,"or as "limited edition lithographs." * Many thousands of bird lovers and ecology supporters paid rather high prices for these inexpensive and sometimes inferior reproductions.

* *All editions are necessarily "limited" in size and all offset printing employs lithographic technology. Thus, any instant printing firm makes limited edition lithographs all day — — but not at such high prices.*

Editions sold out, and prices went up as the prints reached the resale market. I find it very interesting that the demand for such dubious undertakings seems to now be subsiding as collectors begin to realize that they have paid excessive prices for signed, inexpensive, calendar—quality reproductions.

Of course, the most remarkable area of growth for the art market of the sixties and seventies has been in the medium of the *original print*. Partly as a result of the work of Tamarind Lithography Workshop in encouraging hundreds of important artists to try this medium, partly as a result of the develop— ment of a number of fine workshops where artists may work together with master printers in making of limited editions, and partly as a result of remarkable growth in public interest in collecting works in the original print media, a situation has developed in which good original prints are now both widely available and widely purchased.

It is relatively simple for an art dealer with modest capital to open a gallery featuring original works by widely known artists, simply by acquiring an inventory of their original prints. Artists in this country seem to prefer the immediacy, color, and scale afforded by the lithographic process to many of the slower, more limited print media, but intaglio prints have also become very important and, for certain schools of artists, serigraphs and woodcuts are widely employed, as well.

A broad variety of written materials is available on var— ious business aspects of the original print, including a number of my own studies written for Tamarind. Also, the National Print Council has issued an excellent publication on the care and collection of original prints by Carl Zigrosser. Now, even those business institutions which were founded to exploit reproductions have begun to realize the difference between an original print and a cheap copy.

While the original print presents an unusual marketing opportunity, it also represents a difficult problem. Many false claims and misrepresentations have cropped up in this field, so much so that the states of New York, Illinois, and California have now entered the arena to circumscribe the promiscuous use of the term "original" in conjunction with print sales.

Even so, exaggerated claims for investment appreciation potential, suppressed data regarding actual edition sizes, and outright counterfeiting are all too common in this field. As discussed more fully below, the novice art dealer, like the novice collector, should be very careful to demand complete documentation and should investigate the reputation of the supplier thoroughly before engaging in any significant bus—iness transactions. The same holds true in the field of other original multiple media as well.

Sculptors often confine their expressions exclusively to the three—dimensional mode, sometimes even to a single material within the field. For works with monumental pro—portions, stone and metal are still widely favored, as they have been for centuries. Their intrinsic strength and beauty, and their other enduring qualities are no doubt the reasons for this preference. Nevertheless, artists work in a variety of other materials, from wood and cast stone to acrylic, hand—made paper, and even corrugated kraft paper.

The choice of materials is often a matter of esthetics — — color, light transmission or reflection characteristics, contex—tual associations, etc. Sometimes the material choice is technological, relating to the ease with which the artist can work the material, its physical characteristics, or its repro—ducibility. Costs, too, can affect the artist's material choices.

In addition to monumental works, many sculptors work in smaller scale, producing objects which are particularly well–suited to interior display. Most assemblage appears to be planned for wall–hung indoor viewing.

Cutting across the conventional media, a growing number of our art dealers, under a variety of stimuli, have elected to exhibit and offer for sale, art works which are not always considered a direct part of the tradition of Western culture in the visual arts. The growing interest in the affairs of developing nations, plus the historical importance of West African art in the development of the School of Paris, have focused attention on the art of cultures which we may find exotic or mysterious. This includes art from Africa, Indonesia, Alaska, Guatemala, etc. Some dealers and collectors have mistakenly called such ethnic works "primitive " although they are generally made by highly skilled artists, often employing materials, symbolism, and esthetic standards which clearly belie the term.

If the word "primitive" has any significance in art, it might be safely applied to the works of naive artists who appear in many cultures, including our own. These men and women generally make art without elaborate techniques, often without formal training. Even here, I believe it might be more appropriate to speak of folk art to describe the output of many self–taught, unlettered artists. Many such works have found their way into the art galleries and museums. Some dealers now specialize in the output of naive artists.

Finally, and in an entirely different key, a number of art dealers have learned that many first–rate artists produce works which might easily be classified as craft in that their works are often useful. These artists make wall hangings and tapestries, sculptured one–of–a–kind tables, desks and chairs, jewelry (unique or multiple), ceramics, and a variety of other objects which are both practical and ornamental.

Like the artists at the turn of the century who worked in England at the *atelier* of William Morris to produce the highly figured rugs, tapestries, hand–blocked wallpapers and book endpapers, the stained glass windows, and the original furni– ture which came to characterize much of the art of the *fin de siecle* period, these artists are often called artisans because technique is significant to them and because their works often have a utilitarian aspect. In the history of art, many of the world's greatest artists were carftsmen in this sense. The Greeks of antiquity had no words to distinguish "art" from "crafts." They simply made art for their enjoy– ment and use.

This issue is of particular importance in our own mech– anized and standardized age. Just as some artists want the museum to function as a place where art "happens" rather than a place where art is enshrined, so, too, other artists want to see art actually employed in the environment.

Site Selection
Where Should Your
Gallery/Studio Be Located?

12. How Close to "the Madding Crowd?"

Artists and art dealers very often are iconoclasts by nature. As independent creative spirits, they tend − − like the poet − − to take to roads which are "least travelled." Georgia O'Keefe left the bustle and whirl of the New York art world fairly early in her career for a much different sort of drama in New Mexico. Her studio—home was built on a hard to reach mesa near Taos, and casual visitors are not encouraged to drop by.

On the other hand, seascape artist—dealer James Peter Cost maintains a studio—gallery in the heart of the rather touristy Northern California community of Carmel—by—the—Sea, not far from the world—famed golf links of Pebble Beach and the Seventeen Mile Drive. His location and the rugged, but much—visited, terrain nearby contribute signi-ficantly to the inspiration of his seascapes, just as in quite a different way, O,Keefe's location and terrain have inspired her subject matter, color, and feeling.

In one case, however, the selection of a studio site was based, at least in part, on a desire to be accessible to a good potential market. In the other case, the site was selected specifically because it was not readily accessible. Clearly, the choice of a gallery or a studio site should be connected to the artist's or art dealer's choice of mission. To find an appropriate site, you must first identify your purposes.

13. What Is Your Business Mission?

If you expect to sell any art works, whether your own or those of others, you must locate your facility in or near an appropriate market. An optimum location will combine an active trading area with interesting and compatible neighbors, accessible transportation, and sufficient parking space. It will be correctly placed for the right quality, quantity, and direction of flow of customer traffic, have adequate visibility, and display an appropriate configuration, size, and condition in its structure.

Almost every large urban, suburban, or resort area will offer many potential gallery and studio sites. Now the most appropriate of these can be selected by applying a series of simple criteria. For example, a gallery representing highpriced major artists would probably not do well in a trading community which attracts lower–income or even mostly middle–income customers. Clients in such areas would not support a gallery featuring expensive works, nor could more affluent customers be expected to travel to it, unless some very special inducements were offered.*

But, if a trading area already caters to people with the target collector's economic level and cultural interests, a new gallery might attract clients not only from the immediate neighborhood, but also from other districts. Therefore, it may be important that the gallery be located in a business area which currently services the upper segments of the economic spectrum.

* One such special inducement is the romantic "legend" of the neighborhood. The SOHO in lower Manhattan and the French Quarter in New Orleans are not "ordinary" slums.

The most desirable customer traffic for expensive art will be found in areas which already house the excellent antique dealers, well established rare book stores, important design—ers and decorators, and other sorts of art—related or craft—related shops, as well as other art galleries. Collectors tend to associate such businesses with high quality, good taste, and originality. They enjoy shopping in such trading areas. I can think of only one gallery which failed in Beverly Hills in the past five years. It was located on a hard—to—find side street.

Two highly specialized trading locations which are parti—cularly attractive to certain kinds of artists and art dealers are located in or near prestige hotels and resort communities. Such areas generally cater to high—income transients who are often potential clients for art works. Thus, Palm Beach and Aspen shelter a number of successful art and craft galleries which operate only during the tourist season. So, too, Old Town in San Diego houses an excellent and successful tourist oriented gallery. Similar centers in cities such as Denver and Albuquerque contain several fine galleries. A fine goldsmith with whom I have worked maintains an excellent studio and showroom just off the main street on Lido Isle in Newport Beach. Her clients visit her here from many parts of the world.

Although too many major hotels in the United States are hosts to galleries which specialize in reproductions and art works of poor quality, there is no intrinsic logic to this curious and unfortunate development. If a hotel supports a fine jewelry store or a first—rate curio shop, why should the neighboring art gallery display *kitsch*? Where good hotels do host legitimate galleries, they seem to do well both in this country and abroad. One of my clients, Louis Newman, has been very successful in his selection of the prestigious Los Angeles Bonaventure Hotel as his gallery site. He represents just a few very fine painters, printmakers and sculptors, on

an exclusive basis. A number of these artists earn a substan—
tial livelihood from his efforts. I can only conclude that the
unfortunate flood of low—grade "picture stores" located in
fine hotels elsewhere in this country is an accident caused by
a few chain operators who simply lack taste.

If yours is a business that is aimed at the client who can
afford only relatively inexpensive works, you probably can—
not pay a high rental. However, if you seek an audience of
sophisticated, extremely individualistic clients, you might be
well advised not to select a high—traffic, popular location
where your potential clientele is likely to be slow to com—
prehend the symbolism or esthetic concerns of your art.

I have come to the conclusion, over the past twenty—odd
years, that no two artists or art dealers have quite the same
objectives or interests. Since their business missions and
methods differ, their facility requirements must differ as
well. Your answers to the following questions may help you
decide your specifications for a site.

If you are an artist:

o Do you sell or plan to sell your own work directly to
collectors?

o Will your sales presentations take place in or near your
studio?

o Will you travel to your client's homes or offices to make
sales presentations?

o Will you work only through dealers? If so, where are
your primary dealers likely to be located?

o What is the present or anticipated range of prices of your
work?

The answers to these questions will help you determine whether your studio location needs to be urban, suburban, or perhaps even rural. I work with an artist who sells a certain amount of work in her rural studio, but she also travels a good deal, contacting dealers in a number of major cities. She lives in an affluent section of central Pennsylvania where she regularly sells work privately to her neighbors. While this is not a major portion of her total sales, it is a very satisfactory situation. Her pleasant, rural site is no impediment to the achievement of her mission.

If you are an artist who is determined, for one reason or another, not to sell your own work directly to collectors, you may decide to locate your studio in a community where the primary considerations are social or even esthetic rather than commercial. One of my finest artist—clients, John Swanson, decided some years ago to leave Los Angeles to do work in England where the environment is particularly well—suited to his own interests as an artist. This would have been very hard to do if John were not well—represented by a strong dealer.

If you are now or plan to become an art dealer, you must decide whether your sales activities require a public exhibition and sales area at the beginning of your career. I often encourage clients who lack adequate capital to begin their selling activities as "private" art dealers, working out of their homes or out of relatively inexpensive offices. In any case, you should consider carefully your answers to the following questions in deciding where your facility is to be located:

o   Who are your target clients? Are they designers and architects, corporate executives, home owners, or apartment dwellers?

o Is the best place to reach them: a very popular shopping center? a tourist community? a fine hotel? an exclusive street near other galleries of a certain kind? an upstairs business office? your own home?

o Will your clients come to you or will you seek them out?

o What is your expected selling price range?

o What is your anticipated annual sales volume?

o Is the work which you are now offering readily accessible esthetically, or is it fairly complex and sophisticated?

o Will you operate some collateral business, such as a frame shop, within the gallery?

A careful study of the methods and biases of potential competitors is useful in selecting a gallery site. Paradoxically, a new art dealer may find the most appropriate site is an area already well populated with other galleries. In such an area, the newcomer can benefit from the established traffic of art collectors and an already defined image for the area related to taste and quality. So, too, artisans who work in the crafts may do better when they are clustered together. The same is true for groups of galleries which cater to designers or for others who belong to the *cognoscenti*.

Inspection of other galleries within any area may show that their proprietors employ a different method of opera— tion, have a different view of their role, and a different approach to the art market than the new art dealer contem— plates. This leaves the field open to the enterprising gallery operator with a unique mission. But even if existing galleries feature related or comparable methods and views, the new dealer stands an excellent chance for success by operating in their vicinity and carrying similar work at similar prices since collectors are generally likely to visit a number of galleries in a given area once they are there. Of course, if one can create a unique institution by offering works of a distinctive and arresting esthetic interest, then the chances for success are even further advanced.

As discussed earlier, the gallery operator might elect to specialize in a particular medium, such as original graphics or wood crafts. This dealer might feature only internationally famous artists or only those artists from a particular region or those holding a particular esthetic view. The dealer may elect to feature art of interest only to highly specialized collectors. For example, dealers may choose to display only the art of local artists or only works related to the American West.

Will non—collectors be encouraged to drop in? Will sig— nificant sales activities occur outside of the gallery? Will the gallery be employed to showcase artists of interest primarily to the more knowledgeable, advanced collectors? Will the collection interest novices? Is the gallery designed to serve the needs of a particular neighborhood? Are some transients expected to become regular clients? It is important to have clear answers to all these questions before selecting a gallery site.

14. Relative Costs — Initial and Operational

No matter how attractive a particular site appears from a competitive point of view, the cost of doing business in it may well be a determining factor in deciding upon its suita—bility. Rentals and property taxes vary considerably and certainly influence the cost of doing business. Thus, certain areas and sites will be dropped from consideration once the gallery owner sets a limit on what can be allocated for these expenses.

I like to start looking for a gallery site by determining the dealer's mission and then projecting the anticipated annual sales volume of the gallery after it has been in operation for more than two years. The appropriate annual rental for a facility should be in the order of six to ten percent of this anticipated future volume.

Many landlords of desirable space want a lease which provides them with a minimum guaranteed rental against a percentage of the tenant's gross sales, whichever is larger. These factors should be provided for in the art dealer's pro—jected profit and loss statement. The landlord's percentages typically range from three to ten percent of gross sales, de—pending primarily on the services which are supplied and the desirability of the site.

Not long ago, I helped to negotiate a lease with a land—lord who seemed at first to be demanding a rather prohibi—tive rental. On closer examination, however, we determined that the sales potential of this site was extraordinary, in terms of the high income range of potential clients. We also found that the landlord was willing to finance the bulk of the needed building renovation costs and that he would accept a modest percentage of the gallery's actual sales in lieu of a guaranteed minimum rental during the formative months of the business. These factors made the facility very desirable indeed.

Among the factors adding to the attractiveness of a site is adequate floor space, critical for an effective gallery oper-ation. Thus, when weighing the alternatives, sufficient space should not be sacrificed for the sake of an excellent location, any more than low rentals should be accepted without due consideration of the site's ultimate usefulness. But the final selection will generally represent the compromise between needs and resources. The determination of needed space is discussed fully in the next section.

Within any trading area, several matters may make one building more suitable than another for a new gallery. Each factor may influence the gallery's future success. The rela-tive importance of any particular consideration is largely a matter of judgment. For example, I recently objected to the plans of a client who was about to sign a lease for a gallery facility in a new shopping center in New Orleans. The center was, without a doubt, well located in terms of the type of potential client it might deliver to the dealer. However, the proposed space was much too small, and the proposed second story location was a poor one. The price was right, as was the traffic, but the location and the space were wrong.

Since the choice of building will affect both the initial and also the overall operating expenses, it is wise to consult a real estate broker who is familiar with the relative availa-bility, condition, cost, and suitability of the buildings and building sites in a given area.

Generally, buildings with a recent history of business failure should be avoided, particularly if the unsuccessful ventures were art related. Such locations may have a poor reputation with prospective clients. They may be shunned by those collectors who like to build long—term relationships with a gallery and its artists.

The problem of ambient noise and dirt levels should also be considered. It will be difficult to operate a gallery in an environment where the neighbors or the traffic conditions are excessively noisy or where contaminants are offensive or destructive. Of course, the same comments may be made regarding street crime incidence.

I am often asked by artists and dealers whether I think they should build their own facility, buy an existing building, or rent. If capital funds are limited, it may seem foolish to buy or build. Yet this can be a very desirable course. I work with a client in Nevada who owns a Western art gallery. She started out in a small rented facility. But, after two years of business growth, she and her husband acquired an old garage building which had been unoccupied for some time but was well located for potential tourist business. She worked with an architect, obtained a satisfactory mortgage commitment, and remodeled the facility to accommodate a very attractive gallery plus four rental stores. Income from her new rentals almost covers the mortgage payments plus the taxes. Of course, she also has the considerable advantage of being able to select her neighbors, to say nothing of the appreciation potential of the real estate investment and the tax advantage of building depreciation allowances.

Another client with whom I have worked for some time is Hawaiian artist, Ed Fawcett. He and his wife operated a gallery, primarily to display their own work in an old former residence on Front Street in Lahaina — — Maui's principle town. After several years, he has completely remodeled and expanded this facility, adding not only new gallery space but also three rental facilities. The original and subsequent in—vestments have proven to be sound.

I must conclude that, whenever it is practical, buying or building is often preferable to renting. Certainly, the mid—town New York dealers who purchased their gallery sites in the '40's and '50's have benefitted greatly, since their rentals would be prohibitive today.

The same considerations hold for artist's facilities which are not primarily used for retail sales. I know several artists in California, Illinois, and New York who acquired property many years ago in which they established excellent studios. Clare Falkenstein, Hans Burkhardt, and Louise Nevelson are good examples. To be sure, their taxes have risen in recent years, but not in proportion to the rentals they would have to pay for comparable studios. And they have had many other advantages as well.

15. Traffic and Transportation

Street—level locations can be particularly desirable for attracting pedestrians to the studio or gallery for early visits. Some potential customers are discouraged from entering a gallery if they must climb a flight of stairs or find an elevator. With a street—level location, the gallery front, signs, and the display windows will stimulate interest and even provide easy identification for return visits. I have worked with an art dealer in Hawaii whose business was rather severely encum— bered by her second floor walk—up location, despite the fact that she had located in what seemed an excellent shopping center. She has now relocated to a ground floor site and is doing much better business.

On the other hand, a well established gallery may find it unnecessary or even undesirable to attract walk—in trade. Certain kinds of studios and galleries may do extremely well even when they are located above the street level or on a side street, in a low—visibility facility. This is particularly true for the highly specialized artist or dealer who is not dependent in any way on casual trade. I have worked with an artist who executes commissions in stone for architiects. Since very few clients ever visit his facility, the convenience of his location is of little importance. But the size of his doorway and his access to strong road beds is very significant.

Except in such special circumstances, a good gallery or studio site should be readily accessible by private and, in some cases, public transportation and should offer conven— ient parking space. These are particularly important factors when potential collectors have the alternative of buying good works from more accessible competitors. Only when an art dealer represents artists whose works are both very desirable and otherwise unobtainable can such issues as accessibility and parking be neglected.

In the case of the new suburban gallery or the dealer who plans to sell a significant segment of works to novice and intermediate collectors, the casual traffic question is much more important. But, the critical site selection issue in such cases is not related so much to the anticipated gross volume of traffic in the general area as it is related to the rate and direction of flow of prospective customer traffic on a given street. Site selection specialists point out that most streets have a "right" and "wrong" side, depending on morning and afternoon traffic patterns, the location of traffic lights, the position of other existing business facilities, and other factors of a geographical or marketing nature. This "right—and—wrong" side concept is also applicable to various segments of shopping centers and for different parts of resort hotel shopping arcades.

Since most art gallery and artist studio sales are conduc—ted in the late afternoon and early evening or on weekends, being located on the street side which has heavy morning and light afternoon traffic would be an error, providing that the dealer, indeed, is seeking substantial business from drop—in traffic. Information indicating the times of heaviest traffic, its direction, and its economic make—up (i.e., customer re—sources as suggested by make of car, etc.) can be obtained for many potential sites from market research firms, newspaper advertising departments, or even from your own personal observations over a period of time.

Except for a few major business communities such as Manhattan, there has been a strong trend across the United States for several generations toward the use of the automo—bile, both for general shopping and for buying of expensive merchandise, including works of art. Consequently, adequate and convenient parking space, whether on the gallery premises, at a general parking lot within easy walking distance of the gallery, or at curb side, is another important consideration in selecting a gallery site. It is useful to advertise the availability of parking space to potential customers. Artists who plan to have clients visit their studios must also consider the issue of parking space.

In certain communities, it has become very desirable to locate a gallery within a fine shopping mall, despite the rela—tively high cost of such space. Thus, the Marjorie Kauffman Galllery has done well in the modern covered mall called the Galleria in Houston. In Honolulu, the fine craft gallery, The Following Sea seems to be flourishing in the world—famous Ala Moana Shopping Center. In such cases, the high visibility and the high income transient and residential foot traffic help to make for significant sales opportunities. The Honolulu shopping center houses two other, quite different galleries, as well. One of these is artist—owned.

16. Renovation and Rearrangement

Most buildings will require improvements and renovation to prepare them for use as art galleries or studios. Buildings which need only a minimum of modification are generally most desirable. In any case, it is wise to consult an architect or builder for tentative renovation plans and cost estimates before signing a binding lease.

A rectangular facility is usually most efficient. This rectangular space should ordinarily have a depth—to—width ratio of about two to one. Ceiling height, floor loading, and other interior factors are considered in the next section. An efficiently laid out, full scale gallery generally requires a minimum overall area of about fifteen hundred square feet. Three or four thousand square feet is not unusual, but, of course, costs a good deal more. Except as a short term ex—pedient, I am seldom willing to agree with a dealer who wants a gallery smaller than fifteen hundred square feet as it is almost certain to prove not really viable.

An area of two thousand square feet is sufficient space for exhibition, office, workroom, storage, and the sales pre—sentation activities with a two—to—four—employee sales operation. Occasionally, in the interest of space and dollar economy, an art dealer will elect to eliminate or drastically curtail all of the activities generally found in an art gallery except for those employed for a joint sales and display area. Such efforts usually prove unsatisfactory. Cramped quarters, poor storage, inadequate private selling spaces can be expec—ted to result in substandard performance.

If the gallery's mission requires a high level of visibility to foot and auto traffic, the problem of exterior signs and their illumination must also be considered. But, many of the finest shopping areas strictly limit the installation of exterior signs. To some art dealers, this is a desirable, prestigious restriction. To others, it means a significant loss of volume. Even where a modest sign is acceptable, limitations on its design, hanging, and illumination should be explored thor—oughly before a final decision is made regarding a proposed site.

The space required for an artist's studio is rather more flexible. Some years ago, Billy Al Bengston did an article for *Art in America* on artists' studios in Venice, California. He found that most of the professionals with whom he talked in his chosen town were using from three to five thousand square feet of studio space. This seems particularly appro—priate for a prolific professional who produces fairly large, unique works. Bengston himself now employs two studios, each containing more than three thousand square feet.

I have met a few artists, however, who manage to create a substantial amount of work operating in relatively cramped quarters. For many years, Joyce Treiman, whose detailed oils are generally large, and whose market is significant in New York and Los Angeles, has worked in a one car garage attached to her home. This is not, however, an arrangement I would recommend. Louise Nevelson's brownstone in lower Manhattan with its four separate studios seems to me a much more satisfactory arrangement. Sam Francis' studio in Santa Monica can accommodate very large works—often exceeding twenty—four feet in length and twelve feet in height.

Facility Planning

17. Identifying Functions

A well planned art gallery or studio should provide a comfortable environment for the people who work in it and for their clients. It should also promote effective sales activities and such other supportive and administrative functions as may be needed to accomplish the mission of the dealer or artist. Too often, artists and dealers fail to carefully analyze their needs fully. Thus, they may squander their resources before opening their new facilities. The results are chaotic and ineffective. If inadequate space is provided for accomplishing each function, or if the space is improperly designed, then that function cannot be performed satisfactorily.

In the planning stages, a pleasing ambiance and an effective gallery or studio design should be the primary objectives. To achieve these objectives, it will be necessary to subdivide the available space functionally. Even the best site will present certain physical design problems. For example, I once worked with a dealer whose new facility was excellent except that he had no show window space. We solved his problem by designing and building two show cases which were attached to the exterior walls and were accessible through the front, via a concealed lock.

18. Private Sales Presentation Rooms

One prime consideration should be to keep certain classes of activities separated. First, an isolated space must be pro—vided for private sales presentations, since, important sales are seldom made on the exhibition floor although they can be lost there. The sales room (or the "closing" room) should be private, comfortable, properly illuminated, and even well appointed. If funds are limited and restructuring of existing doorways, halls, walls, or supporting beams is not practical, suitable modification of existing spaces might be achieved with the use of portable or permanent room dividers. Such a compromise is better than no private selling space at all.

Private sales rooms are used in most fields that require direct contact, discussion, and careful consideration. Thus, the sellers of *haute couture,* rare coins and stamps, good furs, commercial real estate, and the more expensive new auto—mobiles, all utilize private sales presentation rooms. They are variously called private salons, closing rooms, private galleries, etc. During the course of the sixties, they became a standard feature in many different kinds of art galleries in the United States.

Whether the facility is a gallery or a studio, whether it is to be used for selling to novices and tourists or to the more sohisticated, advanced collectors, if a private selling space is not first provided and then properly employed, the sales results will be relatively poor. The reasons for this will be discused more fully later in the *Handbook* when selling is considered in detail. On many occasions, I have had the experience of installing a private sales room in an existing gallery or studio. Used conscientiously, it always improves sales significantly.

19. Allocating Space

A full— scale gallery normally requires five major classes of activity areas: exhibition, sales, storage, support, and administration. In addition, some dealers may wish to add a separate shipping and receiving area, a framing or fitting area, and an exhibition preparation area. Most of these activities, in turn require a separate allocation of space; however, it may be possible to combine shipping with receiving or framing and support with the exhibition preparation areas. The total space required for an effective gallery will be influenced by the number and type of activites to be carried on simulta— neously at the gallery as well as by its operating procedures.

The table below illustrates a typical breakdown of gallery space adequate for a three or four—employee facility, with appropriate ratios for the various areas. The gallery layout illustrated elsewhere in this section utilizes slightly different figures predicated on more specialized conditions but main— tains comparable relationships and separations of functions.

Allocation of Gallery Space

Area	Space (sq. ft.)	% of Total Space Available
Public Exhibition Floor	600	30
Private Sales Presentation (2 rooms)	400	20
Storage — Inventory	200	10
Support — Workroom	300	15
Administration Offices	300	15
Miscellaneous — (hallways, washrooms, etc.)	200	10
Total	2,000 sq. ft.	100%

An appropriate allocation of space for an artist's studio might generally require considerably less public exhibition space. However, an additional allowance will be needed for space in which an artist can design and fabricate art works. I find that an easel artist generally needs four to six hundred feet for this purpose — more if models or elaborate set—ups are employed.

An artist engaged in making sculpture, original prints, photography, batik dyeing, potting, or any of a host of other activities will, of course, require considerably more work space. But an artist's requirements for a sales presen— tation room, storage facility, office area, etc. are quite com— parable to those of most dealers. Artists who do their own framing, crating, shipping, etc. will also need adequate space for these functions.

One element often overlooked or underestimated in planning an artist's studio is storage for finished work. Stor— age racks capable of holding more than a hundred paintings are often needed, and artists who work on paper often need twenty or more print cabinet (plan file) drawers for such work.

In a gallery, sales activities are of two distinct types: Floor display sales and private presentation sales. The first requires an exhibition area. The actual amount of space needed here depends on the maximum number of people who can be expected to view an exhibition at any given time and the maximum number of works to be exhibited.

20. The Need for Public Space

Assuming a peak attendance of sixty to eighty people during a special exhibition opening, about six hundred square feet of display space might be allocated in a twenty by thirty foot area. This amounts to an allocation of ten square feet or less per person and suggests that larger receptions are not too practical. On the other hand, the space is quite adequate for more casual viewing and will probably accommodate twenty to thirty wall—hung or free—standing works without over—crowding. Additional wall—hung art works might be mounted on specially placed movable partitions, discussed below.

As a rough, overall guide, the public exhibition area in a gallery should occupy between thirty and forty percent of the total space available. A larger allocation is seldom justified unless the gallery's exhibition program has some non—sales function. Public exhibition areas in an artist's studio seldom require much more than twenty percent of the space available.

In some galleries, where space is adequate, it is wise to allocate a certain segment of the public exhibition space for a semi—permanent exhibition of works by a number of gallery artists and a separate segment of the space for solo exhibitions. I find that, through the use of movable partitions, it is possible to vary the relative size of such segments to accommodate solo exhibitions of different sizes.

An interesting practice has developed in recent years in some galleries of displaying a handful of works by each artist represented in the gallery on a semi—permanent basis. Thus, the Circle Galleries will systematically show three to six works by an artist in a three—sided cubicle devoted solely to that artist's work in each of its facilities. This space remains dedicated to an artist even during another artist's solo exhibition.

Of course, there are some art dealers as well as operators of what I like to call "picture stores" who will intentionally overhang their public spaces. I know a reputable graphics dealer in the SoHo in lower Manhattan whose exhibition space is filled from floor to ceiling. Another fine art dealer, located near my own home in Brentwood, follows the same approach, interspersing works of different quality, price, and esthetic interest. Craft galleries seem even more susceptible to overloaded exhibition spaces. As a result, public exhibition spaces often become high—cost storerooms. I strongly object to this practice, and I cannot find any evidence that it leads to increased business.

Only a fraction of a dealer's or artist's inventory should be exhibited at any one time. Showing too many works gives a studio or gallery an unsightly, cluttered appearance and tends to confuse potential collectors. When a client wishes to examine a more comprehensive selection of some artist's work, or when the seller sees that this is appropriate, a special sales presentation appointment should be arranged. This will give rise to the second, and more important, private phase of sales activities.

21. The Need for Private Sales Space and Storage Space

Sales presentation rooms should be located in an area away from the more heavily trafficked sections of the gallery or studio. Ideally, each room should be one hundred fifty to two hundred square feet in area—large enough to hold a salesman, two or three clients and the necessary furniture and fixtures for showing the artist's or dealer's art works. The gallery layout shown in this *Handbook* employs only about one hundred seventy square feet per presentation room and still allows ample space in which the salesman may move around plus sufficient depth for perception of most two and three dimensional art works. If larger groups of customers are anticipated or if space is available, another thirty square feet might be allowed.

Art work not on display should be stored in a nearby storage room accessible only to gallery personnel. A two hundred square foot area will adequately hold a variety of such works. Oils and acrylics,whether fully—framed or only on stretchers, should be stored vertically in racks designed to prevent more than one or two works from leaning against another work. This can be accomplished with judiciously placed braces and standards. I like to use corrugated card—board in addition, to keep abrasion at a minimum. I also like to carpet the bottoms and the side braces on these racks to further reduce potential damage. Carpet shop remnants are very suitable for this purpose.

Prints, drawings, and art photographs should be stored flat in specially designed cabinets with sliding drawers, in blueprint or plan files, or in solander boxes. Drawers should never be overloaded as this can cause damage to expensive original works. Since prints can be seriously damaged if they roll up at the edges and catch on the inside top of their drawer,

I generally use a strip of heavy mat board to cover the top of the print pile in each drawer. Many sellers of expensive reproductions individually pre—package every signed and numbered print before shipping it off to their retail outlets. While this increases the need for drawer space, it reduces damage. I find that art photographs and serigraphs are easily scratched. They should be stored with a protective covering.

Wide variations in temperature and humidity can also be damaging to canvasses and fine, handmade papers. A separate, completely closed storage room permits economical handling of both factors through installation of appropriate heating, air conditioning, dehumidifying, and other control equipment. A uniform temperature of 68°F. — 72°F. and a relative humidity of fifty percent is generally recommended to avoid deterioration of the stored works.

Three—dimensional objects, including sculpture and many craft objects, are best stored in crates or in corrugated cartons, designed to keep out dust and to prevent damage from abra—sion or impact. These crates and cartons may be held on shelves or stacked one on another, depending on their size and weight. Of course, they should be carefully placed to minimize breakage and abrasion, and they should be clearly identified for easy access.

In fact, all art works should be carefully identified before they are stored, and an index or storage plan should be main—tained showing exactly where everything has been placed. In a good storage facility, it should be possible to find and re—move a work quickly and easily without endangering any of the stored objects or exasperating the seller at a time when emotional control may be very critical.

When certain extremely valuable works are being stored, the facility may require a fire—retardant, walk—in safe. Such equipment is expensive but often justified. Also, off—premise storage in a bonded warehouse can be an appropriate practice for economically holding works not currently needed, but the dealer should carefully inspect a proposed facility and identify all the charges (including the "in—and—out" charges) before placing works in public storage. In major cities, such as New York, Chicago, and Los Angeles, specialized art transportation firms offer excellent storage facilities. A new do—it—yourself trend has developed which provides private locker space at quite modest costs, but I would hesitate to use such facilities for storing valuable works unless I was very certain that good security was provided.

22. Using the Workroom & Framing Space

A workroom is needed in which works may be prepared for shipment. The room may also be used for a variety of other useful purposes, including the storage of tools, office supplies, crates, pedestals, and shipping materials, and for the temporary storage of works arriving at or leaving the gallery or the studio. Approximately three hundred square feet of workroom space will accommodate a work table, plus tool and supply cabinets, wall shelves, mat boards, glass, moldings or assembled frames, shipping materials, etc.

Where space is at a premium, certain storage materials such as corrugated cardboard and wrapping papers may be stored in a rack over the work table. Heavier objects may be kept under the work bench. A covered container should be employed to safely store dunnage materials such as excelsior or foam pellets. I generally store easily mislaid tools on peg—boards on which their outlines have been traced. This en—courages people to return the tools to their proper place.

Many art dealers and artists have discovered that they can do a fair amount of their own custom framing using only a modest space and investment in framing equipment, by employing the services of a "chop" service. This is a frame fabricator who sells, generally at wholesale, a variety of wood and metal moldings, mitred to size, and even pre—assembled. Some of these organizations also furnish a wide variety of framing accessories including strainers for the backs of sec—tional metal moldings, liners, mats cut to required inside and outside dimensions, and even fabric—covered mats. By using such services, dealers and artists can minimize floor space needed for framing as well as the investment required for custom framing since their own functions are thus reduced to mat cutting, glass cutting, and fitting works into frames. In some cases, even mat and glass cutting can be eliminated. Some of the larger nation—wide molding and "chop" firms regularly advertise their services in such publications as *Decor* and *Art Dealer & Framer.*

23. Administrative Space

Sufficient office space should be available for adminis—trative and clerical functions. An average of seventy five square feet per employee will generally prove quite adequate. However, if the artist or dealer plans to do advertising layout and publicity, catalog design, mailing list maintenance, and extensive direct mail programs within this facility, additional room will be needed.

If possible, a gallery director should have a private office of one hundred fifty to two hundred square feet for privately conducting business with selected clients and artists. Where it is needed, this office may double as an alternate sales pre—sentation room. There is an unfortunate tendency in the art gallery field, as in many small businesses, to overstate both the size and the grandeur of such a private office. Office facilities should be fairly modest in size and in decoration.

24. Incidental Spaces

The gallery or studio layout should provide for at least one toilet and lavatory, a drinking fountain, cloakroom or rack, and heating and air—conditioning equipment. As mentioned earlier, air—conditioning is desirable to prevent deterioration of works. At the same time, it is a stimulant to business and to employee morale during warmer months. Sometimes air conditioning and heating equipment can be mounted on a roof or in some other off—premise facility.

It may be advisable to plan for a separate service entrance. A truck—high loading dock leading into or nearby the work—room will be particularly convenient if any significan amount of freight—forwarding is anticipated. Most delivery trucks in this country are designed to accommodate such docks.

In some cases, future space needs may be anticipated before plans are completed and the final layout is designed. Excess floor space, intended for public area expansion or for added private sales rooms, may either be screened off or em—ployed for temporary storage, or it may be used as extra work space. Some leases provide that the artist or dealer gets first option on additional building space as it becomes available. New buildings may also be designed with adequate founda—tions and footings to permit later additions.

25. Decor, Furnishings and Fixtures

In order to do an effective job of space allocation, the size and placement of furnishings, illumination, and equip—ment must be considered carefully. Although the total cost of decorating a gallery or a studio will vary according to your individual taste and policy, an outlay of $12 – $15 per square foot constituted a good average figure in 1978 when this *Handbook* was written. Since this is a sizeable expenditure, the services of a professional store planner might well be sought, especially if the gallery owner or artist is unfamiliar with decorating techniques, materials, and subcontractor sources and costs. Idealy, this planning will be done for a fixed fee and will include detailed written plans and specifi—cations plus supervision and coordination of the work.

All furnishings should blend with the gallery or studio decor so that the overall impression is consistent with and appropriate to the display and sale of fine original art. This includes careful attention to the coordination of textures, materials, colors, floor and wall coverings, and window decor. If necessary, private sales presentation rooms should be cur—tained or draped to assure against intrusion.

Decor in a gallery or studio may take one of two basic alternative approaches. Some facilities for showing and selling art are both brightly colored and boldly illuminated. For example, the Grace Borgenicht Gallery in Manhattan uses abundant floodlights, light—colored walls, and light—colored floors to create a crisp, if cool, contemporary atmosphere in which art is easy to encounter. The feeling is immaculate, bright, and uncluttered.

The opposite approach is employed by Wally Findlay in his galleries in such communities as Chicago and Beverly Hills. It involves the use of dark wall and floor coverings and soft textures, combined with carefully placed spot lights to create a rather striking, extremely dramatic effect. The best lighting in the facility is reserved for the works themselves, and it has a rather theatrical quality which, when it works best, contains suggestions of an almost religious nature.

I like to use the bright, open approach in situations where the general gallery or studio ambiance might otherwise seem a bit gloomy. Thus, a studio that is located on a dark corridor or at the top of dimly lit stairs should be bright and airy. The principle problem with this emphasis is that some art works need warm background colors, soft textures, and very dramatic spot lighting. For this effect, darker, earth toned settings work best. A good compromise consists of a brightly illuminated, light colored public exhibition area, coupled with more warmly decorated private sales rooms.

On one occasion, I worked with a designer who used warm floor colors and textures, combined with ivory walls and broad floodlights to produce a public exhibition space which is both warm and bright. From time to time, the dealer switches from floodlights to spotlights to dramatize certain works in this facility.

26. Gallery Equipment

A new, full–scale gallery operation will require the following furnishings:

— Office desks, with and without typewriter stands. A convenient size is 60" by 32".

— One chair and desk space for each full–time employee.

— Filing cabinets, four or five drawers, letter size.

— Bookcases or over–desk shelving, if space is at a premium.

— A large work table, about 4' x 8' for the workroom.

— Another table, about 3½' x 6' should be provided for any presentation room where original graphics and drawings are shown. Two unframed 30" x 40" works can be con– veniently displayed side by side on this table.

— An auxiliary table on which other graphic works can be placed temporarily is also useful in the sales presentation room.

— Any room which is used to show framed works should also contain a display easel of a kind illustrated in this chapter.

— Comfortable easy chairs are recommended, rather than sofas, for sales presentation rooms.

— A modest table and chair or stool should be available in the storage room to facilitate filing, preparation of sales presentations, and study of works.

- The print cabinets may also be provided with useful table tops.

- An upholstered bench might be provided in the public exhibition area to permit temporary seating for two to four visitors.

Basic operating equipment for the gallery includes tele—phones, typewriters, an adding machine, a duplicating or copying machine, a slide projector, standard width four or five—drawer filing cabinets with locks, and a medium sized, fire—proof safe. One filing cabinet should be fire resistant to protect valuable records. The safe should be equipped with drawers, a money chest, and shelves, so it can be used for storage of certain valuable papers, as well as money.

The workroom should have a portable fog or spray type fire extinguisher, a metal tool and supply cabinet, and metal or wooden shelving. Multiple tier, floor—to—ceiling open section shelving is strong and conserves space. Such shelving should include a bottom shelf starting near but off the floor plus two other shelves. The tallest of these three shelves should be closest to the bottom. Dust may be kept out of this area by provision of a floor—to—ceiling canvas or poly—ethylene dust cover, manipulated with pulleys. A sail—maker or awning fabricator will design, build, and install a canvas cover, but a handy person can fashion one out of a polyethylene painter drop cloth readily.

27. Conveniently Hanging Two–Dimensional Objects

The traditional method of hanging a framed picture or other two dimensional objects in a home or office involves the use of nails and hanger hooks. But this system is rather time consuming and not very flexible for a studio or gallery. It also creates unsightly pock marks on walls. A variety of approaches and devices have been developed for coping with this problem.

Probably the least satisfactory of these methods involves the use of peg boards of the kind employed commonly in hardware and drug stores for displaying notions. Special hangers are available from suppliers of store fixture accessories which fit the evenly spaced holes in these peg board panels and permit hanging of objects in a variety of locations with relative ease. Of course, the boards and their holes are quite unsightly. I have visited some art galleries and artists' studios where an attempt had been made to resolve this problem by covering the board with a coarse textured fabric such as burlap or hop–sacking. This is fairly satisfactory since the hangers can be fitted into the peg board through the fabric, but it is only suitable in a very informal setting. It works particularly well for displaying many objects in craft galleries.

An older method of eliminating the need for putting nails in walls involves the use of a molding near the ceiling from which hooks may be suspended. Traditionally, these "S"– shaped molding hooks were connected to similar hooks with picture wire and these assemblies are used to support the art works. The wires are rather unsightly and some artists and dealers have employed relatively transparent heavy duty fishing line instead.

In Los Angeles, the people at the Ankrum Gallery use a system of rigid metal rods, hooked at the bottom and bent at the top to fit over the molding. This system is not "invisible," but it has the advantage of being quick, convenient, and rather inexpensive. Of course, the rods can be painted the color of the wall to make them less visible. Ms. Ankrum uses rods of several different lengths to accommodate works of different heights. Two rods may be used to support heavier works.

A simple improvement on this method involves no hook at the bottom of the rod. Instead, the lower five inches of the rod is threaded, and a wing nut is then assembled to the threaded portion. This nut can then be rotated up or down the hanger rod to provide a fine adjustment which might not otherwise be available. The picture wire on the back of the art work is then hooked on the wing nut.

Probably the best designed picture hanger rod is the patented device, custom fabricated by Ken Lynch of Wilton, Connecticut. The Lynch rod uses a molding hook at the top of the rod that is custom fitted to your own molding shape. The rod itself is square in cross–section rather than round and carries a slide which provides fine variable adjustments and a simple self locking mechanism. The bottom end of the rod is rubber tipped to protect walls and canvasses. With this system, I have seen complex solo exhibitions, of thirty works or more, which might otherwise have required as much as two days to hang properly, arranged and hung in a matter of less than ninety minutes.

The Louis Newman Gallery uses the Lynch rods in a most ingenious way. They had a cabinet maker mill out a special hanger molding for them which is connected to the wall by spacers placed twenty four inches apart so that the back of the molding stands almost an inch away from the wall. Then, the hanger rods are hooked on to the back of the molding rather than the front. This, of course, reduces the visibility of the rods rather considerably.

Alternate Picture Hanging Systems

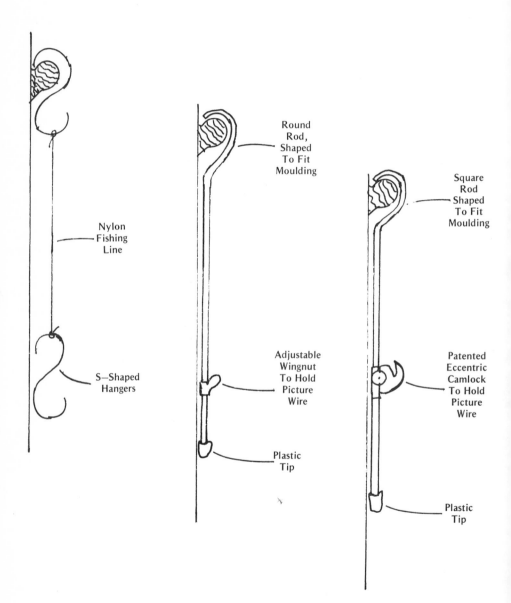

Nylon Fishing Line

S—Shaped Hangers

Round Rod, Shaped To Fit Moulding

Adjustable Wingnut To Hold Picture Wire

Plastic Tip

Square Rod Shaped To Fit Moulding

Patented Eccentric Camlock To Hold Picture Wire

Plastic Tip

28. Building an Exhibition Easel

The device employed for displaying art in private sales rooms should not be an easel of the type which is regularly used for painting an art work. Such painting easels require considerable manipulation. An exhibition easel must be easier to use. More properly, it might be a specially contrived display easel consisting of an "A" frame, built of plywood, and inclined about sixty degrees above the horizontal plane.

Any artist or dealer who is handy can build a display easel. If not, you may have one fabricated by a carpenter or a cabinet maker. The "A" frame should have two sides, like a sandwich board. The entire easel may be mounted on casters so that it may be turned or moved out of the way when it is not needed. On one side, a ledge should be located approximately thirty inches from the studio or gallery floor. A similar ledge on the other side may be located closer to the floor to accom—modate larger works. The easel's ledges should locate the center of attention of most works just a little above eye level of the seated visitors. The entire framework may be covered with a neutral carpeting to serve as an inobtrusive background for framed or unframed works.

A client of mine in Albuqurque built a modified version of this easel for the sales presentation room of his own art studio, confining both ledges to a single side of the easel. Another client with a difficult front—to—back viewing pro—blem designed a couple of hinged ledges which hang on his studio wall and serve the same function as the portable easel. An alternative display easel has been fabricated for some art dealers out of quarter inch acrylic. Even though this is a very modern looking material, it has the defect of being none too strong, and it is also quite susceptible to scratches.

29. Signage

If one singular facility—designed shortcoming consistently pervades most of the galleries and studios I have visited in the past twenty years, it is inadequate signage. Dramatic artists, dancers, and musicans like to see their names in lights. But, the most flamboyant visual artists tend to shrink at putting up even barely adequate signs. Apparently, if they think about the question at all, they feel that good signs are "pushy." I cannot agree. I feel that artists and, of course, art dealers should constantly remind their visitors where they are and what they are looking at.

In a well designed gallery, I would expect to find at least one well illuminated, clearly visible, legible exterior sign with the full name of the gallery. The sign might be internally or externally illuminated. I hope also to see some sort of sign telling me what is going on inside and encouraging me to "come on in." Once I enter the store, I would like to see, once more, a legible, dignified sign which tells me where I am and that I am welcome. In an artist's studio, it is sometimes appropriate, particularly if strangers are expected, for a photo of the artist at work to be prominently displayed. If this is a good photo, it will give the client some idea of the artist's appearance. This could be very useful at a crowded reception or studio sale. In a gallery, I like to see the gallery's name and logotype on every card identifying each of the art works on display so that I am constantly reminded that I am in the "ABC" gallery, if that is where I am.

When a special exhibition is in progress, a temporary sign or banner should explain whose work is on display. If the show is a group exhibition, the entire group or the theme shculd be identified. At a solo exhibition, a client of mine once made a blown—up photo of an excellent review and mounted it on card stock for placement in the gallery window where many pedestrians stopped and read it from top to bottom. This is an old show business stunt, but it works, and it is very appropriate to the best interests of artists and art dealers.

I recently had occasion to meet with a dealer/client whose wildlife art gallery regularly suffers from a sharp drop in business volume annually during late Spring. We worked out a large, temporary outdoor banner announcing a sale on cus—tom framing. This simple sign produced increased traffic and business volume (including increased art sales) sufficient to erase the business loss.

A Typical Art Gallery — Just Under 2000 Square Feet

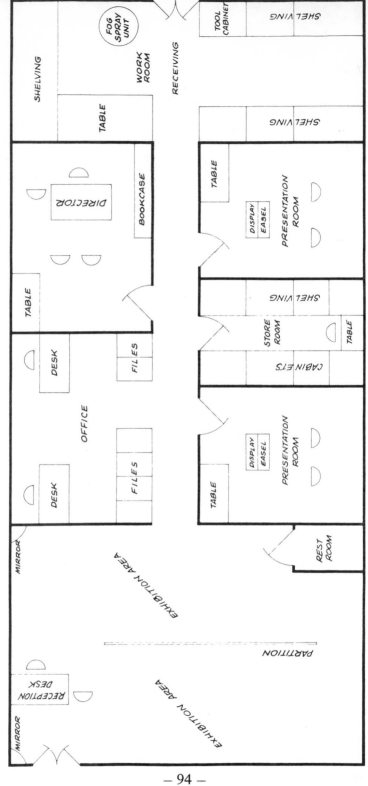

30. Developing a Scale Layout

A carefully planned layout is essential to the operational success of a gallery or studio. While such work may be per—formed by an architect or a store designer, many artists and gallery owners will want to work out the initial phases on their own. Good preliminary layouts along the guidelines offered below can save time and money and can assure that the final result is practical as well as pleasing. In any case, the following layout and design criteria should be observed by anyone planning to work in a studio or operate a gallery.

Flow of traffic within the facility is an important consid—eration. It can be simulated by means of flat scale models or templates which will show the size and location of movable walls, equipment, and furnishings, as well as the adequacy of aisles, placement of fixtures, lighting, workspaces, and acces—sibility. Templates may be prepared in various ways. They are easily constructed from index card stock, Bristol board, acetate, or from other durable materials. Some templates may be purchased from blueprint or art supply houses in the form of cut—out plastic, pressure—sensitive stencils, or as part of a layout planning kit.

The templates should be carefully scaled to match the layout drawings, reflecting the relative sizes of equipment and furnishings as they will be employed in the available gallery or studio space. Since these elements are basically all rectangles, they are not difficult to make. In designing a template for a chair and desk, space should be included for the rectangular area in which the chair is located, including space for pulling the chair back. So, too, in preparing a tem—plate for a print storage file, space should be provided for pulling the drawers fully open.

Before the templates can be used to establish the best arrangement and traffic flow pattern, a properly scaled layout of the proposed studio or gallery floor space should be drawn. Quarter—inch graph paper (sometimes called quartile paper) may be used for such a layout as it provides a handy scale: one—quarter inch equals one foot. Blue print supply houses also sell drawing paper with "fade out" blue lines scored eight to the inch. Again, every inch stands for four feet. So each small square here represents a six inch square. On such a drawing, a plan view of a man or woman would occupy something less than one inch in width.

The basic floor plan layout should indicate the location and dimensions of all permanent structural features of the proposed studio or gallery. These should include: exterior and interior bearing walls and posts, windows and doorways, doors (including their swing), utilities, power and telephone outlets, fuse boxes, heating and air—conditioning equipment, lighting and plumbing fixtures. Any proposed structural additions or modifications, such as new permanent, non—bearing interior walls or partitions to provide work or display areas may be represented on the layout with colored or with broken lines. Sometimes, light and air fixtures are shown on a transparent acetate or mylar overlay after the basic layout has been completed.

After the basic layout has been drawn, the scale model furniture, movable partitions, and equipment templates should be tried in as many arrangements as are needed to identify the most functional arrangement. They can be attached to the basic layout with doubled—backed, pressure—sensitive tape, available from most stationery and art supply stores.

Once a tentative plan has been formed, traffic flow should be simulated on the layout around the templates of furniture and equipment. One might even test traffic flow by moving scale model people through the layout for various anticipated activities, such as exhibition openings, tours, lectures, and sales presentations. In some cases, it will be useful to construct a scale model elevation view of certain areas such as exhibition walls. This can be very helpful for determining whether overhead light fixtures will or will not cast shadows of spectators on the work.

Two factors of importance in planning a studio or gallery layout are the need for privacy and the need for accessibility of the various areas to the people who will be using them most often. Confidential areas, such as sales presentation rooms, private offices, workrooms, and storage areas, should be out of the general public areas of the gallery.

The appended drawing illustrates a gallery layout suitable for a full scale, three or four employee operation. Privacy, accessibility, and overall efficiency are all provided. Furniture, equipment, walls, and doorways have been indicated.

For the convenience of the gallery's clientele, the exhibition area is near the main entrance. Note that double doors are indicated, wide enough to accommodate even rather large works. A reception desk is also located so that it is immediately accessible to visitors entering the gallery. Carefully placed curved mirrors, obtainable from supermarket supply dealers, are located in the exhibition area to permit a clear view of the entire area from the reception desk. These mirrors offer a means of exerting visual control and supervision over activities in the more remote sections of the display area.

A non—bearing movable partition is shown which divides the exhibition area into two smaller rectangles. This partition effectively increases the available wall space for exhibition of works. Other locations for partitions are possible for further increasing the available wall space. For example, several four foot wide partitions might also be placed along certain of the permanent walls at six or eight foot intervals to create a series of three—sided cubicles for showing works of common inter— est — — by a single artist or on a single theme.

Movable partitions may be of several kinds. I have a client in Las Vegas, Nevada whose art gallery is rather high— ceilinged. She employs scenery flats for increasing her wall space. They are made by nailing square moldings and center braces to the backs of four by eight plywood panels. Instead of attaching the panels to form a straight line, she has them connected to each other with door hinges and set at oblique angles of one hundred and twenty to one hundred and thirty five degrees. Each pair of panels is further secured with braces temporarily nailed across their tops. This is a very flexible and ingenious arrangement.

A somewhat more elegant, but still fairly inexpensive and highly flexible system was designed for the Louis Newman Galleries and is interesting. These panels are only seven feet three inches* high by four feet wide. They are covered front and back with a vinyl coated fabric. A channel at the top of the panel accommodates custom designed Lynch hanger rods. Each panel has two flat feet which extend approxi— mately twelve inches in front of and behind the panel. These feet are made of brushed metal about a quarter inch thick and four inches wide by twenty inches long. They are welded to rods which run vertically up into the panels providing enough stability so that the partitions are truly free—standing.

* *Some building codes prohibit movable panels which are taller than seven feet.*

Twenty partitions provide one hundred and sixty feet of linear wall space — — enough to accommodate about forty good–sized art works in a wide variety of easily arranged configurations from the straight line shown and the cubicles discussed above to more complex patterns, including Y's, X's, and triangles.

In the illustrated layout, the offices are centrally located, providing ready access to the rest of the gallery. One of the sales presentation rooms is reached through the main office area; the other can only be entered from the back hallway. This provides maximum privacy for sales presentations.

The storage room is located adjacent to both sales pre–sentation rooms and near the offices. Because of its location, sales people can obtain additional works readily if they are needed during a presentation. The storage room in this layout consists of two sections: a general storage area equipped with a table and chair and large filing cabinets and a security storage section which can only be entered from the general storage area and is kept locked unless in use by authorized personnel.

The workroom is at the rear of the gallery to minimize disturbance of other gallery activities. It is large enough to serve as a temporary storage area for incoming and outgoing art works and has a wide service entrance for deliveries and shipments. It can also be employed for fitting and assembling frames and perhaps even for mat cutting, but it would be inadequate for a full–fledged frame shop, which would require room for molding, storage, saws, glass cutting, etc.

Once a satisfactory preliminary layout has been drawn up, a final version should be prepared by the architect, designer, or builder. If the gallery owner made the preliminary layout, the designer or builder should be provided with a written description of the layout objectives and any special features which must be incorporated into the final plans.

Ideally, the gallery owner will try to bring an architect or builder into the planning activities at an early stage in order to benefit from this professional's experience with building codes, costs, and projected time schedules for accomplishing the work within a reasonable time period. The architect or the builder may also be used to obtain the necessary building permits and approvals from local authorities.

31. Security

The operators of any retail sales facility must anticipate the possibility of internal and external theft, fire, and van—dalism and take protective measures against these pernicious problems. Some common types of protection are: subscrip—tion to a fire and burglar—alarm system which is installed and monitored by a bonded, outside organization; installation of time locks which identify, through coded keys, who opens a door and when; and doors designed to lock automatically and internally. Strategically—placed mirrors, as described earlier, allow supervision of activities in the exhibit area, while the security storage area should have only very limited accessibility. I often recommend bonding employees who handle valuable art works and significant monetary sums.

Officers of municipal fire departments will be glad to furnish free advice regarding the selection and placement of fire extinguishers. They are also very helpful in explaining how to call in fire alarms and how to best guard against fires. If the fire and police organizations have visited your facility, they can be more helpful in an emergency.

All these security measures should be considered during the gallery layout planning stages so that the most appropriate type of equipment can be selected as an integral part of the layout. They should be operative as soon as employees and an inventory of art works are on the premises. In addition, all art works should receive numerical identification on arrival and records noting their movement in and out of the gallery must be kept meticulously. I like to insist that no art work moves in or out of a studio or gallery except with appropriate paper work. Invoices are excellent for this purpose. Memos tend to get mislaid or discarded.

Burglar alarm systems are employed primarily as protec-tion against intrusion during the night and on non-operating days by unauthorized individuals. The best systems sound a silent alarm at a central office when a window or door is opened or when a light beam or ultrasonic beam is broken. Some systems sound an alarm at the facility. This serves to alert anyone in the neighborhood to the intrusion – sadly, including the intruders. Still other systems are also designed to detect and report smoke or fire.

No professional artist or art dealer can afford wholly to be without insurance. The most useful form of protection is, curiously, often less expensive than many lesser forms of insurance. This is an Inland Marine All Risk Fine Arts policy, available through any experienced casualty underwriter. I am constantly amazed and chagrined at the lack of experience in this field of many otherwise fine insurance agencies, and recently I have been recommending that artists and dealers use the services of one of the specialist firms which advertize in the art press.

32. Zoning

The gallery should be located in an area which is officially zoned for commercial use by the municipal zoning authority. Some communities zone their commercial activities by sub—categories to protect independent, small businesses against encroachment by larger retail organizations. I have seen a few fine galleries which located in industrial rather than commercial facilities and many artists choose to do so.

Occasionally, an artist, a private dealer or artists' agent will decide to locate in a strictly residential area because of the rather private nature of this person's business. If this artist or dealer does not employ signs which are incongruous or prohibited, and does not offend the landlord or neighbors with excessive traffic or noise, such business activities are seldom hampered by regulatory agencies. Thus, a number of artists and private dealers in major communities currently operate successfully in facilities which are not, speaking strictly in terms of local regulations, available for use in commerce. However, since their efforts are not objectionable, they have had no difficulties or complaints for many years.

33. Leasing Conditions

In examining a proposed studio or gallery site, the art dealer should seek evidence that the facility is watertight and weather proof, that ventilation is adequate, that windows, doors, and ceilings are in good repair, that plumbing facilities, including water and waste lines, are in good working order, that heating and air—conditioning equipment are adequate and operative, and that the landlord's future responsibilities regarding such matters have been clearly defined.

Most commercial property is rented on the basis of the price per month per square foot of usable interior space. It is wise to check dimensions after they have been quoted and to refigure prices in terms of the user's own measurements of usable space, since quoted figures are often exaggerated or misleading.

After a lease has been accepted by the artist or gallery owner and the landlord, the artist or dealer can expect to invest a significant sum in renovation and even money in establishing the location in the minds of potential clients. Usually this investment should be protected through an option which may be included in the lease and which permits its extension at the tenant's discretion. Thus, a five—year lease might provide an additional five—year option under the same rental terms. Some lease renewal options provide a formula for escalating the rent if they are exercised. Even so, they are generally advantageous once the artist or dealer is well established in a facility.

34. Illumination

Galleries require better and more flexible illumination than is needed for most commercial facilities. A uniform standard of 100–foot candles at eye level, especially against the display walls, is appropriate. Typically, department stores feature only 60 to 80 foot candles in their display areas. Further, the gallery's illumination should permit an accurate reading of subtle color differences.

Several manufacturers now offer so–called daylight or "full spectrum" flourescent tubes, but these have light dif–fusers and, therefore, are seldom adequate for gallery use. Other manufacturers have produced lines of fixtures for in–candescent spotlights and floodlights which are specially designed for gallery installations. These fixtures can be employed in conjunction with specially designed power–supply tracks to permit easy relocation and regrouping of spots and floods. While such fixtures are more expensive than conventional incandescent or flourescent installations, they provide flexible and effective lighting and are, therefore, well worth the extra expense.

In locating power tracks and light fixtures, the gallery planner must avoid or at least minimize the possibility of undesirable shadows and glare. Viewers standing about 22" before a work on display would inevitably cast shadows on the work if the light fixture were only two feet above and slightly behind their heads. On the other hand, if the fixture were three and a half or four feet higher, the light from the fixture could easily bypass the viewers, casting shadows on the floor. Thus, the ceiling height in the gallery's display area should, when possible, exceed ten feet. This provision generates larger, more useful wall spaces as well.

Some artists and art dealers employ floor—mounted spots and floodlights to produce special illumination for certain works. To do this, one needs a variety of convenience outlets in the facility baseboards and sometimes even in the floor it—self for works which may wind up on portable partitions and free—standing sculpture pedestals.

I often encourage artists and dealers to run tracks for track lighting in a "U" configuration or in a double "U" configuration such that the light fixtures are never more than seven or eight feet apart. Care should be taken to wire such tracks on more than a single fuse or circuit breaker to im—prove the prospect of uninterrupted lighting in the event of an overload.

35. Floor—loading & Wall—loading

Where the art dealer plans to show unusually heavy sculptures, the bearing capabilities of the floor and the wall in the display areas need special attention. Floors are normally stressed to carry only one hundred fifty pounds per square foot, and most walls cannot accommodate objects weighing more than a hundred pounds or so. Thus, special provisions may be needed, including floor and wall bracing.

Varieties
Of
Sales Activities

36. Acting vs. Waiting

As we have seen, art reaches the collector along a wide variety of routes. It may be sold by artists, their spouses, their friends, or by people who call themselves "agents," or "consultants," salespersons, auctioneers, designers, decorators, dealers, gallery directors − − and even by other collectors. Whoever sells an art work, the transaction is almost never a "passive" function, as is the selling of movie theatre tickets or ice cream, where the attendant simply dispenses the tickets or the ice cream and takes the money.

Indeed, one of the primary differences between the mass market and the art market revolves around the fact that most mass marketed goods and services are so completely pre—sold that little or no sales effort, as such, is required at the point of sale. In supermarkets, sales clerks have long ago been re— placed by stock clerks and check—out attendants. In many modern department stores, employees are more often wrap— pers and cashiers than sellers. The selling function in mass marketing situations is accomplished by advertising and other promotional efforts, designed to create demand for a product or to encourage brand loyalities and stimulate purchase urges. But, in the art market of our society, an active effort must be made by a seller — — not simply in advance of the formal sales situation — — but at the actual point of sale. Otherwise, the art will probably not be acquired.

There have been many unsuccessful efforts undertaken by major merchandisers to alter the art acquisition process. As mentioned earlier, probably the most notable failure was the Sears and Roebuck venture of the middle sixties. At rather considerable expense, this giant organization proved — at least to its own executives — — that art does not lend itself well to the relatively automatic sales promotion activities which Sears and others have used for several generations to merchandize hardware, auto insurance, ladies ready—to— wear, and stuffed animals.

Since collectors of art work are attempting, as we have noted before, not to *join* a group through their art acquisi— tions, but rather, to *differentiate* themselves, from the all too common mass, they have a natural, built—in resistance to mass merchandizing methods. Collectors want to meet the artist, talk about specific works with dealers, examine differ— ent works, develop their taste more fully, touch the creative spring from which art derives, quite directly.

They tend to respond poorly to such mass merchandizing activities as mail order or television advertising campaigns and even more poorly to passive sales measures such as self—service sales displays. Many dealers, even more artists, are confused and angered if "the public" does not freely and consistantly woo them. But art must be "sold," it is not simply "bought." The dealer who opens a store near another art gallery, stocks it with works of art which are hopefully different in some respects from those available elsewhere, and then sits and waits for clients to arrive with funds in hand is doomed to almost certain disappointment. Like the process of making art, the process of selling art involves a conscious effort, an attention to detail, and a deep—seated belief that the seller's "product" is truly worthy of the attention of a special seg—ment of society. There may be exceptions, but I have yet to encounter them.

In the remainder of this section of the *Handbook,* the reader will encounter a rather comprehensive listing and analysis of the kinds of selling activities which may be em—ployed in bringing art to collectors. Not every artist or dealer will want to employ every one of these activities. For some artists and for some dealers only one or two methods of selling will be advisable. For others, a combination of half a dozen methods will be needed.

37. Casual Business

To be sure, a good business location which provides a fairly steady stream of highly qualified potential clients is a very valuable asset to the art dealer. Therefore, my friends at Trailside Galleries in Jackson Hole, Wyoming and in Scottsdale, Arizona have been very selective about setting up their gal—leries on the city square in Jackson Hole and in a good corner of a very fine shopping mall in Scottsdale.

They sell excellent Western art, and these attractive loca—tions have enabled them to casually meet a large number of individuals who find this particular kind of art work very much to their own liking. A less interesting or less accessible location would, no doubt, reduce the sales opportunities of these astute dealers. But their remarkable success is only partly related to their fine locations. What happens when a potential client finally reaches their galleries is nothing less than a "one—on—one" encounter. The owner or one of her expert assistants, in this case as in so many others, must take the time to develop the interests of their clients. Sales are regularly made on the floor of the gallery, but much more often, especially in the case of really important transactions, sales are made in private sales rooms. I find that this is true in the cases of all the most successful dealers. As the late founder of the Maxwell Galleries in San Francisco once told me, "Our most significant sales are made under fairly formal circumstances, off the gallery floor."

38. Private Sales Presentations

Since the process of buying art is a rather singular, personal affair, it is best conducted in a private sales room where the casual gallery visitor cannot intrude and where the ambiance is intimate and homelike. The structure of this room and its importance have been detailed in the section on Facility Plan—ning. An artist who wishes to sell art to collectors, like an art dealer, needs a private sales room.

Locating and identifying prospective clients can be done on the gallery floor or in many other public and semi—public places. We will consider the problem of finding and qualifying prospects in the section on selling. But once a qualified pros—pect has been located, this person (plus spouse if appropriate) should be encouraged to make the time for a formal, private viewing of a body of works. Also, such invitations might be extended to certain collectors in advance of an exhibition opening or even to certain casual visitors to the gallery. One might invite someone encountered at a party or at a museum function to come to a private showing. In any case, the artist or dealer who tries this approach will soon realize that private sales presentations to qualified prospects will produce more consistent results than any other form of sales activity.

In the section on Selling, we will examine in detail pre—cisely what happens in a private sales presentation including methods for focusing attention on specific works, heightening interest, identifying and handling problems and objections, and closing sales. Such methods may be employed in any sort of sales activity, but they are best used in the private sales presentation.

One special variety of private sales activity occurs when a client is seeking a commission to create work that does not already exist. Whether the artist is interested in portraiture assignments, in murals, or in major works for public places, the sales presentation will usually take place in the client's home or office and generally involves the use of a portfolio, discussed elsewhere in this *Handbook.* In these cases, we generally are seeking, during the course of the presentation, for an opportunity to submit a proposal rather than an out— right sale. The issue here is one of interesting a client in assigning you or your artist to do something that does not exist. This can be done best when the client first has a clear picture of the artist's abilities and interests as exhibited in the portfolio, plus a clear picture of precisely what work is under consideration. This statement of objectives, methods, etc., is the purpose of the proposal.

39. Private Sales Parties and Benefits

Quite a different kind of sales activity is the sales party. This form of sales activity, which seems to have originated in the housewares field in the Twenties, and has been carried out with great success by the Tupperware Company, works very well as a device for selling art works of a wide variety of price ranges and of many levels of sophistication. I know a young, relatively unknown artist in Southern California who is supporting herself in some comfort on the basis of the private sales parties which she and her husband conduct per—iodically. I also know a private art dealer in Manhattan whose primary sales activity is a monthly, rather elaborate sales party.

Generally the artist or dealer finds a willing host or hostess. This may be a relative, friend, or collector who wants to help, or it may be the program chairman of a church or synagogue auxiliary or the director of funding for some worthy cause. The party is usually held in a private home at a particular time and place or in the social hall of a church or organization and those invited are friends of the hostess or members of the organization. Unlike a gallery exhibition or studio sale, the art works shown at a sales party are or seem to be available only for a fairly short time span. They are not all exhibited at once. Instead, the invited guests are seated and shown works one at a time as at an auction. They are told a little about each work as it is shown, and they are encouraged to select those works as they are shown which interest them most. Prices are announced in a review at the end of the showing. Of course, this procedure is a small—scale variant of the famous annual Cowboy Art sales, where potential buyers view the works, have dinner, and then vie to be first in offer—ing to buy a particular work.

In general, private sales parties should not be set up for large groups. Twenty is a good—sized group, but thirty can be rather unwieldy. Each guest should be supplied with a note pad and pencil on which to mark the names of those works which are of greatest interest. They may later wish to circle the items which they wish to acquire, put their name and address on the reverse side of the card and turn it in with a check. If two or more people want the same unique work, they may toss a coin or draw lots to determine who gets this work. Of course, more than one person may acquire a mul—tiple original work.

The key to the private sales party is the feeling that the offerings are indeed special and worthy of interest and ac—quisition. I once worked with a Guatemalan folk craft dealer who has developed his private sales parties to a rather highly sophisticated level. He often sets up parties for groups of potters and weavers and others who are in a position to appreciate the quality of the works he offers. He will generally show slides of the villagers making their ceramics, weaving their fabrics, using their dance masks, etc. This part of his presentation requires thirty to forty minutes. The presenta—tion of objects takes another thirty to forty minutes, and the completion of purchasing transactions rounds out about two to two and a half hours.

As in Tupperware parties, guest participants at private sales parties often ask for permission to conduct their own functions at subsequent times. Of course, many first—time buyers become art collectors and regular clients of the seller.

40. Solo and Group Gallery Exhibitions

The most readily identifiable art marketing activity is the solo or group exhibition. A good deal more is said elsewhere in this *Handbook* about such functions which are commonly used as a means of focusing attention on a particular artist or group of artists.

I know artists whose only sales occur at such exhibitions, and I know dealers whose only sales activity is the exhibiton and the related exhibition opening. Such functions can be useful sources of sales, but they can also drain the resources of both artist and dealer. I feel that over—emphasis of exhibitions is really rather unfortunate since they are not the most effective method of stimulating sales.

Essentially, an exhibition is a good attention—getting device. It is fairly easy to get free media time and space for an exhibition. As I discuss elsewhere, some of my clients have had excellent success with publicizing solo and group shows and even more spectacular attention arising from their "theme" shows — — exhibitions where the work deals with an interesting or important subject. On the other hand, the dealer or artist who depends too heavily on exhibition pro—grams will almost certainly miss many fine sales opportunities. Exhibitions are expensive and time consuming. They should be used sparingly, and they should never be any more than a significant part of the overall marketing effort.

41. Studio Shows and Sales

Artists will often tell me that their friends and business associates "do not buy art." As a result, they feel that they cannot successfully conduct a studio show and sale. Others have told me that their community is not interested in art. Of course, if this were true a studio show and sale would, indeed, be impractical. Fortunately, I have found that very few people in our culture are without the funds to buy art and that no community lacks an interest in acquiring art works.

The studio show and sale is just about the simplest of all art sales activities. The artist, often assisted by a spouse or a friend, develops a mailing list of friends, relatives, and others using methods discussed in detail elsewhere in the *Handbook*. An invitation is sent to the people on this list and the tele—phone is used to reinforce the invitation.

Most studio sales are weekend affairs. Light refreshments may be served, and potential clients are urged to stop by at any time over a period of hours ranging from mid—morning to early evening. The works are hung as they might be seen in a formal exhibition, and a desk or table is provided on which sales can be written up.

Ideally, I like to use a private sales room even at such in—formal functions to improve sales opportunities. If your own studio is not well located or if it is not suitable for a studio sale, you might wish to borrow a home or another studio. Properly promoted, this sort of activity works well for a wide variety of artists.

I work with an excellent artist who claimed that her early studio sales were very disappointing failures. As her reputa—tion grew and as her own confidence developed, her studio sales improved. She annually sells many thousands of dollars worth of art and her collectors look forward to each event.

42. Contract Sales

Some artists and some art dealers specialize in selling art to business institutions. Others sell to private collectors and to businesses as well. The executives of such organizations may wish to acquire high priced, unique works done by well established artists or they may buy a group of relatively inexpensive works. They may be seeking to simply decorate their walls, or they may have more sophisticated objectives. Major companies such as Standard Oil of Indiana, the Chase Manhattan Bank, and IBM regularly collect fine art. So too, relatively small firms of attorneys, doctors, dentists, architects, and small manufacturers collect art. The savings and loan companies, insurance underwriters, accounting, and real estate firms collecting art are numerous enough that corporate collecting today roughly equals private collecting in annual dollar volume.

Again, finding and selling this type of prospect demands an active sales program — in this case one generally requiring a rather modest investment level — as elaborate showrooms are not needed. Since business institutions buy art more often when they are building a new facility or relocating to new offices, if you wish to sell to such customers, it will be useful to know who is building and who is moving. The periodic construction reports now issued in almost every community (sometimes called the Green Sheet or the Dodge Report) will tell you the details of any building permit which has recently been issued in your area. Building contractors and subcontractors subscribe to such reports as a means of identifying bidding opportunities. Usually the type of building, estimated cost, architect, and responsible party will be identified in these reports. If you see that a certain bank has retained an architect to put up a new branch in a suburb near your place of business, you may wish to contact their project manager. He may tell you that the art for the proposed new facility will be acquired through a certain design firm, and you may then track down the head of this firm.

Once you identify the key party, you should send a letter and a brochure with a request for an opportunity to make a presentation of your work or your portfolio. In some cases, you will find that the designers are working with an unrealistic budget or that they find that your work is not appropriate to this particular installation. In other cases, you will get an opportunity to submit a proposal for a purchase order for a number of ready—made works, or you may even be invited to propose a special custom assignment. Generally, your indi—vidual sales to institutions will be larger in value than your individual sales to private collectors although they may be a bit harder to get, especially at first.

Another good source of institutional sales prospects can come to you through friendly commercial real estate contacts. Realtors often know when a professional firm plans to relo—cate and, once again, you can send a letter plus a brochure, followed by a phone call asking for permission to show your art work to the key person of the firm or agency which is relocating.

Of course, businesses buy art even when they are not relocating or building new facilities. I have a client who makes art in Florida which deals with the Florida landscape and the Gulf Coast. He and his wife have found that system—atically contacting business and professional people in their state results in sales of unique works, multiple originals, and special project assignments. His sales from these contacts have recently begun to significantly exceed his sales to private collectors.

Such sales are often called "contract" sales because they are generally based on a purchase order issued by a company after a presentation has been made. This presentation is often accompanied by a written proposal — sometimes containing a few alternatives. Occasionally, institutions work more in—formally, but they more often award contracts to artists or dealers.

Some agencies will even award contracts for the purchase of art on an open, competitive bid basis. In this case, the institution's buyer will generally invite several artists or dealers to meet with the appropriate planners in preparation for the submission of concrete written proposals, aimed at filling the organization's need for art. Guidelines are generally laid down regarding scale, media, price range or budget, etc. Curiously and encouragingly, the lowest bid is sometimes rejected as inadequate to meet the institution's need.

43. Auction Sales

Art may be acquired at three different kinds of auctions. First, there are the well established art auction houses – firms like Christie's and Sotheby Parke Bernet – which maintain showrooms in a few major cities. These firms will regularly auction a wide variety of fine art, including contemporary art. They can provide a useful secondary market, that is, a market where collectors or heirs may liquidate a collection or sell individual works. Generally, the works offered for sale through such outlets are by well established artists of the present or earlier eras.

These auctioneers will usually offer related works at a single sale: French Impressionists, German Expressionists, Hudson River, Ash Can – a collection of any of these schools may lend itself to a specialized sale – if enough works can be assembled. So, too, contemporary American and European original graphics might be offered. In most cases, this type of auctioneer is acting as an agent for the owners of the works and takes a rather modest fee, such as fifteen percent of the proceeds, when and if a work is sold. Of course, no one can guarantee that an auction sale of a specific work will bring a ready buyer at the right price. But, a system of "reserve" prices is usually available from the better auctioneers to pro–tect the seller against unacceptable losses. Whenever a seller elects to set a reserve price, this usually means that the auctioneer will receive a fee whether the work is sold or not.

While the activities of the major auctioneers are widely publicized and often laced with drama, most artists and art dealers have little to do with them except for certain special–ized dealers in master works who use them as a possible source of supply for their own particular specialty. Thus, a dealer in turn–of–the–century American art might wish to bid on a Thomas Cole if it were to come on the auction market. For this purpose, he might send a sealed mail bid, send someone else to bid at the auction, or even attend himself.

A second kind of sale is offered by the on—going antiques auctioneers. They regularly include art of nineteenth and earlier centuries by artists who are not particularly well established. Landscapes, figure studies, still lifes, and nudes often show up at such auctions. Here the contemporary artist and dealer have very little involvement indeed. Only rarely will such auctions attract collectors or art sellers of any appreciable seriousness. Art in such situations is basically an adjunct of the antique business; although forgotten but worthy artists sometimes are found at such auctions.

On the other hand, a great deal of contemporary art is sold at various kinds of charity auctions. These range in quality all the way from excellent to terrible in quality and legitimacy. Thus, the public broadcasting institutions will often use their own facilities for widely publicized televised sales where the proceeds benefit the institution. I am almost always loath to advise artists and dealers to contribute works to such functions since the organizers are generally unwilling to protect their donors against "dumping" which is the name given to unprotected auctioneering. If an artist donates a work worth $600 (for which no tax benefit is available under the current Federal tax law) and if the auctioneer has no re— serve price system, the work might be sold for a ridiculously low figure, a small net gain to the "good cause" which has neither investment nor reputation at stake, but a destructive publicly—acknowledged loss to the artist.

Even worse, from the artist's point of view are the pro— motional auctions, often held under the auspices of church and synagogue organizations where promoters offer mislabled reproductions, shoddy Asiatic imports, and other forms of *schlock* art on an auction basis. Why heads of fine, reputable institutions, especially religious institutions, allow themselves to endorse such shoddy merchandizing practices, I cannot tell. I know the head of a fine synagogue auxiliary in Westchester County in New York who annually raises a very large sum at an art auction where only excellent, *bona fide* original art is offered. At this function, the artist's interests are discreetly protected by a system of reserve prices. Since legitimate methods and good art succeed at benefit auctions where they are used properly, the shoddy practices of others can only be explained in terms of ignorance and avarice.

Incidentally, it is not unusual for unscrupulous promo— tional auctioneers to "salt" the collections which they offer with a few genuine (sometimes even "important") original graphics so that they can claim to offer "original lithographs, intaglios, and *other* prints," not mentioning that the bulk of their offerings are photo—mechanical reproductions which are essentially colored posters and calendar or magazine quality illustrations, produced at a commercial printing company by the familiar four color, half—tone process.

44. Prepublication/Pre—Exhibition Offerings

If art works are expected to outlast mere man (*vita breva, ars longa*) and if art works actually improve in value over a period of time as artists and art dealers generally maintain, then there is no place in the art world for "clearance" sales or special reduced—price sales of any sort. In the section of this text which deals with pricing art works, the danger of unearned discounts and other forms of price—cutting is con—sidered more fully. At this point, it should be noted that such practices are usually counterproductive since they seldom produce satisfactory sales results and are often harmful to the best interests of both artist and dealer. The very term "sale" suggests merchandize which is not quite right — — left over, soiled, factory seconds, and slow—moving goods are liquidated at sales.

But art collectors often feel very attracted to special offers which *precede* a price increase. A number of artists with whom I work regularly release their original prints and multi—ple three dimensional objects on the basis of an original offer which is available only for a limited time. On a certain date the price will be automatically increased. For example, an original lithograph in an edition of one hundred works might be initially offered at $225 for a period of three months, with the price scheduled to increase to $250 at the end of this period. The price of an impression from this edition might again be advanced to $300 when the remaining portion of the edition has been largely depleted by prior acquisitions. Certainly when only twenty works are still available it would be appropriate to announce an impending price increase as a spur to sales.

Some sculptors will offer the first few bronzes in their edition at an introductory price, increasing the price on a fixed schedule over the life of the edition. Of course, such sales promotion activities presuppose, first, that the art works in question have some sort of ready clientele. It could be most embarrassing to offer an edition at an attractive intro—ductory price where there are very few buyers and even more embarrassing to have a fixed schedule of increases which does not get exercised because the first few works do not sell. A sales offer that fails can be damaging to an artist's ego and to a dealer's stature. Therefore, I recommend this type of sales activity only where the artist has an enthusiastic following of collectors who enjoy the status of "insiders."

Prepublication offers are, of course, the logical and eco—nomic obverse of a discount selling policy. Instead of telling the client to buy works now at a special, reduced price, we are suggesting that the client should buy now before the price goes up. Initially, I felt that this procedure would only work with art works that are produced in some multiple form. I am happy to report that it can be employed for artists who work primarily with unique works as well. Thus, an artist who is planning a studio show and sale or a dealer who is planning a solo or group exhibition might announce a special, pre—exhibition offer to the artist's or dealer's best clients under the terms of which a collector may select a work at any time prior to the public showing at a special price.

Several of my clients have offered a five percent early purchase allowance. One offered ten percent with excellent results. Of course, the collectors were asked to leave the works on display for the duration of the exhibition. But they could not possibly conclude that they were being asked to buy seconds, slow—moving or obsolescent works. Again, such a practice works best where artists have a significant and active following.

45. Special Projects Sales—Commissions

As reported above, in my own rather extensive experience with artists and dealers of many kinds, I have found that approximately half the money spent on art annually in the United States is spent by business institutions of one kind or another. Many directors of business organizations and a fair number of private individuals, as well, need art of a kind which is most effectively made to suit a set of specialized specifications. For example, a bank manager may want works which deal with the geography or history of the community his institution serves. A dentist or psychologist may wish to acquire works which display certain familiar, relaxing, non—abrasive sentiments. A board of directors may wish to exhibit a bust of the company's founder.

In each of these cases, they will probably elect to acquire the services of an artist who will undertake to meet their own particular needs. In the art market such transactions are often called "commissions," although I prefer to call them "special projects," since a commission can mean many other things in business, including the sum paid to an art seller as an incentive for making a sale.

Regardless of what we call them, these transactions involve furnishing art which does not pre—exist. When the art must be "custom—made" rather than "ready—made," I find that the selling process involves a few additional steps. First, as in the case of any art sales transaction, we must identify a qualified prospect − − someone who has a well defined or conscious need for art. Next, in the case of special project art, we must try to develop this "need" to a more full—blown statement. Where will the work be located? What is the ambient traffic, lighting, decor, activity, etc? Does the client have a budgetary allocation? Such things should be discovered before the next, most important, step occurs. This is the preparation of a proposal.

I do not advise any artist or art dealer to ever attempt to offer a presently non–existent work for sale until a formal proposal has been prepared. For artists and art dealers who work with business institutions and for those who wish to obtain portrait assignments, a good looking, well developed proposal is critical. Many art dealers without galleries or other business accoutrements do well because they have designed their professional activities to encourage a large number of Requests for Proposals (RFP's) from architects, designers, and others.

The proposal for a special project will often be delivered in a colorful folder. It will include a letter of transmittal which briefly recapitulates the nature of the proposed project, a budget, which indicates the price, required down payment, estimated start and finish dates, progress payments, and any other significant financial considerations, a rough sketch of the facility, showing the proposed work in approximate scale with relation to its surroundings, and (most important) some sort of preparatory drawing or model of the work to be done. The degree of detail offered in the proposal will be a function of the importance of the project to the seller and the amount of time the artist can afford to make available.

A client of mine, making his first proposal for a pair of murals in the reception area of a large toy company, supplied a simple perspective view of the room with the works indica–ted, plus a scaled–down preparatory water color sketch of each proposed mural. He also furnished a full scale sample detail of the proposed work. A sculptor with whom I work once furnished a fine color photo of a small model of a pro–posed outdoor work of monumental scale. The photo included a mock–up of the adjacent building, the surrounding garden, and even scale–size people and trees. In the photo, the entire scene was dramatically illuminated for the purpose of cap–turing the intended feeling of the proposed work.

When the artist's services are in great demand, it is often possible for the artist to request some sort of payment for preparing a proposal. If this is not the case, I will generally recommend a certain modest speculative investment to get things started. I find that if the talent is there and the client is genuinely interested, the results are worth the effort. I once worked with a very accomplished portrait artist whose works moved up in price from an average of $300 per assign— ment to a range of $3000 to $10,000 in a period of less than a year. At the same time, demand for her work increased significantly. Her two most significant changes in sales activity were the development of a good portfolio, as described in the section on Aids, and the development of an effective proposal presentation routine.

From time to time, an institutional buyer will wish to issue a purchase order to cover the transaction. In this case, the proposal should be written so that it may be quite readily quoted in the client's purchase order. The section on Agree— ments later in this *Handbook* provides a fairly useful outline for a proposal which may be turned into a purchase order.

46. Festivals, Malls, and Expositions

For many generations, American county fairs have pro—vided pavilions where art can be shown, judged, and purchased side—by—side with needle work, baked goods, and even prize heifers. Such fairs are hardly the "proper" ambiance in which to view art. The lighting is usually terrible, the folk—holiday crowd is seldom in a serious mood, and the tendency to equate the efforts of artists with the activities of 4—H Club members can be demeaning, to say the least.

And yet, for many fair visitors, the opportunity to see art is a rather unusual one. So too, for many artists, the opportunity is significant. The idea of the open air or covered mall art festival, which began at the county fairs has spread in recent years to become a major enterprise. In California, Florida, and other states, I have been able to identify a few hundred active promoters who regularly conduct from three to twenty—five short term sales annually. They generally run their functions from Thursday through Sunday, and they tend to operate in shopping centers, malls, parks, and parking lots. I know an operator of a large restaurant in Claremont, Cali—fornia who has an open air art sale of some sort every week—end during good weather near his parking area.

The format of these mall shows or art festivals, as they are usually called, varies. In most cases, the participating artist pays a modest fee to the promoter. This may or may not go partly to the owner of the property and partly to promote attendance at the sale. In addition, the artist is often asked to pay a modest portion of sales receipts to the promoter. When all works well, everyone profits; but when the location or weather is poor, when the offerings are ill—chosen, or when the neighborhood is simply over—run with competitive festivals, the only profit is made by the promoter.

I do not usually recommend that serious artists undertake the rigours and risks of the festival/mall circuits, but for certain artists they have proven very profitable, and for others they have been a good entry point into the art market. For example, there are a number of painters who regularly earn enough each summer at the outdoor Laguna Art Festival in Southern California to support themselves for the remainder of the year. I know a traditional realist artist who earns close to $100,000 annually at a series of carefully selected mall shows.

Although rather low—priced figurative work generally sells best at such shows, hand—crafted jewelry, simple pottery, and highly decorative abstract art also does well, as does some naive art and some craft. The two most critical factors seem to be these: First, the esthetics of the work must be readily accessible to casual viewers. Symbolism, contextual and narrative references, if present, must be simple enough to be quickly appreciated. If deeper or secondary factors are also present in the work, they cannot be relied upon to generate sales as strolling, casual shoppers will seldom take the trouble to relate to subtle cues. So too, subtle design and color relationships may well be destroyed by poor lighting and otherwise difficult viewing conditions. The second factor of major importance is price. The collector who buys art at fairs or festivals is almost always a novice and is seldom prepared to pay prices in excess of a few hundred dollars.

Since I know legitimate artists who are earning significant incomes by touring to various mall shows and festivals, I cannot, to be fair, recommend that artists should avoid such shows altogether. But the return, at best, is usually low in comparison to the time and energy required, and I always urge my own "sunshine artist" clients to get off the street just as soon as they can manage to do so.

One artist with whom I worked had an extraordinary experience in the festival shows. He is handy with wood, and he designed and built a handsome portable display booth, complete with a small lectern—shaped stand on which he mounted a guest book. When visitors admired his rather mysterious—looking paintings, he often asked them to sign his guest book, whether they seemed to be likely buyers or not.

Subsequently, he used a color post—card of his work to invite these people to studio sales and to private sales pre—sentations. His results in the more formal sales situations were considerably better than they had been in the mall since the viewer now had a chance to relate to the works in more business—like circumstances. For him, the festivals became prospecting opportunities rather than sales activities.

A number of publications specialize in reporting on the festival and mall scene. Many promoters advertise in the *Sunshine Artist,* published in Florida and even more advertise in *West Art,* published in Auburn California. Other arts publications such as *Art Week, American Artist, New Art Examiner,* and *Art News* carry a few listings in each issue.

47. Sales by Cooperatives and Museums

There is, of course, nothing illegal or immoral about the sales activities of non–profit (that is, taxfree) instituitons. Such organizations range in size and importance from the Metropolitan Museum with its own international marketing activities, mostly devoted to replicas, reproductions, etc., down to the *ad hoc* alternative exhibition activities of a few relatively unknown artists who have banded together to open a store front gallery.

Even though most states have a special section in their corporate legal codes providing for the incorporation of cooperative societies, artists seem generally to have avoided utilizing this format. Instead they have formed unincorpor–ated, voluntary membership societies. Such organizations are, however, not as efficient or as safe as incorporated non–profit cooperative societies which were originally designed to serve farmers, utility distributors, and many other producers of products and services. A producers' cooperative should not be confused with a consumers' cooperative. The difference is that in the first case the producers band together to reduce distribution costs, combine capital, and regulate their mar–keting activities, while a consumers' cooperative involves customers getting together to improve their own purchasing power.

The voluntary, unincorporated artists cooperatives with which I have worked have seldom sold very much art. Instead, they have tended to open their doors to more artists than they could intelligently and tastefully display. One motivation is that these artists contribute time and money to help cover the expenses of operation. In return, the association usually retains a very small portion of the proceeds of sale – – from ten to twenty percent. This system means that the sales and promotional activities are often inadequate and, in short, that these organizations are little more than self–governed vanity galleries. There are many notable exceptions, of course. The Detroit Artists Market with its professional staff and active sales program is a good example.

If the founders of an artists' cooperative are serious enough to raise the necessary capital, regulate their standards, and employ professionals, they should be able to do as well as any profit–oriented art dealer might do with the work of their members. In other fields, from oranges and poultry to power generation and distribution, the coops have outstripped their more traditional competitors.

48. Direct Response Selling

Selling merchandise or services of one kind or another through catalogues, with the aid of magazine request coupons, and telephone campaigns is as old a sales method as the parcel post and telphone systems themselves. Such giants of the marketing field as Montgomery Ward and Sears and Roebuck found in the nineteenth century that a nicely—illustrated mail order catalogue, coupled with carefully designed order forms would generate sales that were otherwise virtually unobtain—able. Thousands of entrepreneurs, large and small, have turned to a variety of merchandizing schemes — — all of them aimed at selling their goods or services without the aid of stores by reaching potential clients at their homes and offices, via the mail or the telephone.

These methods have been refined in modern times with the development of computerized, highly selective mailing campaigns, sometimes coupled with wide—area telephone campaigns to sell camping equipment, ladies' garments, and insurance, even (very effectively) for soliciting political campaign contributions. Even though the techniques vary, the fundamental idea is quite simple. The seller has a pro—duct or service which has a fairly significant potential clientele. An "offer" of some sort is developed. For magazine campaigns it may be a special introductory subscription rate or a series of lavish prize drawings. A pre—paid direct reply envelope is generally included with the offer letter or brochure.

In some cases, following Sears and Montgomery Ward, a variety of items is offered in the same communication. These items may be related. Thus, the Dover Book people will often offer several dozen book reprints on a particular theme in a single mail packet. So, too, the major department stores will offer a variety of linens or Christmas items in a single brochure. In recent years, the offer letter has often been coupled with a special telephone campaign to spur positive response.

Sometimes, the offers are sent only to a select customer list or to holders of credit cards with particularly good credit ratings. On other occasions they are sent to special interest groups — — the owners of certain models of automobiles or residents of certain neighbcrhoods, the subscribers to certain magazines or to supporters of certain religious, political, or philanthropic causes.

Some offers are sent only to respondents of special interest coupons which have been placed in selected magazines or newspapers, *The New York Times Magazine, The New Yorker,* and many of the high fashion women's magazines are regularly employed by direct response sellers with catalog offers. The ads may also offer a key item such as a bracelet or a sports cap. Buyers will receive the item *plus* a catalogue.

In a well planned direct response campaign, a variety of coupons, media, lists, and offers may be tested and carefully evaluated before any significant money is spent on a sales program. Organizations which specialize in list rentals of many kinds generally are willing to cooperate by renting just a few thousand names from their larger lists for such testing purposes. A selected listing is appended at the end of this section.

These organizations, ranging from list compilers with hundreds of different lists to institutions such as the American Library Association which rents its own list as a fund raising device, are all described in detail in *Direct Mail Standard Rates and Data,* a directory of mailing lists which is organized by subject headings much like the Yellow Pages.

Using this directory, an artist—client of mine once found a list compiler who was willing to rent her a list of all the architects and interior designers in Southern California, together with telephone numbers as well as addresses. My client paid several hundred dollars for this list. She then developed a personalized letter which was sent with a color brochure and followed up with a phone call. In this case, no sales were made by mail or phone — — only presentation appointments were made. But the program worked very well, and my client has developed a series of clients of her own on a basis of this undertaking. Many of them have remained regular sources of assignments.

As for direct response sales of art, as distinguished from such simpler prospecting efforts, a number of firms in the art market have tried these methods, but few have succeeded. In New York, the Martha Jackson Gallery, and in Los Angeles, the Felix Landau Gallery tried circularizing priced catalogues of original graphics in the mid— sixties with rather indifferent success. Landau sent out a series of loose—leaf pages with several works illustrated in black and white on each page. Jackson used a combination of color and black and white illustrations, but usually the pages contained ten or more rather small illustrations. I was told that the offering was sent to old customers and occasionally to architects and de—signers, but I found the offer itself was rather unclear. No order form was enclosed. Terms of sale were not stated. I got the impression that both of these enterprises were being conducted as a part—time endeavor of the gallery staffs. Not surprisingly, the offerings were abandoned in a fairly short time.

On the other hand, Roten Galleries, Associated American Artists, Original Print Collectors, Ltd., and Christie's seem, over the years, to have developed their own direct response sales programs to a highly successful level. Over the past fifteen years, their catalogues have become more professional looking, their order forms and offer letters have gotten clearer, and their method of finding prospects is more sophisticated. Roten regularly publishes a coupon ad containing two rather different images − − one featuring a very well known artist, the other showing an interesting subject. The prospect is asked to qualify his interest by paying a dollar for the cata−logue. This of course, does not cover costs, but it winnows the prospects to a fairly serious group. The catalogue gen−erally contains work of various levels of sophistication and prices vary widely, as well.

Associated American Artists, Christie's, and Original Print Collectors follow similar tactics; although their offerings are quite different. AAA sends out new catalogues about every quarter. Like many direct response sales programs, they seem to have found the means to eliminate prospects from their lists when no purchase is made over a measured period of time.

As you can see, such sales programs require a good variety of works, a fair amount of capital, and a great deal of art sales expertise. I have noted with mounting interest that very few organizations possess these special capabilities. As a result, many such programs fail. In fact, my own dead storage files are filled to the overflow point with direct response sales programs that apparently did not result in adequate sales and were abandoned in the trial stage or shortly thereafter. I have seldom advised a client to undertake such a program since many others, including the one listed above where the artist used her mailing list not for sales but for prospecting, are less expensive and more certain to produce satisfactory results. I believe that only well−financed, experienced wholesalers and publishers of multiple originals are really in a position to utilize these specialized sales methods successfully.

Selected Cultural Mailing List Sources

Addresses Unlimited
  14760 Oxnard Street, Van Nuys, California 91401
    118M Los Angeles Cultural Patrons   213/873—4114

Dependable
  425 Park Avenue South, New York City 10016
    175M Art Connoisseurs   212/679—7160

Dunhill International
  444 Park Avenue South, New York City 10016
    110M Buyers of Art Works   212/686—3700
    220M Museum Patrons and Members
    47M Art Show Attendees
    5M Museum Directors, Curators, Presidents

Fulfillment Associates
  155 Allen Blvd., Farmingdale, New York 11737
    52M Metropolitan Opera Guild   516/249—0860

Names Unlimited
  352 Park Avenue South, New York City 10016
    100M Theatre Guild Members   212/686—2454

Response Mailing Lists
  39 Pine Drive, Park Ridge, New Jersey 07656
    134M Cultural Buffs   212/752—5350

Sales Promotion Services, Inc.
P.O. Box 257, Tiburon, California 94920
    90M California Professionals   415/388—2271
    (Arch., CPA's, Drs., Attys., etc.)

Zeller and Letica
  15 East 26 Street, New York City 10010
    4.8M Artists, Collectors, Critics   212/685—7512
    1.7M Art Museums

See: *Direct Mail Lists—Rates & Data,*
    Standard Rates & Data Service   312/966—8500
    5201 Old Orchard Road, Skokie, Illinois 60076

49. Renting and Leasing Art

Many non—profit art organizations maintain art rental programs. A few very sophisticated art dealers offer art leasing. The difference is highly instructive. An art rental program is generally one in which a museum or cooperative (I know of only one business institution which offers to rent art) furnishes one or more art works for a relatively short time period to individuals or executives of businesses. The works are usually consigned, framed by the artist, to the rental agent, and they are usually not very expensive works. Typically, a work with a retail price of under a thousand dollars is rented for three or more months for three percent of the selling price per month or fifty dollars, whichever is larger. The client must have established credit and agree in writing to return the work in good condition at the end of the rental period. In most cases, a purchase option is included in the agreement. Thus, the rental is really a sort of low obligation trial purchase with the initial rental as a down payment.

Although these programs do, indeed, produce some in—come for both the artist and the seller, the money involved is rather miniscule in comparison to the effort needed to accomplish the sale. I seldom find any real justification for such programs although they are often justified by well meaning administrators as easy ways of introducing art to new collectors. I feel this approach is timid, often fruitless, and involves a high cost of sales if the value of the voluntary sales effort is considered at all. I also worry about how such works are safeguarded and insured while out on rental.

Leasing, or more properly, lease—financing, is really quite another matter. Many corporate executives are advised by their tax specialists that art is a "bad buy" because it cannot be depreciated. That is, a corporation may not recapture any part of its expenditure for art as a business expense as it may depreciate its expenditures for typewriter, delivery trucks, or office furniture.

To avoid the cash—flow implications of non—depreciable acquisitions, some corporate collectors prefer to arrange a lease—financing agreement with a third party. In such an arrangement, a leasing company, or even the selling gallery, obtains clear title to the work from the artist or dealer. It then negotiates a lease with the corporate collector under the terms of which the collector agrees to pay the owner of the work an amount equal to the selling price of the work plus an appropriate interest charge on the owner's investment over a period of three to five years. At the end of this time, when the leasing owner of the art has been repaid the cost of the art plus the interest on the investment, the owner may agree to continue to lease the work to the corporate collector for a rather nominal annual sum. Now lease payments are fully deductible as a cost of doing business, providing that they are not tied to some sort of purchase option. Therefore, lease—financing can be an attractive method for a corporation to acquire art over a long—term period with the federal govern—ment sharing the cost of the acquisition in a form of tax forgiveness, treating the art as if it were a rented truck or computer.

Several art dealers offer such leases as an alternative to outright purchase. From time to time, I have encountered art sellers who thought that this was a powerful selling tool since their competitors did not have it available. However, it is not a significant competitive advantage since any cor—porate collector can arrange a lease—financing agreement with any financial agency which is in the leasing business, providing the collector's credit is adequate. Therefore, a corporate collector can, in effect, lease any art work it wants to lease, regardless of whether a special leasing service is offered by the seller.

A leasing firm in Chicago developed a special art leasing division in the mid—sixties, but quickly abandoned the project when its executives discovered that they were educating clients to an interesting scheme which was readily available from many other sources once it was clearly understood.

50. The "Visiting Fireman"

Early in my career as a consultant to artists and art dealers, I worked out a most remarkable art marketing activity with Margo Leavin, who was one of my first art dealer—clients. While she has since become a major force in the art market, at that time she was a struggling private art dealer, based in her small home near Beverly Hills. Margo, with my help and encouragement, planned a sales trip to Chicago where she stayed in a fine hotel suite for a period of about ten days.

In advance of this trip, she contacted her own friends, and anyone else she was able to get a referral to, who might be interested. She sent letters, made long—distance phone calls, and set up appointments in advance. On her arrival in Chicago, she made additional phone calls. Although she was not then a particularly well—established dealer, her art work included some excellent examples by fine California artists, who were not often seen in Illinois.

Margo Leavin worked hard on this project, not only in Chicago, but in preparation for the trip. One architect, whom she tried to reach, was particularly elusive. His secretary intercepted all calls with a statement that her employer was "in conference." But Margo persisted in attempting to reach him, and he turned out to be the best customer of all.

The trip proved to be a great success. Ms. Leavin sold more art in ten days in Chicago than she had sold in the prior two months in her home city. Of course, she had novelty on her side since the works were all new to this community. She also was able to honestly indicate that her potential clients had only a limited time in which to view the work and make their decisions.

I have recommended this "visiting fireman" activity to many other art dealers and artists over the past two decades. It works with varying degrees of success, depending primarily upon how good the seller's preparation has been, together with such other factors as the quality of the works offered and the quality of the approach made by the "visiting fireman." One of my current clients, who is a private dealer of considerable achievement, regularly visits New York, Dallas, Houston, and several other cities annually on this basis and manages to sell a good quantity of rather high–priced work on each trip. His annual volume would do credit to an art dealer with a much higher overhead.

51. Wholesaling

Any artist who places work with any sort of retailer for subsequent sale to a collector is "wholesaling" that work. Since a wholesaler is simply someone who sells through other outlets, any art dealer who sells work through another art dealer or through a designer is essentially also a wholesaler.

As we noted earlier, the wholesaling activity is still rather new to the art market and a large number of artists and their dealers do not fully understand it or its implications. However, wholesaling is the basis of most merchandizing in the United States, and I believe that it will become increasingly important through the eighties as more artists and others learn to cope with the process.

Not too many years ago, as we have indicated, fine art was sold almost entirely by a handful of local retail galleries, the largest number of which were located in Manhattan. As the market grew and significant galleries were established in many other communities, the need and opportunity for art wholesalers developed quite logically.

Many of the newer galleries are furnished at least in part with an inventory of art works acquired from one of the major whoesalers — — firms like Roten Galleries in Baltimore, Associated American Artists, and Brooke Alexander in New York City, Lublin Graphics in Connecticut, and Fidelity Arts in Los Angeles.* Such firms generally distribute the works of very well known artists, although they also offer works by lesser known artists.

In addition, many of the original printmaking workshops† which developed in this country during the sixties and seventies publish editions by making special arrangements with artists for rights to works which the workshop operators can distri— bute, in addition to those works which they print on a custom basis for artists and their dealers. In the New York area, Universal Limited Art Editions, Elinore Ettinger, and Tyler Graphics; in Los Angeles, Gemini GEL; in Chicago, Landfall Press; and in San Francisco, the DeSoto Workshop: All of these organizations and many more function as wholesalers of art works. In the three dimensional field, the same situa— tion obtains. Such orgainizations as Classic Bronze, located in California; Modern Bronze and Roman Bronze in New York, among others, commission sculptors to create editions which they cast. They then wholesale the finished works to art dealers, paying the artist a flat fee or a royalty.

* *Fine Arts Market Place,* published by R.R. Bowker of New York carries a useful, if not complete, listing of print publishers and wholesale distributors.

†I compiled a rather comprehensive, but still incomplete, listing of original print workshops which appeared in the October, 1976 issue of *American Artist.*

An artist who can paint or draw well can usually learn to make fine original prints. Such artists can then work with a master printer to make editions, or they may work in their own studios on their own presses. So, too, any artist who works in stone or wood can readily acquire the skills to work in clay or wax and can then work alone or with a foundry or work—shop to make bronzes or other three dimensional multiples.

I am continuously confronted with the artist or dealer who wishes to expand the available supply of art works through some system of non—art reproduction. Commercial printers are readily available with offset printing equipment capable of turning out four color process "prints" of the kind generally found in art books, calendars, and posters. A significant industry has developed in this area. Some artists are content to sell reproduction rights to established distributors of reproductions such as the New York Graphic Society or Harry Abrams. Firms of this kind sell works to decorators, frame shops, furniture and department stores. They sometimes pay the artist a flat fee, and on other occasions, they also pay a royalty as well. Few artists (to my personal knowledge, only two in my many years in the art market) make any significant amount of money in this way. The business of selling inexpen—sive reproductions is a risky one; however, many merchants have done well with it. There are significant firms in most major cities who print, frame, and sell reproductions in large quantities for a variety of purposes.*

* Many such firms are also listed in Bowker's *Fine Arts Market Place.*

Art Marketing Handbook

The differences between original prints and reproductions are discussed in the section of this *Handbook* on Business Ethics. Contrary to the wishful thinking of many uninformed artists and merchants, few images lend themselves well to mass reproduction. The color quality is usually poor and the fine points are often blurred. I have never been able to find *any* reason why artists should confuse themselves and their public by numbering and signing reproductions as though they were original prints. Regardless of the high selling prices and low production costs, the wholesaler/publisher of reproductions seldom pays any significant sum to the artist for reproduction rights. An informed, capable artist can usually make a good deal more by finding a way to wholesale real art, including multiple originals.

This is true in spite of the fact that some wholesalers of multiple originals like to buy works for as little as one—tenth to one—twelfth of the expected retail selling price. Of course, many wholesalers are content with a more modest share of sales proceeds.

Here, as elsewhere in business transactions, the "proper" division of the proceeds depends on many different factors. Logically those artists who contribute most to the process should get most. A wholesaler who invests little or no capital and does little to publicize or sell the work is really not entitled to a very large share of the collector's dollar. One who is instrumental in financing and promoting an edition is entitled to more, while a distributor who can successfully sell many editions at good prices in a short time may be entitled to an even larger share.

So too, an artist whose reputation and following make the sale of original prints or multiple bronzes relatively simple should expect more from the proceeds of sale than one who is virtually unknown. Also an image which has broad appeal by virtue of its originality or the depth of mood which it evokes might demand a better price for the artist than a work which is more specialized in its significance.

Like any other legitimate business activity, wholesaling involves a sharing of responsibilities, risks, and rewards. It is not a field of endeavor in which every artist or dealer must participate, but it can be a very useful part—time activity for many artists and dealers, as well as for full—time specialists.

I have a client in the Pacific Northwest who gave up his retail gallery to organize a strictly wholesale facility. He and his associates carry art in several media by a number of first rate artists. They call on dealers and designers in Washington, Oregon, Idaho, and Montana, and they participate in several trade shows annually, as well. This firm has been performing a valuable service for its clients and finds its new endeavors very rewarding. This group has combined its wholesaling function with an excellent framing operation, a combination which is particularly valuable to certain of its clients.

The activities of wholesalers differ from those of retailers in several notable respects. First, they tend to spend more on advertising. Thus, Fidelity Arts produces and distributes a fine color portfolio of reproductions of available works to help promote their inventory. They also advertise works by artists, whom they represent exclusively, rather heavily in the art press.

Finally, like the other specialized wholesalers, together with publishers and art dealers who are in a position to wholesale their artists' work, they participate in trade shows (as does the Northwest wholesaler mentioned above.) Trade shows are quite new to the art scene and deserve special consideration.

In other fields of sales activity, it is a regular practice for manufacturers and their distributors to exhibit new models and current lines at annual or semi–annual displays where the audience is limited to interested retailers. For example, the key executives of the housewares industry conduct a trade show in several major cities twice a year. So, too, the giftware industry has special trade shows in several cities periodically.

For many years, an annual international exhibition aimed primarily at art dealers has been held in Basle, Switzerland each summer. American wholesalers are now heavily repre– sented at this trade show and more American art dealers attend every year, looking for new artists and new sources of supply. The international flavor of this fair makes it parti– cularly attractive.

A newer trade show has been developed in Washington, D.C. which has been held in the spring in recent years and seems to be thriving as wholesalers and retailers learn to use the occasion to buy and sell art works, meet each other, and otherwise extend their own command of their activities. The Washington Art Fair has featured speakers, demonstrations, and other activities to augment the displays. At quite a different level, the Professional Picture Framers of America hold an annual national convention and two or more regional conferences each year in various locations. These meetings are featured by seminars on framing and related topics and are usually also accompanied by a trade show at which wholesalers show art works as well as moldings, matting materials, and other materials of particular interest to framers.

I am often asked what trade discounts are appropriate to wholesaling activities. Although many wholesalers and more than a few artists do not like to talk about it (their reasoning always makes me suspect that they feel there is something reprehensible about wanting to make a profit) the trade discounting problem is really a rather simple one.

We must start by determining the appropriate retail price for the work. Remember that we are talking about sharing the client's money. Once the retail price has been determined, we can allocate a portion of this figure to the retailer. The remainder must be divided between the wholesaler and the artist. In the case of a multiple original which is not made entirely by the artist, we must also consider an allocation for the workshop or foundry.

The appropriate discount policy for retailers is discussed in detail elsewhere in the *Handbook.* It will generally vary between 40 percent and 50 percent of the retail price, de—pending on whether the works are consigned or purchased. I regularly encounter a situation where an artist is represented informally by a retail dealer who develops, sometimes rather casually, an opportunity to sell that artist's work through another retailer. In such cases, artist and the first dealer decide to offer the second dealer a portion of the first dealer's forty percent. This is a poor sales incentive and only works well in the short run. Operating expenses being what they are, a dealer − − whether primary or secondary − − who settles for ten or twenty percent of the retail price will almost always lose money on the transaction. This is not a totally unreasonable situation if it involves accommodating a client now and then, but it will certainly not work in the long run.

If the actual retailer retains forty or fifty percent of the proceeds of the sale, the remaining sixty or fifty percent might be divided between the artist and the master dealer or whol—saler on a sixty—forty basis when the wholesaler is consigning the art work and on the same basis if the work is being sold outright. Let us consider an example: Artist Jimmy Canto makes some intaglio print editions in his own studio at his own expense. He consigns some of these original prints to a wholesaler named Jones. They agree on a suggested retail price of $250.00 per impression for these works. Jones places some of these works on consignment with dealer Abel, and others are sold outright to dealer Baker. Whenever Abel sells a work, he pays Jones $150.00 (sixty percent of $250.00.) When Baker buys the work outright, he pays Jones $125.00 (half of $250.00.) In each case, Jones acts as an agent for Canto, since Jones actually owns none of these works. Jones keeps forty percent of the net proceeds and pays the remainder, amounting to $95.00 and $75.00 each for the Abel and Baker transactions, respectively. If Jones had been willing to buy the works outright from Canto before wholesaling them, he might have demanded a better deal. As it is, he keeps forty percent of sixty percent or forty percent of fifty percent— — a modest sixty or fifty dollars, respectively in these cases.

As suggested earlier, some wholesalers will buy all or part of an edition from an artist or from a print workshop for the purpose of wholesaling works which they own outright. If Jones had been willing to buy Jimmy Canto's works outright, he might have offered between one—fourth and one—twelfth of the retail price for the works. In this example this would amount to a figure between $20.00 and $62.50.

Now there are artists who will thoughtlessly announce to their wholesaler (sometimes even to their retail dealer) "I am not interested in the price you get, I want such—and— such a fee for this work for myself." There are wholesalers who are only too happy to encourage this attitude. Usually each party to this game of blindman's bluff is trying to outwit the other. The artist thinks that he will sell his works to all— collectors, dealers, and wholesalers alike — — at substantially the same prices, forgetting that collectors who buy through retailers will almost certainly find out – – sooner or later –– that they have paid a great deal more than their friends paid for a similar work by the same artist. The wholesaler thinks that he is going to "buy very cheap and sell very dear" – – a process that will cause the artist's affection to wane rapidly when it is learned that the wholesaler has retained more than a fair profit on the transaction.

What is a "fair" profit? Simply one that appropriately compensates the wholesaler for the risks taken in terms of funds and efforts expended. If a wholesaler publishes an edition of an artist's work, paying the workshop's cost and the artist's fee in advance, that entrepreneur should generally expect to acquire the edition for a total cost of between one–fifth and one–tenth of the retail price. Thus, an impression from an edition meant to sell for $250.00 might cost the wholesaler twenty–five to fifty dollars, including the artist's fee and the workshop's costs. The wholesaler must expect to furnish additional funds to promote and otherwise distribute the works, of course, but in this case, the artist has taken no risk and invested none of the needed funds, so the wholesaler is certainly entitled to a fairly respectable reward.

The problem is much more difficult when the artist and the wholesaler are faced with a workshop or foundry cost which, in itself, exceeds twenty percent of the anticipated retail price. In such cases, I generally recommend that budgeted fabrication costs be deducted before a split of the anticipated proceeds is made between the artist and the wholesaler. For example, if the artist is a sculptor planning to create an edition of twenty bronzes, he might make a deal with our Mr. Jones of this kind: The artist and the wholesaler jointly participate in the cost of making the mold and in the cost of casting and finishing the first article, which will be retained and used as a selling sample until the edition has been sold out. Jones will show this sample work to art dealers in various communities, taking orders where it is appropriate. Suppose that the mold cost is $2000.00, which amortizes in this case at a rate of $100.00 per casting. Suppose that the casting and finishing cost is an additional $100.00 for each work. If the work retails for $1000.00, then the foundry cost, per work is precisely twenty percent of the selling price (to be sure, the selling price may escalate, but we will not consider that in this example.)

Now, if dealer Abel buys a bronze outright for $500.00, we may subtract the $200.00 cost and divide the remaining $300.00 on a 60/40 basis between artist and wholesaler. In this case, the artist would net $180.00 and the wholesaler would net $120.00. Of course, they would pay $100.00 to the foundry for the casting and they would reimburse them—selves for a portion of their mold investment by dividing the other $100.00 between them.

If the work is consigned to dealer Baker, the resulting $600.00 would be distributed in the same manner with $200.00 set aside for casting and mold costs, and $400.00 divided on a 60/40 basis. Again, if the wholesaler wishes to absorb all the costs and all the risks, paying the artist a fixed fee or a royalty, then it would be reasonable to expect a better portion of the proceeds to remain in the hands of that wholesaler.

One final word remains to be said regarding wholesaling. The basic interpersonal business problems of responsibility, promptness of payment, etc., are magnified when more than two parties are involved in a transaction. If Mr. Jones places Jimmy Canto's work on consignment with dealer Abel, all may go well. But the responsibility for insuring the work, returning it in good condition if it is not sold, and paying for it promptly if it is sold, must be clearly identified. For now, we must remember that such issues cannot safely be avoided. Secondary dealers must be willing to accept an appropriate share of responsibility for the works entrusted to them.

Promotion

52. Can We "Pre—Sell" the Artist's Work?

Outside the art world, most products and services sold to customers in our fast moving, contemporary mass market are at least partially "pre—sold" before the client thinks about making a specific purchase decision. A sizeable literature exists regarding the many subtle and overt techniques which may be employed to create an awareness of a product's desirability and virtues or to engender a favorable pre—disposition towards, or a reliance on, a particular brand name, personality (in the case of entertainers) or ideology (in the case of politicians.)

Whether these potential clients are to be offered a new automobile, an art work, a political candidate, or a different viewpoint regarding our ecology, an organized force must seek them out, gain their attention, and encourage a friendly recep— tion. These motivating forces: advertising, taste—makers, political parties, fund raisers, even art critics and curators, are all fundamentally "promoters." They use various communi-cations media and various kinds of appeals to win adherents to their viewpoint. Obviously, such powerful methods can be an important force for good as well as for evil. A great deal depends upon the values and the honesty of the promoter.

If a curator, working in concert with a prominent member of a museum board, decides to resurrect a long—forgotten chapter of art history or if a critic undertakes to rewrite or simply to re—evaluate an established aspect of art history, the ensuing interest and attention can be extremely significant in the art market. The remarkable restoration of the value of the works of artists of the Hudson River School during the sixties and the increased demand for the works of these artists was preceded by a shift in position by a few curators who previously had been grudging in their willingness to even store major works by Cole, Church, and their circle. The shift was coupled with a critical "discovery" that these very realistic, figurative painters who were often treated with contempt by critics in the fifties, were really the "forebears" of the action painters of the New York School. The logic of this develop—ment may not be impeccable, but the economic significance is unmistakable. Since such strange examples abound in the recent history of art, we must conclude that no one can expect to make any real headway in this field who has not mastered the fundamentals of promotion.

Advertising and publicity are two different varieties of promotion. The first is purchased and available to just about anyone who can afford it; the second is more informal and is not generally acquired for cash. Both are essentially pre—selling tools. They may be employed with finesse or baldly and in either case, still lead to great success. But they may also be used so crudely or so obtusely that the effort proves meaningless or even counterproductive, undermining the very response which the promoters were seeking. Promotional efforts are extremely significant aspects of every kind of marketing endeavor.*

53. What is the Aim of an Art Promotion Campaign?

Successful promotion in the arts usually will give the prospective collector significant information about artists and art works. It also stimulates a consciousness of interest and need, encourages a positive attitude toward purchasing, and informs the prospective collector regarding appropriate and available courses of action. Large—scale marketers of items intended for mass consumption outside the arts regularly spend a rather large portion of their anticipated annual business income on promotion. One—fourth or more is not uncommon in promotional budgets for shampoos and break—fast cereals. Only a few consumer products receive limited promotion and still enjoy significant acceptance in the market. The Hershey Company's chocolate line is an exceptional case. Their products still enjoy wide popularity after years with almost no active promotion.

* *Marketing is sometimes used incorrectly as a synonym for selling. It is more properly the sum of several different kinds of activities, including promotion, research, planning, pricing, and "intelligence" (the nice word for spying on the compe—tition) as well as selling. Since this is a specialized marketing* **Handbook,** *each of these functions will be examined in turn. Market research, the study of who buys and why, and market intelligence, the study of what others are doing, receive less attention than the other marketing functions because very little has actually been done in these areas in the art market to date.*

While the resources of the artist and the art dealer are generally much too limited to permit large—scale expenditures, the promotional problems of the art world are not entirely unlike the problems faced by many producers of consumer products. Artists and art dealers must make potential clients conscious of the value of owning art in general and aware of the existence of certain esthetic points of view and of certain art works in particular. They must also attempt to favorably predispose prospective clients toward these works. And they must encourage the collector to undertake certain expendi- tures to their own benefit and to the benefit of the collector.

One of the major shortcomings of the art market is that too little effort is directed by artists, art dealers, and others at encouraging non—collectors to acquire original art. This promotional avenue is a significant potential source of great gains for the art market in general. It would take cooperative effort, not unlike the energy employed to promote travel, sports, and the virtues of milk or orange juice, but it could be done simply and effectively.

The American auto industry has long understood the desirablility of generally promoting interest in and use of its products on an industry—wide as well as on a brand name basis. Thus, in addition to their familiar and recognizable advertising programs, they are very cooperative with film and TV producers who wish to use their cars, and they are equally cooperative with secondary schools, where driver—training is a popular subject. I see no reason why art dealers' organiza- tions and artists' organizations would not contribute greatly to the welfare of their members by encouraging more regular and more intelligent use of contemporary art in the motion picture and television industry plus more attention in the high schools and colleges to the many advantages of art collecting — — a subject which could easily be introduced in art history and art appreciation classes.

There are, however, many important differences between mass market promotion and promotion in the fine arts. Individual artists seldom seek or need a large market with vast numbers of collectors. More often, their images have a limited, highly specialized audience. Also, an artist's annual output is never very large. Even prolific printmakers number their works in the hundreds, not in the tens of thousands. Further, the appropriate clientele, and the best methods for reaching it, for one artist can well be completely different from the proper clientele and logical approach for another artist.

So we cannot expect that the same promotional methods used to build interest in or preference for a particular brand of hair dryer could be directly transferable to the marketing needs of the art world. The pre—selling objectives of the artist and art dealer are normally quite different from those of the mass market. The typical small appliance promotional campaign might be aimed at generating and maintaining wide—spread brand loyalty across the nation, plus a feeling of need for a particular device. But the promotional effort used for interesting an individual in becoming an art collector in the first place, and the kind of publicty program which succeeds in stimulating a collector to take an active interest in a particular artist or art dealer in the second place, must be much more precisely directed. Acquiring art is, after all, a highly individualistic affair. I like to think that most art acquisitions are matters of taste, refinement, and specialized interests.

Of course, everybody "needs" art, probably a good deal more clearly than everybody "needs" a hair dryer. I have yet to hear that an art collector's hair fell out simply because of an acquisition. Still, not everybody can benefit from acquiring a certain work by a certain artist because not everyone has the same taste, level of development, or sense of relevance. Further, when we think of buying a work of art, popularity, utility, and economy are not and should not be the primary factors determining our selections.

Pre—selling the art works of a contemporary artist may involve: gaining recognition among a small group of specialists, achieving acclaim from a few critics, collectors, or curators, collecting testimonials from these individuals in the form of remarks, purchases, or awards, and − − more important − − gaining a certain public exposure for these reactions so that a somewhat larger group of collectors and others who may agree with this "starter" group will have the opportunity of learning that these events and judgments are, in fact, taking place.

Not everyone will be equally impressed by an artist's work. A rather modest few may be moved so favorably that they develop a predisposition towards acquiring a work. But a significant number of any artist's potential clients will be within such a group if the effort is successful. In this respect, promotional efforts are useful to the art world. They can help establish and then help enlarge an artist's following.

For example, suppose that a talented young graduate of a professional art school named Mary Frescobaldi submits a number of her works to several important exhibition jurors. Suppose further that some of her works are accepted for inclusion by these jurors in exhibitions. If, in addition, critical reviews in the art press or the metropolitan press mention these works favorably and a few important collectors see and then acquire some of them, or if a few works are awarded a prize of some sort, then this artist's career has been measurably "promoted." Frescobaldi's reputation is enhanced. Future works are now, to some degree, being "pre—sold."

Now further, suppose that the community newspaper serving Mary's home residence runs an illustrated feature story on her recent achievements. Clearly, this added exposure extends her "image" to a wider public. If similar events occur in several communities or in a major publication, then the "pre—selling" is more wide—spread, and a regional or national market is possible. In this instance, promotion is simply a function of communicating the facts about the artist's growing recognition in such a manner that the communication process itself contributes to the growth of the artist's market.

News items regarding the events which help to promote the artist's reputation include: the winning of a prize, the receipt of a commission, the announcement of a solo exhibition, or the acceptance of an honor or a fellowship. Feature stories might deal with the works of a particular collector, the application of a new or little—used technology, or the views of an artist regarding personal attitudes or perceptions. Feature stories may also deal with the artist's subject matter life style or views regarding nature.

But what starts these promotionally useful opportunities? Different artists may employ a wide variety of approaches, but, as has been noted, the young artist should not avoid the competitive juried shows. With all their limitations, such exhibitions are an important entry point for the little—known artist into the art world. They can serve the same basic function employed by an artist who participates in solo or group exhibitions in an art dealer's gallery. They call attention in a meaningful way to the artist's image. For the artist who lacks a dealer, a studio sale can also provide the same pro—motional opportunity as a solo show. It brings the artist's image into direct contact with potential collectors, and it also offers a basis for promoting wider interest in the artist's efforts.

54. Two Successful Examples

Two of my best clients recently engaged in separate promotional campaigns, in different parts of the country which I think might be very instructive. The first, Florence Putterman, a Pennsylvania — based artist with a fast—growing reputation, has been both assiduous and successful in devel—oping a nation—wide following for her watercolor abstractions and her sophisticated original prints and monotypes. She regularly researches competitive exhibitions which are suitable to her media and esthetic interest, carefully selecting a few dozen entries each year that are particularly appropriate. To be sure, she is very proud that Clement Greenberg, a critic of major importance, juried her into an exhibition in New England and then awarded her a prize. But more important than the prize is the promotional opportunity. This and similar significant achievements are featured elements of Putterman's short biography.

This artist, at my suggestion, once took the logical step of sending a personal note of appreciation to a juror who was a curator of a fine municipal museum near Washington. The juror responded by offering Putterman a solo exhibition in his museum. This, too, created valuable promotional opportunities. On the occasion of a gallery show in Los Angeles, a local art critic wrote an excellent review in one of the metropolitan newspapers. Putterman extracted key elements of that review for inclusion in a color brochure which illustrated and further promoted her work. I am de—lighted to note that Putterman's home market has improved and expanded, at least in part, because of her visible success outside her own mid—Pennsylvania circle. Note that none of these individual activities is particularly novel or difficult in itself. But they add up to an extremely effective promotional campaign when they are combined.

Another fine client with whom I work, Hal Stowers, lives on the Florida Gulf Coast and makes watercolors and original prints which capture the essence of the swampy wilderness near his home. Because of the subject matter and Stower's success in handling it, he is frequently able to place color illustrations of his work in periodicals which promote an interest in Northern Florida, and he has had excellent success with feature stories regarding his views on the importance of the wilderness. Here, too, the promotional activity has pre— pared the ground for an increased following for the artist's work, which is beginning to find its way into a fair number of non—Florida collectiors.

For Stowers, as for other artists, each successful activity becomes the promotional basis for others. When he was successful in selling his work to a Florida bank, this helped to form part of a promotional campaign which led to sales in other banks in other places. Feature stories were reprinted and used outside their original audience orbit. Every success becomes a reinforcement for every other effort.

55. Promotion to Which Audience?

Many artists (even more art dealers) believe that they must somehow "innovate" in order to attract attention to themselves. Others prefer to adapt their talents to currently "popular" or perennially "acceptable" themes and styles. Viewed by themselves, each of these approaches is wrong. Artists should neither innovate just to attract attention nor follow the fashion of the day just because it enjoys ready acceptance. They should try to develop individualistic styles and images, equally independent of prevailing fashions and the compulsion to be different. If the work which an artist is producing is honest, well—done, and esthetically interesting, a market can be found for it. The marketing problems of the artist begin with the identification of that objective market and then proceed to the promotional efforts required to make contact with the individuals who constitute that market.

Some artists may find, as they study their own work and talk about it with their dealers and others, that a particular community or circle of acquaintances does not contain sufficient potential clients for their works. They must then seek other areas of contact — — areas which contain the right kind of collectors. In many cases, without special effort, art cannot be sold to non—collectors, no matter how well the artist's work is respected.

So, also, art of a particular medium, scale, esthetic bias cannot generally be sold to clients whose fundamental interest is pointed in a different direction. Hard—edge abstraction is of little relevance to the householder whose home is a small museum of authentic early Americana. Apartment dwellers have little reason to consider acquiring a sculpture of massive dimensions. Not everyone relates to "magic realism" in the same way. An artist whose images reflect an angry or bitter point of view may have trouble finding clients who are im—pressed enough to want to share the artist's anguish. Artists must find their own particular communities of interest and then promote their special viewpoint within it.

Certain artists will decide that their works are primarily of interest to architects and builders rather than to individual collectors because of factors of scale, materials employed, or subject matter. They might conclude that their works will primarily interest institutional and business collectors because of their esthetic orientation. In each case, the artist or the art dealer must define appropriate market segments. Where are a particular artist's collectors likely to be found? What common interests do they possess? Why would they want this type of work in their collection? These questions can seldom be posed successfully before a coherent body of work has been conceived and executed, but they are very appro—priate afterward.

To be sure, I prefer to see an artist working with an image which is wholly his or her own, but regularly I meet artists whose interests and abilities are so diffuse that their work is frankly confusing to their audiences. In a few cases, I have advised artists to work in two fairly different directions with their talent, aimed at two quite different kinds of collectors. More often, I will encourage an artist to focus attention more narrowly on a particular variety of image — — one which has a clearly perceptible following. This audience is seldom vast. It may be sophisticated in a particular direction or interested in a certain subject matter, but it is definable.

Once an artist's particular market is fairly well defined, we can better deal with the problem of reaching it. If one wants to devote a major portion of one's life to creating large illuminated fountains, one must expect to gain little in the way of commissions from entering juried watercolor exhibitions. Such an artist's best clients will most probably be institutions rather than householders. This artist needs to make contact with contemporary architects and commercial builders who might be able to integrate these fountain designs into their own plans and structures.

An architect might be expected to attend a competitive exhibition of sculpture or of sculptural designs, but we would probably not often find this person looking for talent at a watercolor annual. More concretely, an illustrated brochure or a portfolio of photos of maquettes, specially aimed at institutional architects, could be expected to produce a number of inquiries and even requests for design proposals. But other promotional activity, aimed at the general public or even at the home—oriented collector, would probably fail.

I think that the most spectacularly unsuccessful catalogue/ brochure I ever saw was one associated with a museum exhibition which centered around some large photomurals of a well established sculptor who works with quite heroic themes and proportions. Since the catalogue designer had difficulty photographically reducing the artist's large works, he selected some rather disconnected close up details in combination with close—up pictures of the sculptor's hands as his illustrations. While the brochure itself was well designed and expensive, it did not promote the sculptor's images or sentiments and, of course, it was aimed at no interested audience in particular.

An artist whose images are fairly representational must realize that getting works into a show at an institution which is well known for its non—objective viewpoint cannot do any significant good. The collectors who may be expected to attend such an exhibition are not likely candidates to acquire this artist's work. They will come seeking something novel and challenging in a particular category of images. They may even be offended by a work which is merely well done and does not partake of their biases.

To summarize: pre—selling promotional campaigns are just as important to the artist and the art dealer as they are to the mass marketer, but they work quite differently. Each artist needs only a small, specialized, intensely loyal segment of the world's collectors for a following, a segment which is probably not shared broadly with a large group of other artists. The artist or art dealer must, therefore, seek a series of promotion—worthy events and activities which by their nature bring the artist's views and works into focus in the eyes of just the right group of collectors and in just the right way. Words and pictures should be combined to generate promotional materials which can be employed in connection with these functions.

56. When Does Advertising Help the Artist and the Dealer?

Since advertising space and time are quite expensive, many gallery operators and artists have concluded that ads should be employed sparingly, if at all, and then for informational pur—poses only. The use of purchased space in periodicals and newspapers by most art dealers seems almost entirely limited to terse announcements of names, dates, and places, rather than to the more familar variety of advertisements which are aimed at creating some sort of favorable predisposition in the client's mind regarding a product, personality, service or cause.

For example, even a small ad for a new play or musical will generally feature selected remarks from critics who en—joyed the show. The basic purpose of this ad is not simply to delineate information, but to encourage increased attendance through the use of testimonials. Even the very august cultural establishments which sponsor symphony concerts and operas have begun to use advertising as a positive force to interest their clients in buying tickets rather than merely holding to formal, often formidable, announcements and calendars of coming events.

The announcement of an artist's last name in bold type, or illegible script, coupled with a gallery's name, a date, and an address is not likely to encourage a worthwhile response. I am puzzled that gallery operators, representing some of the most creative elements in our culture, should be so consis—tently uncreative in preparing their advertising copy. They seem somehow to have avoided the issue of why they are advertising, altogether. Thus, they will seldom employ color although this is a key to most of their artists' output and despite the fact that the cost of color advertising is dropping.

I am particularly appalled with the continuing use of "reverse" ads (white letters on black backgrounds) in the specialized art magazines. While such ads can be very dramatic, the type is often too thin or small to be legible, and the design quality is often as dismal as the copy is unattractive.

Further, most art dealers have not yet found a way to utilize television consistently although a work of art can be appreciated visually more readily than verbally. In my own experience, it is fairly easy to get free time on both public and commercial television for artists and their work, providing one takes the trouble to suggest interesting talk show segments, provocative program themes, etc.

Another class of promotional failure in the arts deserves special mention. I call it "panic" promotion. Thus, I recently received a brochure from an artist seeking the support of collectors. It was written in a petulant tone. The copy indicated frustration, anger, and disappointment − − traits not at all in consonance to the proud, virile images with which this artist represents himself in his work. "The world admits a need for art," he intoned, "but seems unwilling to extend its support." Such hand−wringing appeals lead collectors to suspect that something may be wrong with the art as well as with the world. We may wish to help distressed and indigent people, but we seldom collect their art.

A variant of this unfortunate, negative approach was recently illustrated when a well established, successul dealer advertised the names of several internationally important artists, indicating that he was "liquidating" his inventory at "fantastic reductions of 40% and 50%." I cannot understand or condone offering works which are worth owning in this manner, and I cannot believe that such approaches generate any valid sales support. Even unsophisticated art collectors are likely to suspect the legitimacy of such an offer.

I am looking forward to the day when art is advertised in periodicals and on television as effectively as are other major elements of our culture, such as automobiles, health research funding, and political causes. As suggested above, one very appropriate advertising campaign would find dealers banding together to encourage more people to collect art, to show them the advantages and tell them how they might start a collection. The effort could readily be justified if it were concerted and well directed.

Advertising and publicity can help the artist and the dealer only when it involves more than informational exchanges. When promotion improves or enhances attitudes towards a particular artist's work, then it is useful. Otherwise, it may be only expensive and even harmful.

57. Brochures

Gallery operators are often quite successful, and more rational, in producing direct mail brochures, a form of adver—tising widely employed to promote attendance at exhibitions and especially to promote crowded (sometimes overcrowded) exhibition openings. I have reserved my own rather negative appraisal of the often limited function of such openings for a more appropriate place in this *Handbook*. For the moment, it should be noted that many of these brochures readily achieve their simple objectives. They do promote attendance at gallery functions, and they do create a favorable predisposi—ion in a selected audience.

Essentially, a direct mail brochure, whether employed by a gallery or by an artist, should include several important items of information aimed at achieving its end. All of this vital information should be presented clearly and without excessive verbiage. The artist's name, the gallery's name and address, the theme or title of the upcoming exhibition, the dates of the opening and closing should all be set forth with appropriate clarity and typographic emphasis.

I feel that it is an error to include in such brochures the artist's complete *curriculum vitae,* interminably listing all schools attended, exhibitions held, and collections containing works. This information is useful to the scholar and should be carefully preserved for eventual use in catalogues of major retrospectives, but it makes tedious ad copy. A few well written, complete sentences giving some interesting highlights of an artist's career will be much more informative because they are more likely to be read and remembered.

The brochure should also contain one or two imperative or hortative statements: "Please join us to see this important showing." "Don't miss this opening," or "Phone for an appointment." In addition, it is very useful to include an illustration of the artist finishing a work or a good reproduction of an actual work plus a straightforward critical comment attributed to a dealer, the artist, a critic, or to some other authority.

Although the brochure need not be expensively printed and produced in full color, it must be legible, neat, and a credit to the artist in terms of the taste and quality it suggests. Since many collectors save these documents for future reference, it should always carry a complete address and telephone number, including mailing zip code and telephone area code.

Some artists and dealers will intentionally avoid any specific dates on their brochure so that they may use it extensively over a significant period. In this case, an added card or letter may be inserted with the mailing to function as an invitation to a specific event. The brochure says something about the artist and the work. The inserted card or letter says something about a specific event or opportunity. This technique illustrates the bimodal use to which advertising and publicity may be directed. It is the difference between strategy and tactics.

58. Promotional Strategy and Tactics

First, is the immediate, *tactical* function of promotion. We wish to guarantee attendance at an opening. We wish to offer an opportunity to come, see, examine, and buy certain works at or before a certain time. "Come to the opening." "Visit this exhibition." Second, promotion can have a more far—reaching, *strategic* function. We want certain classes of collectors to be aware of an artist's existence and importance. "Hal Stowers is alive and well and working very successfully in Crystal Beach." Or, we want collectors to be impressed with the growing acceptance of the artist's work. "L.A. art critic Betje Howell says that Florence Putterman's work is unique." In these cases, we want a result of an intermediate, strategic rather than an immediate, tactical nature.

It may not be quite as important that the collector come to a particular event as it is that a favorable view of the artist become deeply—rooted, assuring and reinforcing broad ac—ceptance by competent critics and collectors. It is possible to produce ad or brochure copy which aims at both tactical and strategic ends. "Come to the opening next Sunday to see the Putterman works which Betje Howell finds so unique." This kind of simple statement, joined to a familiar gallery logotype works at many levels at once.

However, when the goals of an advertising campaign are not clearly set forth in the mind of the advertiser, sizeable investments can easily be wasted. A full—page ad in a recent issue of a national art journal illustrates this point rather well. The copy consisted of a large, diagonal scrawl — — the illegible signature of a fairly famous artist who was currently enjoying an important exhibition at a major gallery. Of course, the scrawl was recognizable to the *cognoscenti,* a handful of collectors familiar with the artist's signature, as well as with the other pertinent facts of the case.

But the collector who could not decipher the autograph, who did not know the unnamed dealer, or the dates of the show, was simply left out. Perhaps this was the real objective of the dealer, but he could have slighted his non—clients more easily and less expensively if no ad had been placed at all. An ad may be simple and direct or even oblique and sophisticated, but its purpose or purposes should always be clear to the intended reader, and an ad or brochure should be designed to expand audience interest not to cut people short.

59. How Does Publicity Serve the Artist and Art Dealer?

Many business—oriented individuals think of publicity as a form of free advertising. Actually, this is not strictly true, first, because it is not always without cost and second because, unlike advertising, the materials of publicity are not readily controlled by their originator. Nevertheless, since the costs of publicity are more indirect, and since those who control the most familiar outlets for publicity are genuinely interested in the work of artists, a good deal more energy is devoted by artists and art dealers to getting publicity than is devoted to preparing and placing advertising.

At its simplest level, the artist or dealer — — for that matter, anyone with an interesting, noteworthy, amusing, or contro—versial story — — writes a press release or gets someone else to do it. The press release may simply announce a forthcoming or recent event of wide interest. In the art world, forthcoming events seem to be more acceptable than those which have already occurred. A release might also announce a recent award or a significant commission. The main point is that information about the news is furnished by the artist or the dealer to the media — — not the other way around. Weekly publications generally need about ten days' advance notice to accommodate an exhibition opening or a studio sale. Monthly publications often need at least two months lead time, especially if color illustrations or display copy is involved.

60. Writing Press Releases

Practical press releases should start by setting forth the fundamental facts: Who? What? Where? When? Why? How? After a few leading sentences outlining the anticipated or recent event, in general, the press release should go on to fill in details. A paragraph on where and with whom the artist studies, some major collectors, prior exhibitions, awards, and honors might be in order. Another paragraph quoting the sentiments of a prominent curator, critic, or collector might be employed. The closing sentence should give a telephone number or an address where further details are available or appointments might be made.

The editor will decide whether the article is newsworthy and will edit it to suit the paper's interest and the available space. Do not avoid giving the *whole* story. The editor will cut out less essential elements if it seems wise. The press release might be accompanied by a glossy 8 x 10 photograph of the artist receiving an award, installing or presenting a work, preparing a work at the studio, smiling at a proud collector, etc. Another photo might actually illustrate one of the artist's works.

Care should be taken to prepare photographs with ade—quate contrast to withstand the poor tonal capabilities of most newspapers and periodicals. On newsprint, light greys tend to vanish while dark greys tend to turn black. Fine lines often disappear entirely in newspaper reproductions. Therefore, the artist should not try to reproduce works with weak contrasts, nor should a photograph be overburdened with too much fine detail. When individuals are present in a photo, they should be accurately identified in a caption, taped to the bottom of the photo. Otherwise, the caption should simply state what is being looked at. It is often wise to recapitulate the essence of the story in the caption. State the name of the work and add: "This and other oil paintings by J. Canto will be on display at the Heritage Gallery in Oak City through December."

The press release is fundamentally a story with some sort of time element to it. Accordingly, it should be submitted in plenty of time to work. If you are planning a Sunday studio sale and want a notice of this event in the prior Friday's paper, find out the appropriate deadline and get your copy in on time. Direct your press release to the appropriate party. Some periodicals have calendar editors. Others want all art related news to go through an art editor. To be sure, you can locate the proper recipient of your release by asking at the editor's office. All releases should be directed to a particular individual.

It is wise to suggest a headline for your release. Always indicate when the release should be carried and whom to phone for further information. When preparing releases for more than one community, it may be useful to consult one of the many directories of periodicals for names and addresses. An excellent, if not absolutely complete, listing of newspapers and magazines that devote space to art news can be found in the latest issue of *American Art Directory,* published by R.R. Bowker.

When an art dealer or artist works regularly on promotion, it is useful to build a file of promotionial outlets, including broadcast as well as printed media. Many commercial radio stations will carry art news as part of their public service announcement programs.

In addition, a promotional file should be developed by every artist, and for each artist seriously represented by an art dealer, containing black and white photos of the artist and of art works as well as biographical and story material. This file should contain good reprints of all published materials as well, including press notices and reviews.

61. Features & Feature Items

A more advanced form of publicity is the feature item. This is not an article based on a press release, but a smaller item of interest to readers. It is usually furnished to a feature columnist or editor by a concerned individual. It might deal with some sort of news. More often, it deals with a matter of human interest – – something noteworthy, amusing, or amazing. Almost every publication carries some feature items in a round–up column written by a columnist who may be specifically interested in art or involved with cultural issues. Watch these columns for examples worthy of emulation.

Magazines, Sunday supplements, newspapers and television stations devote a fair amount of their resources to public service and public interest subjects, including the fine arts. A full–length feature article or a television visit to an artist's studio, a gallery, or a "happening" is almost always good copy. That is, the activity is novel and unusual enough to stimulate audience interest. Professional publicists are often able to develop good ideas for such features and special pro– grams. Of course, any imaginative individual can, with a little thought, do the same. But try to develop a feature concept in enough detail so that it may be evaluated by a media person who knows little about art.

Once a concept has been developed, it should then be presented to the managing editor of the periodical or to the producer or the program director of a television station for consideration. Where an influential public figure, a prominent collector or architect, is involved, this may be the proper person to make the presentation.

Features are also employed by such specialized media as the art magazines and the metropolitan newspaper art pages. In these cases, the critics and editors who select the materials are harder to reach because they are literally inundated with suggestions and material, including proposals from powerful curators, advertisers, and collectors. Thus, theirs are the most difficult publicity channels in which one can make progress.

Somewhat more accessible, but often very important to the reputation of an artist, are the metropolitan women's editors and their counterparts on the staff of the women's magazines. Somehow the notion has gotten abroad that, since most purchasing in the United States is done by women, so, too, art – – culture in general, for that matter – – is a proper subject for women's pages and journals.

I have no conclusive evidence proving that women do most of the art collecting, and some evidence suggests that they do not, but nevertheless these are useful and prestigious avenues of publicity. A good proposal for a feature directed to the women's editor is likely to receive a very sympathetic audience. These specialists are particularly interested in re—porting social functions which are attended by "notables" and in discussing in public the art acquisitions and interests of "social lions."

Again, however, as with advertising, it is possible to con—fuse ends and means in building a publicity program. If the end is a strategic enhancement of interest in an artist's general reputation, image, and works, then it would be useful if these were presented to the kinds of people who can best relate to such works. These might be architects or they might be affluent collectors.

What counts most here is the expression of interest and involvement of these specialized audiences. This interest is often more important than the endorsement of a critic or of a famous collector who has no peers and, therefore, sets no real patterns for others to follow. Promotion in art should be selective, directed, and carefully designed to achieve specific ends.

I once had two artst—clients who managed to get a great deal of attention for their forthcoming joint exhibition, in spite of the fact that they were relatively unknown, simply because their theme involved broad public interest. They created a collection of paintings, drawings, prints, and sculp— ture based on the people who live in Venice, California — — a rather unique enclave of the Los Angeles beach community. Because the theme was so interesting, the Santa Monica paper, which serves Venice, devoted the cover of their weekend supplement plus a two—page spread to the story. Three of the television channels found sufficient interest to arrange interviews with the artists where slides of work were shown, and, of course, just about the entire community knew about the show and its artists because of these feature presentations.

While subject matter can often form the basis of an effec— tive feature story regarding an artist's work, other approches (called "hooks") can be equally valid. I have had two clients — — one an artist with her own art studio and retail gallery, the other a once rather unknown novice art dealer — — who used the identical ploy in quite different contexts. The first story was about an artist who lives upstairs of her studio and gallery. The second was about an art dealer who lives in the back of her gallery. Both features were beautifully illustrated in color, ran over four pages and actually reached millions of readers in a major metropolitan Sunday supplement. Both led to many useful business opportunities as attested by the fact that these women are much better established today than they were. In neither case did anyone have any "inside" connections with the editor of the periodical. They simply had an interesting idea for a feature, and they presented it to the right publication. Notice that such features generally are not time related and can be used in a variety of situations by an editor.

62. The Great Dangers of Over—Promotion

Thus far, I have been discussing advertising and publicity as useful tools for pre—selling the artist's work. When they are properly used and directed, they can indeed enhance the artist's career. But they are not always used in this straight—forward manner. Historically, and more particularly in the post—World War II era, certain collectors, curators, and art dealers have discovered that great power and economic ad—vantage can be wielded by those who successfully promote the careers of artists.

Accordingly, large sums have been spent, sometimes quite cynically, by promoters to bolster an artist's name, image, and price structure. The mass media and the major magazines have been employed, in combination with the antic efforts of friendly museum curators. Once these promotions succeed, and prices are sufficiently inflated, the artist's sponsors have been known to "unload" their works on an unsuspecting public as actual sales or else as tax—deductible donations to museums, based on inflated market prices.

Having exhausted their supply of works and their profit opportunity, the promoters then have withdrawn their ex—pensive promotional support and gone on to oher artists where the potential gain was still great. Seldom does such a promoter buy an art work from an artist whose reputation is firmly established and whose prices have reached a substantial level. And seldom does such a promoter retain the works for long.

Only a few artists can withstand the whiplash of such a meteroric build—up, followed by rapid withdrawal of support. They find themselves in high fashion during a brief season, and then quickly the fad shifts, and they are suddenly out of vogue. The artificially stimulated demand is now vastly diminished, and the artist is suddenly dropped, left in a pre—carious position at the top of a steep decline.

A professional artist needs promotion, but not the kind which builds a career too rapidly and artificially and then leaves the artist dangling without a valid consituency. The best promotional effort is a carefully planned, deliberate, long—term program, based on developing sincere collectors who will generally stay on as the artist's image matures and expands even as prices rise. Such a program underscores the proposition that good art is never a series of passing fads, but rather has the power to interest and attract long after the movement of which it was a part has lost its original novelty.

63. Are Artists Freaks?

Another equally dangerous avenue of publicity is open to almost any creative person. One can simply assume an out—rageous character or appearance. Artists in recent generations have adopted many unfortunate ruses, aimed at seeking the public eye and ranging from spray—painting one's hair silver to shooting oneself in public or even to self—mutilation. All of these devices lead to attention since the people who control the media seem to enjoy promoting almost any activity if it is sensational enough.

A difficulty arises, however, in that public attention is not being focused so much on the artist's work as an artist but rather on the artist as some sort of freak. The publicity values and opportunities are considerable, but the respect of the serious collector is often withheld. I am rather pleased to note that even certain of the rock performers who have popularized this approach to broad visibility are now moving away from their freakish behavior. In the long term, it seems always to be counterproductive.

Promotional
Sales
Aids

64. The Function of Sales Aids

Merchants have learned over the past fifty years that there is a great deal more to successful marketing than a useful item or service and an attractive promotional and sales program. Particularly in the art world, where the client is asked to dis—tinguish between fine, generally intangible criteria on the basis of qualities which are more often felt than measured, a sound program of advertising and publicity, coupled with the pre—sentation of interesting, provocative art works is not in itself enough to generate consistent sales. An increasingly important component of marketing in the art world is the promotional sales aid. A sales aid is any material which can be employed by a sales representative to help the client to better appreciate and relate to the artist's work or the dealer's abilities.

However, one of my biggest problems as a consultant to artists and art dealers arises from the mistaken notion that good promotional materials are somehow a substitute for sales efforts. In many mass marketing situations this is, indeed, the case. For example, there are firms which sell popular and even classical record albums on television, using no other sales activity than the media ad itself. So, too, many items are sold through the simple device of a special point—of—purchase display bin. As a general rule, art cannot be sold this way, as many experienced merchants have learned to their own great cost. First, art in almost all cases must be experienced directly before a collector can decide to acquire it. Second, collectors seem to greatly enjoy the direct contact with artists and art dealers that is impossible when art is offered through an ad, a display, a catalogue, or over the broadcast media. Promo—tional materials can be used to increase the awareness by and improve the attitude of a collector regarding an artist's imagery or reputation. They can be used to encourage attendance at specific sales—oriented functions. But promotion is almost always an aid, never a substitute, for art sales efforts.

The simplest promotional sales aids are very often most effective. A number of these are listed below together with a few which are more complex and sophisticated. It must be remembered that these are linkages, designed not so much to produce sales as to heighten interest and improve general understanding on the part of the client.

Brochures and invitations were considered briefly in earlier sections of the *Handbook*. They are examined more fully here, together with a number of other promotional sales aids.

65. Photographs

Considering that art is almost always primarily a visual experience, the well designed and executed photograph can be a valuable sales tool, extending and reinforcing our visual grasp of particular artists, their work spaces, and their work.

The artist may be shown in the studio, in the field, or otherwise at work. Many collectors find it easier to relate to a work when they have some concrete ideas about the appearance of the artist. So, too, the notion that the artist has a serious or an interesting physiognomy is important to many. For this reason, art dealers feature photographs of their artists in their promotional brochures and in their exhibitions. Further, photographs of work—in—process, studio interiors, famous collectors, and any unusual gallery situations can be employed as promotional sales aids.

I am often appalled at the poor quality of the photography employed by artists and dealers for promotional purposes. When an artist, art dealer, or collector is photographed for publicity purposes, a good deal of care should be taken to assure that the tonal range of the picture is not too stark. Good lighting and proper balance between foreground and background are critical. A picture is indeed worth a thousand words, but the cause can be lost if the picture contains the wrong words or if the words are unintelligible.

Any amateur can learn to take good indoor and outdoor photos, and many professionals are available who already know how to do this. First, it is important to plan the design of the photo; next, adequate and appropriate lighting must be provided. Many hasty photographers use flash or strobe equipment where diffused light is needed. The "hot" spots on the surface of a delicate sculpture or on the glass of a framed watercolor will destroy the usefulness of the photo.

I work with a client who uses photographic prints as a small scale substitute for brochures and color postcards. He regu—larly prepares a montage of color views of recent commissions. These are assembled, together with captions and a point of contact, and then printed by a color lab for distribution to a fairly small group of potential clients. Good color prints can be purchased at reasonable cost in quantities of one hundred or more, and the total cost is considerably less than my client would pay for a printed color brochure. The brochure would, of course, be more economical if larger quantities were needed.

66. Slides versus Photographs

Inexpensive color slides and photographs are very often employed to show works not in the art dealer's possession and not easily transported to the client's premises. Sad to say, the color of these reproductions is often inadequate, and their small scale can make them a very poor substitute for the original image. Unless the artist or dealer can manage professional quality photographic prints, it would be wise to avoid them entirely.

So, too, with slides. Unless they are of good quality and can be projected under excellent viewing conditions, they are seldom worth the expense. When these conditions can be met, they provide an excellent opportunity for the collector to better visualize an artist's works.

I am often asked about the relative merit of photographic slides and prints for showing the artist's work. A large num—ber of competitions open to relatively unknown artists provide for screening or even judging by color slides. This is very convenient for the judges and relatively inexpensive for the contestants, but it is often extremely unfair. In many cases, a poor slide will cause an art work to be rejected that would otherwise be quite acceptable.

Photographic color prints are much more amenable to inexpensive color correction because most modern color labs are equipped with computerized color correction equipment. To use this equipment to the best advantage, the artist or art dealer should always insist that the work being photographed has, taped outside its own boundaries, a color guide and a gray scale. These standards can be purchased in a camera shop and serve to assist the laboratory technician, who can adjust the computer to print more blue, less yellow, darker, etc., using the color guide and gray scale as reference points.

Of course, if outdoor film is used with artificial light or if flashbulbs over—illuminate certain areas of the work, no laboratory can correct for such gross errors. I generally re—commend shooting pictures of art out—of—doors in diffuse light. I have also found that the new ASA400 color print film is rather effective for indoor shots of art work, since it operates well without special tungsten lamps or flash bulbs.

When color photos of art works or installations are to be used in portfolios, I usually like to see them mounted on neutral—color mat boards larger than the prints so that they may be handled without being readily marred. In some cases, I also recommend an overmat or a cover to improve the appearance of the illustration.

67. Business Cards, Stationery, Logotypes & Labels

A subtle, but simple and pervasive, sales aid finding increasing employment in our visually—oriented culture is the tastefully designed business card and the interesting letter—head. For the sales representative who is based in a private residence or calls on institutional collectors away from a gallery situation, the initial customer contact is primarily through a letter or a business card. These should suggest something about the sales representative's taste, design sense, and interest in esthetics.

They need not be elaborate or expensive, but they must be legible and well planned. Often a letterhead or a business card will exhibit a distinctive logotype which is repeated in other printed studio or gallery material. This may be a spe—cially designed monogram or a distinctive type style. It may be a stylized figure, suggestive of an aspect of the art world, or it may be a reworking of a signature. It serves to identify the artist, the gallery, the collection, and a point of view regarding art.

A good business card will state the name of the individual and his or her occupation, *viz:*

Mary Frescobaldi
Artist

or:

James Canto
J. Canto Gallery

It will then state all the basic contact information including: address and telephone, including zip and area codes. I prefer to use a light weight card stock as clients seem to retain these more readily.

Letterheads and envelopes should carry the same basic information and should be printed on good quality (partially rag) paper. The envelope should carry the legend "Address Correction Requested" in the lower right hand corner. This instructs the post office to notify you whenever a letter has been forwarded, so that you can keep your own address files up to date.

Every art work should have a non–removable pressure sensitive label on the reverse, attached to the mat or frame and indicating the name of the artist, art dealer, medium, size, name of work, etc., as well as address and telephone. Similar labels may also be used to accompany works on exhibition, but these may be removable.

68. Reprints

Critical notices and reviews by critics in metropolitan newspapers and elsewhere can be easily reprinted at modest cost. Most art dealers and artists keep scrap books containing their publicity and advertising materials. But such material is not a useful sales aid since it cannot be carried away by a client. It is a good practice to reproduce, electrostatically or with photo–offset methods, certain press notices and feature articles when they are pertinent.

Such reproductions may be sent routinely to an artist's collectors. They may also be employed to assist in a sales presentation of an artist's merit. I have helped clients to assemble press notice brochures containing a collection of reprints of several related press notices. These are particularly useful for follow–up mailings during and after exhibitions. Since newsprint half–tones will reproduce poorly and often generate *moire* patterns, it may be more effective, in preparing reprints, to furnish the printer with glossy prints of the original photographs employed in preparing the news article. The printer can then make fresh half–tones for use in the reprint.

It is also possible to modify the scale of an illustration in making a reprint to better fill the space. In fact, I have from time to time found it convenient to enlarge the type used in a reprint, as well, to improve legibility, and I have used a fifty percent half–tone in copying large headlines to reduce the boldness of such areas in reprints.

In any case, always be sure to indicate that the copy is being reprinted from a specific publication and date and also always add a point of contact to the reprint, consisting of the name, address, telephone, etc. of the artist or dealer. Thus, the reprint is fully self–sustaining.

69. Documentation

Letters and certificates indicating the provenance and originality, methods of fabrication, and conditions of prior exhibition or prior ownership of a work are often duplicated and made available to prospective collectors. Some dealers package this material handsomely and deliver it to a customer with each newly acquired work. It may be useful to an art collector for tax and insurance purposes, and it heightens interest not only in the new acquisition, but in collecting art generally.

Two useful forms are shown here. The first is designed for employment with a unique art work, and the second will apply to the documentation of a multiple original, whether two or three dimensional. To illustrate this, the completed documentation for a monotype by Martin Green is appended, as is the completed documentation of an original lithograph by Florence Putterman. Note that this sheet is signed by Master printer Ernest De Soto, as well, as by the artist since the work was created by Putterman with the active collab–oration of De Soto.

Unique Work of Art

Certificate of Authenticity
Documentation

Title of Work . . . .

Dimensions . . . . . . x . . . . . .

Medium . . . .

I hereby warrant that the unique work of art described herein was created by me. This work was conceived on or about . . . . , 19 . . . . and executed on or about . . . . , 19 . . . .

It consists of: (Describe materials employed in some detail: e.g. "Grumbacher oils on Belgian linen" or "Reinforced polyester resin, cast in a specially constructed plaster mold") . . . .
. . . .
. . . .

Finishes employed: (Describe in detail: e.g. "Two coats of Damar Varnish" or "Hand rubbed patina") . . . .
. . . .
. . . .

This original work of art is in no sense a copy, duplicate or reproduction of any other art work but represents my own original creative expression. It exists only in this unique state. It has been signed and dated by hand. I was assisted by . . . . in the . . . . portion of this work.

Date . . . . , 19 . . . .
                                                    Artist

Multiple Original Work of Art

Certificate of Authenticity
Documentation

Title . . . . Medium . . . .
Dimensions . . . . x . . . . Edition Size . . . .
Description of Work: . . . .
. . . .
. . . .
I hereby warrant that the multiple original works of art described herein
were created by me and executed with the assistance of:
. . . .
. . . .
These original hand signed and numbered works were conceived on or
about . . . . , 19 . . . . and were executed in
. . . . , 19 . . . . They consist of: (Describe images briefly in
terms of forms, colors, and methods employed.)
. . . .
. . . .
. . . .
Materials employed: . . . .
. . . .
Record of the edition: (For original prints, identify all existing or
planned works in the edition, including printer's proofs, trial proofs,
artist's proofs, standard proofs, cancellation proofs, etc. For sculpture
and hangings, identify castings already finished or planned, weavings
finished or planned, etc. Indicate whether special states exist. Indicate
identification system employed.)
. . . .
. . . .
. . . .
All other (proofs/castings/hangings)* have been destroyed. The (plates/
cartoons/molds)* employed to make these works have been (effaced/
destroyed/stored until the edition is completed, at which time they will
be effaced/destroyed).*

These multiple original works of art are in no sense copies, duplicates,
or reproductions of other art works but represent originals of my own
creative expression. They are strictly limited in number, as detailed
above, to a total of . . . . works.

Date . . . . , 19 . . . .
                                                    Artist

*Choose one term

– 188 –

THE ERNEST F. DE SOTO WORKSHOP
San Francisco, California 94103

319 IIth Street
415/863–3232

Artist: Florence Putterman
Title: Canyon Series III
Printed between 11–8–77 and 12–23–77

DSW Edition Number: 32
Paper Size: 22 3/8" x 30"
Image Size: 22 3/8" x 30"

A nine color lithograph printed as follows:

The images were drawn with Korn's litho crayons and Korn's rubbing stick, and in the case of the washes, with *Charbonnel Encre Bessinsteurs Lithographique.* Deletions were made with solvent and etching out as with abrasives and erasers. The image on Run 1 is a transfer with additions. Images were drawn on lithographic limestone or aluminum plates as indicated.

Run 1: Alum. plate — *Indian red:* Leaf brown, Trans. base—Hanco; Bismark brown — S & V, Umber ; Leaf brown, Trans. base — Hanco; Bismark brown, Oriental green — S & V.

Run 2: Stone — *Ochre 1:* Trans. base, Leaf brown, Opaque white — Hanco; Chrome yellow, Oriental green, Stone purple — S & V.
Ochre 2: Same as Ochre 1 plus Policy Orange — Hanco.

Run 3: Stone — *Green 1:* Thalo blue green, Opaque white, Trans. base — Hanco; Oriental green, Chrome yellow — S & V.
Green 2: Process blue, Opaque white, Trans. base — Hanco; Bismark brown, Oriental green, Chrome yellow — S & V; Orange; Stone purple— S & V; Policy orange, Trans. base, Fire red, Leaf brown — Hanco.

Run 4: Alum. plate — *Dark green:* Process blue — Hanco; Oriental green — S & V; Purple/Brown; Chrome yellow— S & V; Leaf brown, Trans. base — Hanco; Stone purple — S & V.

RECORD OF PRINTING:

1	*Bon a Tirer* on Arches Buff	75	Numbered Edition
1	Shop Record on Arches Buff	1	Cancellation Proof
2	Printer's Proofs on Arches Buff	Ø	Publisher's Proofs
Ø	Artist Proofs	Ø	Presentation Proofs

All other proofs and impressions have been destroyed. The aluminum plate/stones have been effaced. This lithograph bears the chop of the de Soto Workshop and Master Printer.

Printers:

Artist:

Date: 12–27–77

Certificate of Authenticity

Louis Newman Galleries
404 South Figueroa Street
Los Angeles, California 90071   (213) 687–3200

Title of work: Monotype Mural for Dr. & Mrs. xxxx xxxxx.
Dimensions: 25 feet wide x 10 feet high (approximately)
Medium: monotype over wood panels

I hereby warrant that this unique work of art, conceived and created in Feb. & Mar. 1978 was installed on 30 March 1978.

The work consists of monotype panels specially shaped to circular contours. BFK Rives roll rag paper stock was used. Printing inks were fabricated by Hanco, Sinclair and Valentine, as well as Cal Ink.   The monotypes were printed on my own etching press using acrylic plates. Several glazes were added with an airbrush.

The separate elements of the monotype mural are mounted on ¾" lumber core mahogany with a 100 percent rag barrier paper between the wood and the monotype paper. Mounting was accomplished with a wheat starch paste (Los Angeles County Museum of Art's formula). Nine panels were cut for this project using a specially–rigged jigsaw on a radial arm. The edges of each panel were finished to match the color of the wall against which the mural has been installed. The panels are mounted on the wall with dovetailed oaken com– ponents attached to each panel and matching components on the wall.

Finishes employed: Krylon Crystal Clear.

This original work of art is in no sense a copy, duplicate or reproduction of any art work, but represents my own original expression. It exists only in this unique state and has been signed in the lower right hand corner.

I was assisted by George Gilbert in both the mounting and installation of the work.

Martin Green, Artist   4/2/78
                                        Date

70. Portfolios

Many artists and dealers operate very effectively with a scrapbook or portfolio in which they have assembled a series of photographs, clippings, letters, notices, biographical notes, awards, etc. Such a collection can be employed to quickly show a professional art buyer, some sense of the scale, images, textures, prestige, and critical reception which are character— istic of an artist's work. This is particularly useful with clients who are considering commissioning a work.

The best portfolios consist of a case which carries a series of presentation boards of uniform size. Attache cases may be used for this purpose, but artist's map cases can be even better since they accomodate larger mat boards. Select the case first and develop the mat boards to fit. Recently, a few firms have managed to adapt telescoping fiber board shipping cases as portfolios, and I recently learned of a fabricator who molded a case of sturdy plastic of the kind used for luggage.

If you are getting started as a private art dealer working out of your home or office, the portfolio boards should display representative examples of the kind of work which is available through you. One board might contain a close—up color illustration of an art work. The next might show a well illuminated, actual installation of works hanging on an office or home wall. Another board might show a detail of a work. To keep the display boards from becoming too dog—eared, it is useful to tape a sheet of heavy paper to the face of each board to act as a protective cover.

If you are an artist seeking commissions from architects and designers or if you are an art dealer representing artists who do such work, your portfolio should contain good examples of "public" art — — that is art which is particularly appropriate for public display. Good mounted photographs of such installations are excellent for this purpose. Where you have actual installations to show, they are preferable, but also useful are photographs of models and mock—ups of proposed projects. It is always helpful to include size references in your photos. These may be familiar scale models of such objects as cars, trees, and people.

I once worked with an artist who specialized in painting rural landscapes which he sells through a number of galleries in different communities. Since his works are large and cumbersome, he decided on a substitute for a portfolio which is an excellent portable slide viewer with its own self—contained screen. Instead of showing mounted photoprints, he shows a wide variety of works and close—up details in a short period of time with this portable viewer. Such equipment is available through audio—visual equipment shops. He was insistent on selecting a unit which has a self—contained screen and can be used effectively in a room which has not been darkened.

71. House Brochures

As suggested earlier, an artist or an art dealer may produce a brochure designed, not to advertise a specific exhibition, but rather to illustrate an ambiance, a capability, or a series of images. Such brochures are usually illustrated and may contain testimonial materials and brief biographies, as well as an address and telephone number. They are particularly useful as companions to solicitation letters.

On many occasions, when working with some relatively unknown artists, I have found that a well designed house brochure, printed in quantities of three to fifteen thousand, produced in color and illustrating the artist's work is an ex—cellent investment. The brochure should be large enough to show work to advantage, and it should be printed on good paper. My favorite format is 11" x 17" printed on both sides and folded to make a four—page 8½ x 11 brochure. I often suggest coated stock and over—all background tints as this sets off the illustrations to best advantage.

In addition, I like to see a brief biography – – which relates primarily to the artist's professional history and mentions several important private and institutional collectors – – in the house brochure. This biography should accompany an interesting picture of the artist either at work in the studio or viewing an art work. Many art dealers make the error of in—cluding long, hard—to—read lists of awards and exhibitions in such a brochure. I once saw an artist's brochure which apparently listed the names of every collector who had ever acquired a work. Such lists are, of course, counter productive since they do not distinguish well between matters of relative importance.

As indicated earlier, the house brochure should contain a point of contact − − that is the artist's or dealer's name, address, and telephone number. I will often advise my clients to print a good number of house brochures with a blank space in this area that can be imprinted by a dealer in another community. An alternate involves using preprinted labels to fit the brochure for use by another dealer.

The house brochure can of course be teamed with invita−tions to serve for several different exhibitions. It can also be used as an introduction to a potential private corporate collector.

72. Invitations

The practice of many art dealers and artists is, as has been noted elsewhere in this *Handbook,* one of concentrating all or almost all time and money on the single sales activity of the art exhibition, and more particularly, on the opening of the exhibition. Invitations to exhibitions are often quite unjustifiably expensive. Thus, an art dealer will spend three thousand dollars or more on a beautiful color illustrated in−vitation which has only a single function, knowing full well that this expense will be hard to justify as an investment without sales of at least forty thousand. I much prefer a simple, if formal, invitation inserted in a house brochure which has other uses.

A compromise which can be quite effective where a house brochure is not available involves an invitation printed in color but not using a four color process. Recently, I worked with a client who used this approach on a major solo exhibi−tion of a sculptor's work. The brochure − invitation was printed, without the cost of color separations, using duo−tones and tinted backgrounds. In this case, the photographs of the sculpture were printed in a process color which approximated the patina of the works themselves. This colored half–tone was overlaid with a thirty percent black half–tone to accent the three dimensional character of the work. The background of the brochure, which was printed in a contrasting, but rather neutral olive green, went all the way to the edges of the paper (bleed printing). The result was a dramatic, modern, and relatively inexpensive illustrated color invitation.

For use with a house brochure, I have often printed the invitation on translucent manifold paper. This flimsy material does not add much to the weight of the letter and permits the recipient to view illustrations right through the invitation.

All invitations, whether to gallery solo openings, to studio sales, or to sales parties, should be more than mere announce– ments. Be sure to indicate that an activity is desired of the recipient. "Please join us." "Don't miss this important exhibition." "Save the date." This exhortation should be followed by a concise, but complete statement of the facts: *Who? What? When? Where?*

Again the printed material should be legible. Text styles that are hard to read should be avoided, together with fuzzy, skinny or light type faces. Important elements such as the artist's name and the date of the function should be larger or bolder than the remainder of the copy. In listing a date, always include the weekday as well as the calendar date: "Sunday, March 30, from 3 to 6." not "March 30, from 3 to 6." When a facility is in an unfamiliar location, add verbal instructions: "Turn left (west) from the Base Line Exit of the Acme Expressway. Travel about two miles on Center Drive and then turn right (north) on to Alfalfa Street."

73. Presentation Folders — Proposals

An art dealer or an artist who submits a significant number of written proposals for commissions or special projects may employ a presentation folder to set off the proposals and give them a distinctive appearance. Most of these folders are usually printed on index stock and often carry the artist's or dealer's logotype. Some are designed to function as file folders as well while others have the appearance of report jackets. They give any proposal a packaged, professional look, and they help prevent the contents from being lost or separated.

A proposal for a special project generally contains a letter to the prospect outlining the main elements of the project. To this may be appended a budget, a schedule, a contract, preliminary sketches, color photographs of a cartoon or of a maquette, a *curriculum vitae* of the artist, and a brief history of the art dealer. House brochures and reprints may also be included.

It is not unusual for an artist or an art dealer to ask for a developmental payment covering or partially covering the cost of preparing a proposal, on the grounds that the efforts in—volved are time—consuming and expensive. It is also not unusual for a creative person to copyright the contents of a proposal before releasing it, to forestall attempts to copy original designs and treatments.

74. Color Postcards

A number of galleries and artists have regularly reproduced a few key works as colored postcards in conjuction with their exhibitions and other sales efforts. These cards are generally printed on coated index stock. A postcard, reproduced in colors which accurately reflect the original work, is seldom inexpensive, but it lends some authority to the claims of the seller regarding the quality of the work. Visitors to galleries or studios, including important collectors, are often pleased to buy several such cards.

The postcards may be produced by two processes. Most commonly, a four—color process is employed. Here, the original work is photographed and then optically separated into four half—tone components — — the three primary colors and black. These separations should then be corrected before the card is printed. Several companies in our major cities specialize in such color postcards and can often do rather good work at fairly low prices.

The other process, called collotype, can only be employed when the work has previously been sub—divided into different colors, as it is when the separate plates and stones of an original lithograph have been individually proofed. Here, each plate is printed in its characteristic continuous—tone color, often producing an excellent reproduction. More than four plates may be used. Only a handful of printers have collotype printing capabilities.

Of course, not all images reduce or reproduce well. The dealer should be careful about selecting only suitable works for postcards. And adequate information should be printed on the back of the card.

75. Illustrated Monographs

A much more costly, but very effective sales aid, is the illustrated monograph. These documents may vary in size from just a few pages with only one or two black and white illustrations to a large book—length essay, fully illustrated in color. Monographs may be prepared in conjunction with a museum show, or they may be published independently by a gallery or an artist. I have worked with a sculptor who published a fine soft—cover monograph jointly with his New York dealer. The book has been extremely useful as a sales aid.

In either case, an art critic or curator is generally retained to prepare the text and select the illustrations while a pro—fessional graphic designer is assigned to select and specify type and paper, to design the cover, lay out the interior, select the printer, and supervise production. These days, most mono—graphs are produced with paper bindings to reduce expense, which is much greater when hard covers are employed. A well done monograph can be of great interest to collectors and institutions and can increase the reputation and market strength of an artist. It is seldom a self—liquidating investment.

76. Slide Carousels

The art dealer may find it useful to assemble a group of color slides relating to an artist's works for viewing in the sales presentation room in a slide carousel or cartridge. Here the focus, scale, and color intensity of the slides can be controlled and the overall impact of the artist's work on the collector can be enhanced. Such displays make an interesting adjunct to a sales presentation. Be careful not to show a client too much. It can be a debilitating experience. Of course, many artists use slide carousels, too.

77. Libraries

Every dealer and artist needs a good art library containing pertinent materials, reference books, directories, periodicals, catalogues, and reproductions of important works. The library may be installed in the studio, in the sales presentation room, or in the dealer's office where it can function as a very useful composite sales aid.

Art museums and art schools often maintain excellent libraries which are available to qualified artists and dealers at little or no cost. While some are much better catalogued than others, they generally contain a great deal of extremely useful information which cannot readily be obtained or assembled from any other source. Showing a client related or supportive materials can be quite valuable in selling an art work. These might include critical and other bibliographical references. They might be art historical or geographic in their nature, but they can be very useful.

78. Films, TV Cassettes and Documentaries

The development and introduction of 16 mm and 8 mm sound film and of television cassettes and cartridges has made it possible to develop relatively inexpensive short movies of professional quality which are extremely useful to artists and art dealers. Such films often encompass six to eight minutes of viewing although some are longer. It can show the artist, the studio, the artist's works in the process of being executed, or in the possession of an important collector. Occassionally, the film will include significant comments by the artist, by an admiring critic, or by a client. Yaacov Agam has developed a series of very effective cassettes which portray certain of his kinetic works. They are excellent promotional aids.

Gallery owners have also subsidized longer films in the form of documentaries. These works generally deal with some particular aspect of the artist's work or interests and may encompass the stages of a major commission or the prepara—tion of a retrospective. Films may also be employed to capture the ambiance at a happening. Skillfully prepared documen—taries have a market in the art departments of colleges and universities, which often rent or buy films to show to art classes. They, in turn, tend to improve the appreciation of an artist's work.

Marketing
Planning

79. The Importance of Careful Planning In The Art Market

As we have seen, a properly conceived and executed promotional campaign can be an important form of indirect contact with prospective clients. But contacts with potential collectors should be only partially indirect. A direct approach can be considerably more productive in terms of finding legitimate sales opportunities for art works. Towards this end, once "pre–selling" efforts have been initiated, the artist or art dealer must begin Marketing Planning. This is a con–ceptual activity in which various avenues for direct contact with potential clients are explored, priorities are set, and effort, and funds are allocated.

In this *Handbook,* as in many other marketing studies and texts, marketing planning is a systematic, coordinated effort designed to establish prospecting and selling goals, and to couple these with specific kinds of sales activities and supportive promotional efforts which are acceptable to the artist and the dealer. In planning art marketing efforts, the artist or dealer must consider the methods which are to be used to achieve these goals and should also seek a way to measure the varied results which can be obtained through the employment of different marketing methods. Thus, marketing planning consists of setting realistic client contact and sales goals, developing different methods of accomplishing these goals, and measuring the relationship between funds and efforts expended and the results which may be obtained, through different approaches.

There are some artists and dealers who feel that their market will, or should, develop more or less automatically, without any planning, as long as their works are interesting, and properly priced. They assume that "somehow" their income from sales will eventually at least equal their expenses. This assumption too often proves incorrect. Many fine artists and dealers do not even cover their own expenses with income from the sale of art works.

In the last analysis, they support their art with funds obtained by working at other jobs or with income from other sources. Such artists and dealers are, in a sense, self—funded philanthropists of art. They are supporting their own work or the work of others, but gaining no significant financial benefits from the activity. Sometimes, the non—financial rewards of being active in the art world are quite impressive. The chance to travel, to meet and work with interesting people, to collect fine works is not to be dismissed as inconsequential.

But, the serious artist and art dealer cannot afford a complacent attitude towards cultivating sales. At best, without marketing planning, sales results will be erratic and unpredictable. At worst, the lack of marketing planning can retard the careers of fine artists and prevent them from ever reaching any significant number of potential collectors. For dealers, unplanned activities can produce frustration, a failure of expectations, even bankruptcy.

To be sure, some sales may occur without planning or even effort, for that matter. Clients are referred by supportive friends and other artists. Customers wander in off the street without invitation. But one cannot live with the illusion that such sales will ever be a significant factor in the art market. They are fortunate accidents which only suggest how truly successful the artist and art dealer might become if realistic planning were undertaken and followed by a vigorous marketing campaign.

Nor should one mistake marketing planning for business trend—plotting, a common confusion among small business—men. Business trend analysis is the study of certain external market factors which might justifiably be considered by the artist or dealer, although such trends are seldom directly responsible for success or failure in the art world. In truth, it is sometimes relatively difficult to sell an artist's work during periods of economic recession. Also, the waxing and waning of fashions in art may notably influence an artist's fortune.

But good marketing planning can help the artist and the art dealer to weather the vicissitudes of shifting business conditions and changing vogues among collectors. Such planning can even produce sales results which are counter—cyclical so that an artist's acceptance by collectors grows even as business in general and fashion in particular wanes or shifts. This is possible because many collectors are relatively free from the more harmful effects of a recession and can move at will into the art market to buy works, even when unemployment is relatively high or the stock market is bearish. So, too, many potential clients (the largest number) stand quite outside the fashionable "in—group" of the art world and are totally unaware of the fickle fads and interests of so—called key curators and collectors.

Incidentally, the most important long–term market trend affecting the acquisition of contemporary art in the United States is a very positive one. This trend − − the very significant and continuing entry of new collectors into the field − − is caused by a general awakening of interest in everything the contemporary artists are doing, reinforced by a prodigious growth in the relative number of families who have significant discretionary income. As reported earlier, the shift of both factors dates from the end of World War II and shows no signs of deteriorating during the eighties.

These circumstances are particularly significant in that they have led to a large, relatively unsophisticated clientele. That is, these new collectors and potential collectors have the desire and the ability to buy art, but they are not predisposed to any particular school or esthetic bias. Their tastes can be developed in a number of fruitful directions, depending on who reaches them and how well their experiences with art are cultivated. And they constitute a largely untapped market.

80. Relating Efforts and Funding to Success

The basic assumption of the marketing planner is that a measurable, reproducible relationship exists between the expenditure of time and money on specific varieties of marketing activities and the sales generated by such expenditures. For example, we may find that a well written letter of solicitation addressed to the right kind of mailing list will produce a certain level of interested response. That is, one hundred personal letters to prospective collectors, properly followed up with an equal number of telephone calls, will produce a given number of opportunities to make private sales presentations.

In my experience, the actual response in such a campaign varies between two and ten percent, depending on the quality of the letter, the quality of the list, and the quality of the follow-up. A repetition of this same kind of effort with a comparable list will, on the average, produce the same rate of success. A larger number of contacts will produce a proportionally large number of qualified prospects.

Certainly, a well designed letter directed to a well chosen list will produce better results than a hastily contrived letter sent to a haphazardly selected list. But, whenever the quality of the marketing effort is held relatively constant, the number of contacts and the volume of sales produced will depend directly on the volume of solicitation and sales promoting activity.

Now every artist and art dealer has many different kinds of marketing activities available at any point in time. Some activities, such as a gallery exhibition, may require a good deal of planning, a fairly significant expenditure, and a lot of cooperation. Other activities, like a private sales party, a studio exhibition and sale, or a private sales presentation to private or corporate collectors, will usually require a smaller expenditure of time and money.

The artist or dealer can discover through experience just how much of a particular variety of marketing activity is needed to generate a certain level of contacts or sales. Of course, one may then improve on this ratio by doing a better job within the marketing activity. Better mailing lists, better solicitation letters, smoother sales presentations will improve the rate of success to be expected from any particular variety of marketing activity. But, again, based on prior performance and on anticipated improvements, it should be possible to predict the sales results which a given level of marketing activity can produce over a given period of time.

81. Solo Exhibitions

The most commonly used art marketing activity in our culture is built around the solo exhibition of the artist's work. Advance publicity for such exhibitions, the opening reception, which is generally held in conjunction with the exhibition, and the show itself, all serve to encourage potential collectors to take an interest in certain works which have been placed on display in the hope that sales will be produced.

As suggested earlier, an exhibition will generally lead to publicity. It is not hard to use this activity as a device for sales promotion, as well. Whether it leads to any significant volume of sales is another matter. I have talked with many artists who were bitterly disappointed at the failure of their solo exhibitions to generate sales.

Through recent decades, it has become fashionable to show only certain of the artist's most recent works, usually those which pertain to a particular series or mood. This fashion is very convenient for purposes of the reviewing critic, but it tends to violate the interests of any artist whose work contains more than one level or interest. It certainly does little for the collector whose own interests, biases, and needs may not be satisfied by the particular series placed on exhib—ition. The collector who appreciates an image which the artist was creating earlier cannot be served if these works are not shown.

I seriously question whether this particular and highly specialized variety of marketing activity is effective enough to justify its being used almost to the exclusion of other approaches by artists and art dealers. For example, I find that solo retrospectives and group shows often tend to produce more sales because they offer a wider variety of images to the public view. The contrasts are helpful to the collector. Also, I find that an artist's studio exhibition and sale, which is generally not so specialized in content, but tends to cover many moods and periods, is also more consistently productive of significant new contacts and sales.

Many successful dealers find that their best collectors abhor attending openings with their curious folkways. These collectors seldom buy at exhibitions though occasionally they will be interested in looking at works in advance of an exhibition. More often, however, the sophisticated collector will want to see certain works independently of any public display.

The dealers often justify their expensive, time—consuming, solo exhibition programs on the grounds that "the artists expect it" and also on the proposition that "it brings new people into the gallery." What the artist needs most from marketing efforts, far more than the prestige of yet another exhibition, is a consistent source of new and meaningful clientele. Further, there are many more productive ways of stimulating potential collectors to come into a gallery or to visit an artist's studio for the purpose of examining and buying art works.

An impressive number of private dealers avoid the formal exhibition approach entirely because they find it wastes their resources while more and more public art dealers are using group shows and other cultural events to stimulate traffic where it seems useful.

The question remains then: is the artist's solo, single—theme gallery exhibition, together with the publicity and opening normally associated with such functions, an effective activity for stimulating sales? The answer seems to be that while it is a method which is widely used, it is often not the most effective source of new or repeat sales available to the artist or dealer. Further, it should never be employed ex—clusively or even as a primary marketing activity.

I have, in fact, observed that the most significant sales associated with a solo exhibition can occur prior to the opening. A number of my clients have planned special pre—show marketing activities designed to make the contents of an exhibition available to collectors who are established clients before they are available to the general public. Such "pre—selling" must, of course, be carefully planned so that the work, lists, letters, and brochures are ready in plenty of time.

In the past few years, I have encountered, on several occasions, a curious competition for gallery time and space arising from the rather arcane notion that an artist's solo exhibition is some sort of sacred ritual. Artists have, on occasion, insisted that no works by other artists be hung during their solo shows and that their exhibition must remain untouched for a month or more. On one occasion, I heard a critic for an art journal decline to review an exhibition because, by the time she arrived at the exhibition two weeks after the opening, two works had been removed, with the permission of the artist and at the request of a client. This sort of destructive thinking cannot help the artist or the dealer to survive. Dealers are often justified in showing a few works by other artists outside of the solo show and in in—creasing the number of other works after collectors have had a legitimate opportunity to view the solo exhibition. In most cases, a gallery owner cannot afford to operate as a non—profit museum would in allocating time and space to a solo exhibition.

82. Private Sales Presentations

The private sales presentation approach already discussed more fully elsewhere in this *Handbook* is probably the most effective method for making contacts, developing new clients, and selling art works. This technique involves writing or talking to a potential collector, sometimes, enclosing or dis—tributing a brochure calling attention to an artist's work, and inviting the collector and the collector's spouse to a sales presentation at the gallery or at the artist's studio where they may study the works in privacy. Unlike the formal gallery exhibition where attendance takes on a social character all its own, at a private sales presentation the prospective collector comes in for the specific purpose of examining art and making purchase decisions.

It is a consistently effective marketing technique and a relatively inexpensive one compared with the high cost of solo exhibitions and their attendant publicity and opening costs. Further, unlike the exhibition method, which requires an elaborate gallery exhibition facility, the private sales pre—sentation method can be employed by anyone with a private room, even a living—room or a studio, including an artist or a private dealer. For the public art dealer who relies on these private sales presentations, solo exhibitions can become an important, but auxiliary function.

Clearly, this method of promoting sales through private presentations requires a certain amount of courage since it puts the artist and the art dealer in direct face—to—face contact with relatively unknown, possibly even hostile individuals. Further, in the case of some artist's images, and certainly in the case of some classes of mailing lists, one might find it necessary to exhaust a relatively large number of names before locating any significant number of qualified prospects. But once such a qualified prospect has been located, the probability of making a sale is rather high. I have been told by well established dealers, such as the late Mr. Maxwell of Maxwell's Gallery in San Francisco, that two—thirds of all their gallery sales are made in private sales presentations.

This solicitation and sales method also requires a certain amount of market research to develop sources of potential clients. One approach involves contacting individuals in a variety of businesses and professions such as law, medicine, dentistry, and building construction, in a particular community on the assumption that a fair percentage of such contacts can be interested in a private sales presentation. A more uncertain approach involves purchasing mailing lists of buyers of art books, subscribers to art magazines, members of arts associations, etc. for specific communities.

Such lists are compiled and sold by mailing list companies. The names of a few of these firms, together with a description of a few such lists, will be found at the conclusion of that section of this text which discusses direct response sales activities. Other kinds of lists are available from mailing list firms in the major metropolitan areas throughout the country.

My own studies show that artists and art dealers working with contemporary works done by capable but relatively little known artists in a wide variety of images can generally make a sale of one work per private sales presentation to a qualified prospect developed from such marketing activities. Ten private sales presentations to qualified prospects can yield an average of ten works sold with an expenditure of consid— erably less effort and money than is required to mount a solo exhibition in which fewer works may be sold.

Obviously, if the artist's reputation is better than average, if the images are more interesting than most, if the prospect lists and solicitation letters are of a very high caliber, this success ratio can easily be exceeded.

I work with an artist who sells his own work out of his studio and currently manages to sell about fifteen works for every ten private sales presentations. He uses sales parties, solo exhibitions, and other marketing activities as well, but they are not as effective for him. Of course, results improve as experience and confidence is gained. Curiously, for all the hundreds of letters in my file, no artists or dealers have ever written to me stating that they have tried this approach conscientiously and found it fruitless.

A number of my art dealer clients have found that private sales presentations can even be made during the exhibition openings and at other social functions. Interested individuals and couples are encouraged to view a work "in more intimate surroundings." One or more works are actually removed from the wall and taken to the private sales room. It will, of course, be rehung after the presentation. The Louis Newman Gallery in Los Angeles regularly employs two private sales rooms during their solo exhibitions and finds that this method pro— duces a very satisfactory success ratio in terms of works sold per sales presentation.

83. Making Repeat Sales and Referrals

An interesting variant of private sales presentation activity involves making contact by writing letters of solicitation to collectors who are already well known to the artist or dealer. It is far easier to write a letter or to make a phone call to someone who has already done business with an artist or art dealer or who is already known to be a collector than it is to contact someone who may not even have expressed an interest in collecting art. An exception is the internationally famous, advanced collector, who is literally inundated with offers and solicitations.

Of course, the easiest person to contact is one who is already a collector of the artist's own work. In this variant, the list of potential clients is smaller, but the percentage of appointments which can be made by properly using such a list is consistently greater. In any case, the marketing activities involved in making appointments for sales presentations with old friends, former clients, and those already acquainted with the artist or the gallery involves a potentially much higher rate of success than can be expected from a similar activity with "cold" contacts.

Still another variant of this marketing activity, which also leads to opportunities to make private sales presentations, involves contacting art collectors who have been referred or recommended by the artist's or dealer's clients and friends. A friend who is interested or a client who is pleased with an artist's work may — — but generally only when asked — — suggest acquaintances and business associates who might be interested in becoming collectors of that artist's work. Again, solicitations where a referral exists are easier to make. And they will probably produce more sales presentation oppor—tunities per hundred contacts than can be anticipated from an equal number of "cold" contact solicitations. In other business fields, vast sales empires have been erected almost entirely on the principle that referrals from satisfied customers make the best prospects for new business.

All of the above suggests that as collectors become more accustomed to buying an artist's work and as the reputation associated with an artist becomes better established, it is progressively easier to make appointments to show and sell that artist's work. Unfortunately, many artists and their dealers, through a curious combination of indifference, cowardice, and sloth, tend to relax their efforts too early in the career of the artist, satisfying themselves with a modest, regional clientele when much broader marketing opportunities are available to them.

They tend to avoid actively seeking new referral contacts, and give up entirely on "cold" contacts, merely waiting patiently for old clients to come forward on their own. When such trusty old friends do come forward, they may be shown only the artist's most current work. Artists and dealers forget that often the greatest interest of certain collectors may be in an aspect of the artist's work which no longer excites the artist at all.

These earlier works which the loyal old collector likes so much may now be consigned to a dusty storage place where they are inaccessible and largely unsalable. Realizing the latent opportunity for developing new clients and new markets or for stimulating old clients to make new acquisitions can be hard work. As a result of their failure to do this work, many fine artists and dealers reach only a small portion of their potential market.

84. Finding Ways of Making Institutional Sales

It has been noted that some artists create works which are of a scale, nature, or medium that suits them not for a private home, but rather for a public place. A new office building, a newly furnished suite of offices, an outdoor shopping mall, a branch bank − − all are excellent prospects for institutional purchasers of art. Here, the appropriate solicitation lists consist of architects, builders, decorators, and designers, rather than individual professionals, art mag−azine subscribers, and art book buyers.

One excellent source of prospects for such institutional works is the "Green Sheet" or Dodge Report which period−ically publishes in each major community the new construction plans, describes their scale, and notes the architect in charge. Other lists, such as the rosters of the local architectural association or the designer's society, are readily available. Some of the best lists are available in the local Yellow Pages, without charge to the user.

A private dealer with whom I work reported that she had difficulty finding copies of the construction reports for her community. I suggested that she contact a builder whom she knew, and he arranged for her to consult his back copies of this useful publication. She noticed that a large state−wide bank chain was regularly listed, with a number of new branches being reported in every issue. It took several weeks to find and reach those responsible for placing art in these branch banks, but she eventually discovered that the firm which had been supplying art was doing a rather unsatisfactory job and, beginning with a few test assignments, she is currently selling better than seventy−five thousand dollars worth of art an−nually to this client.

85. How and When Marketing Planning is Accomplished

Artists who are not represented by an art dealer or are represented only in certain very limited market areas should do their own marketing planning. Occasionally, they may call upon a spouse or a good friend for assistance and advice. Art dealers have a larger, but fundamentally easier job since they may combine the names of the collectors and friends of col—lectors of all their artists with their own lists.

Regularly, new list sources should be sought and revision of old lists should be made. At least once every six months, one should replan marketing activities for the entire year ahead, refining, reviewing, and finalizing those sales activities which lie within the six months just ahead and laying the basis for functions which require longer range planning than can be accomplished within a six—month period.

Planning should always be done with an eye to the prac—tical experience of the immediate past, as well as in terms of new opportunities for the future. The number of solicitations and contacts previously made, the results achieved from those contacts during the prior six or twelve months, should not limit the artist's or dealer's future plans, but they should certainly act as a guide in terms of what has been accomplished and what functions need improvement or reorganization along more effective lines.

Once a plan for the next twelve months is established, a calendar should be drawn up on which anticipated events and scheduled targets may be recorded. These should include data for the development and completion of new or revised mailing lists, deadlines for the preparation or revision of promotional and solicitation letters, schedules for mailing these letters and making follow—up phone calls, dates for the preparation of publicity releases, feature articles, and illustrations, deadlines for the development of brochures and catalogues, and for entries in juried competitions, participation in group exhibitions, and preparation of solo shows, studio sales, private sales, and sales parties.

Where an event cannot be set down precisely in a time—table for lack of certain information, it should be listed to the side of the calendar, and a deadline should be set for finally calendaring it. Thus, it may not be possible to say a full year in advance precisely when a brochure will actually be ready for distribution. But it should be possible to determine that the design and specifications for the brochure, the quantity to be produced, its cost, and its date of publication will have been determined no later than a specified date, say, three months prior to the start of a certain campaign. By that time, these items should be ready for detailed and more precise scheduling and budgeting. Art dealers should prepare a twelve—month marketing plan at least every six months for every artist represented more than casually.

Artists and dealers who engage in wholesaling in more than one community should use marketing planning programs to prepare for sorties to distant cities, aimed at finding new outlets and establishing a market outside the artist's home. These undertakings generally require significant planning. I work with a private dealer who plans three to five sales trips annually. In some cases, he functions as a wholesaler, working with other art dealers. In other cases, he works directly with art collectors. He always arrives in a community which is expecting him, with a definite schedule of appointments already established.

86. Using the Marketing Planning Sheet

An artist or art dealer who works in different media or with different classes of art has a number of different sets of marketing problems. A separate form of the kind shown on the next page should be used for each time period planned and for each medium in which the artist or dealer is active. A summary sheet may be used to summarize the contents of the separate planning sheets.

Where marketing planning is being done for a one–year period, three forms should be prepared for each class of work. One of these covers the nearest three–month quarter, the next covers the second three–month quarter, and the third, the last six–month period.

The artist or dealer should begin by filling in all the in–formation which is already known, such as the number of works of this class which were sold during the same period of time for the twelve months which has just been concluded. The average selling price per work sold in this medium during that period should also be recorded, together with the number of works of this variety sold per hundred sales presentations made during the period, and the total number of sales pre–sentations in which works in this medium were shown to prospects during the period. This information can be extracted from carefully kept appointment calendars and from sales invoice records. The latter will be discussed more fully later in the *Handbook*.

On the summary marketing planning sheet, the total number of contacts which were made for the purpose of making sales presentation appointments should be recorded, and the number of personal contacts made for the same purpose, together with the prior year's budget for advertising and promotion, figured as a percent of total sales generated.

Marketing Planning Sheet

Use a separate sheet for each medium planned.

Oils/Acrylics . . . . Original Prints . . . .
Water Colors . . . . Sculptures/Assemblages . . . .
Mixed Media . . . . Monotypes . . . . . . Other . . . .

Sales Objectives

. . . . . . works in this medium to be sold during this planning period.

vs. . . . . . . works in this medium sold in same period, prior year.

$ . . . . . . , average selling price per work in this medium.

vs. $ . . . . . . , average selling price per work in this medium, same period, prior year (increased by . . . . %).

Success Ratio

. . . . . . number of works expected to be sold per hundred sales presentations, same period, prior year.

. . . . . . number of works sold per hundred sales presentations, same period, prior year.

Activity Rate

. . . . . . sales presentations needed to achieve new sales objective.

vs. . . . . . . sales presentations actually achieved in this medium, same period, prior year.

Solicitation Rate

. . . . . . letters and calls needed to produce . . . . sales presen—tations per period.

. . . . . . personal contacts needed to produce . . . . sales presen—tations per period.

vs. . . . . . . letters and calls generated for this purpose, same period, prior year.

. . . . . . personal contacts made for this purpose, same period, prior year.

Supporting Promotional Programs

Anticipated sales volume from this medium
for this planning period . $ . . . .

. . . . % of anticipated volume allowed for
advertising and publicity.

Total promotional budget for this medium
and period: $ . . . .

Marketing Activity Schedule Sheet

	Week Number												
	1	2	3	4	5	6	7	8	9	10	11	12	13
a) Prepare Brochure Copy and Layout													
b) Prepare Photo — Illustrations & Color Corrections													
c) Produce Brochures													
d) Prepare and Place Feature Stories													
e) Prepare and Issue Illustrated Press Releases													
f) Prepare and Revise Mailing Lists													
g) Prepare . . . . Letters for Mailing													
h) Make . . . . Telephone Follow–ups/Contacts													
i) Make . . . . Private Sales Presentations													
j) Conduct . . . . Sales Parties													

If these historical figures are not available, it is probably because poor records have been kept or because sales efforts have been relatively sporadic. Beginning with the first formal marketing plan, a simple calendar diary should be established in which, as the events occur, one may record the number of solicitation letters sent out on each day, the number of phone calls made, the personal contacts made, the number of sales presentation appointments made, the number of works sold at such presentations, as well as the dollar value of the sales made. To make marketing planning even more effective, the artists or dealers should summarize their actual experiences, weekly or monthly, so that performance and results may be compared with plans. As goals are realized and expanded, their usefulness becomes clearer. When targets are not being met, this should be a spur to greater effort, more effective work, and more realistic future plans.

For example, consider an art dealer who sold $40,000 worth of oils and acrylics during the course of the twelve months which just concluded. If the dealer sold a total of fifty works, then the average selling price in this category was $800.00. If the same dealer made a total of sixty sales pre—sentations of works in this medium, counting each effort, including repeats to the same client, during the year, then an average of 50/60 or five—sixths of a work was sold at each private sales presentation. This amounts to a rate of more than eighty—three works sold for every hundred sales pre—sentations made. If this dealer had sent out six hundred letters and made six hundred phone calls to arrange the sixty sales presentation appointments, then ten contacts must have been made for each appointment which materialized.

Now suppose that this dealer is determined to improve upon last year's sales performance in this medium over the prior year by a factor of one hundred percent. That is, this dealer has decided to sell eighty thousand dollars worth of oils and acrylics during the next twelve months. This is not a particularly difficult goal, but it requires consistent effort and good planning, as well as an adequate and diversified inventory of works.

To begin, the dealer should carefully reexamine current selling prices. It may be decided that an average of $800 per work is no longer appropriate. If prices were increased by an average of ten percent, the dealer could be receiving an average of $880 per work. In that case, to generate an income of eighty thousand dollars for the new year, the dealer would need to sell about ninety—one works.

It may be that this dealer feels the success ratio can be improved, as well. That is, it may be possible to increase the average number of works sold per hundred sales presentations. Certainly, as a dealer gains experience and makes appointments only with fully qualified prospects (a concept discussed more fully in the sections on selling) and as more effective sales presentations are made, the dealer can expect to sell more than eighty—three works for every hundred presentations. Some collectors will buy more than one work at a time. Old clients and referrals are more likely to buy than new contacts. My own "norm" is one work sold for every private sales presentation.

But, to keep the marketing planning conservative, this dealer may decide to base the new plan on the older, proven success ratio. On the basis of history, approximately one hundred and ten sales presentations will be needed during the course of the year in order to sell ninety—one works. Of course, if the dealer actually manages to improve on the effectiveness of these presentations, more than the targeted ninety—one works will be sold. In this case, the dealer will exceed planned volume.

Next, the dealer must determine the solicitation activity level required to produce one hundred and ten private sales presentation opportunities. In the prior year, this dealer found it necessary to send out ten letters and make at least ten phone calls or personal contacts for every sales presenta—tion appointment it was possible to arrange. Again, it may be that with superior letters, improved lists, and an increased level of referral business, as well as more repeat contacts with established collectors, the dealer may find it easier to achieve the target of one hundred and ten sales presentations in the year ahead.

But presuming that no improvement will be made in any of these rates, the dealer should schedule eleven hundred letters and calls at least of the quality made in the prior year, as this is the solicitation rate that was needed to produce one hundred and ten sales presentation opportunities during the year. The chances are very good that if this many solicitations in the form of letters, calls, and personal contacts are made, that, in fact, the dealer can expect to generate more than enough private sales presentation opportunities and more than enough sales to double the prior year's volume.

Next, the dealer must divide this anticipated marketing effort into smaller, more manageable time elements. The three month period, which begins in October and ends at the year—end, might reasonably include thirty—five or even forty percent of the total planned effort since this is a major buying season. July, August, and September might include only twenty percent of the planned activity because summer vacations reduce sales opportunities for some in certain communities. The remaining forty or forty—five percent of the plan could be divided equally over the remaining six months.

The dealer will, during all these periods, be working almost twice as hard at showing and selling works as was necessary to generate the lower volume of the prior year. Remember, however, that as reputation and effectiveness improve, it will not take the same effort to maintain the same sales level. Prospective clients will become easier to reach and interest. But any significant new increase in level will require added effort because new clients will be needed.

Once the dealer has decided that it is possible to produce a specific sum, such as eighty thousand dollars, in sales volume through a specific marketing plan, the advertising and pro—motion program which is appropriate to support this level of sales activity should be developed. Many successful gallery owners spend as little as three to four percent of their annual anticipated sales volume on promotion (not including exhi—bition costs). Where a radical change in volume is anticipated, as it is in this example, a considerably greater proportion might be needed for the desired result.

Suppose the dealer in our illustration decides to set aside eight percent of anticipated sales volume for advertising and promotion. This means that the gallery should spend $6,400 during the course of the year on promotion. This sum might be spent entirely on one or two color brochures illustrating the artists represented by the dealer who makes oils and acrylics and containing a few significant critical comments. Such brochures might be employed as companions to the solicitation letters. Promotional funds might, alternatively, be spent developing a publicity program designed to get positive, critical attention for the dealer's artists and to place illustrations of work in certain local or national art publica—tions. In this case, some promotional funds might be allocated to high quality photographic illustrations to be furnished, together with appropriate press releases, to the pertinent publications.

For example, the dealer might contact metropolitan publications to interest them in running an illustration of one of the works with a suitable credit line or caption. If the dealer supplies several different 8 x 10 black and white glossies, this would be an appropriate promotional expense. The preparation of color separations for color illustrations is much more expensive. A thousand dollars or more might be required to produce just a few properly corrected color separations to be used in an art publication to illustrate an artist's work. The dealer might also seek the assistance of an art curator or a free lance art critic to prepare captions or comments for such illustrations. Sometimes these specialists are compensated for such efforts.

Once the dealer has completed a marketing plan for the quarter, half year, and year ahead, the specific tasks related to this plan should be calendared. These include the prepar—ation of solicitation letters, mailing lists, etc. A partial list of typical marketing tasks is appended in the Quarterly Marketing Schedule Sheet. This sheet should be used as a graphic reminder of specific tasks to be accomplished. The illustrated form is designed to aid in accomplishing three months (thirteen weeks) of a marketing plan developed for the dealer discussed in this section. Readers will, of course, want to adapt the style of this sheet to their own purposes. They will want to develop similar forms to cover other time periods.

In the example just considered, we discussed an art dealer's plans for the sales effort associated with oils and acrylics. The same dealer might need a different plan for original prints and another for sculpture or watercolors. Of course, every artist needs a set of marketing plans as well, whether that artist is represented by dealers or not. The artist who is also a wholesaler needs a special marketing plan to deal with wholesaling activities.

Locating Qualified Prospects

87. Contacting Potential Collectors

For many active art collectors, the beginning of their interest in acquiring works coincided with an introduction to an artist or a dealer. Serious collectors and novices to the field often share an interest in meeting "new" and "upcoming" artists as well as established professionals. As any artist's recognition grows, as a dealer becomes better established, new opportunities will arise for meeting collectors. These meetings might take place at a museum exhibition, at a reception sponsored by the dealer's own art gallery in behalf of the artist, at a show of another artist's work, or at an artist's studio exhibition and sale.

To meet potential collectors, the aspiring artist and dealer must learn to "swim in the waters" which art collectors and would—be collectors inhabit. If you regularly attend museum exhibition openings, gallery openings, and other social func—tions in the art world, you will inevitably encounter many collectors. Such opportunities abound for the artist or dealer who is judicious in the allocation of free time. By joining art museum associations and listing their names with the major galleries, they can generally pick from a variety of functions those which seem most promising.

Art collectors of many levels of sophistication may also be found in more prosaic places. For example, an artist's attorney, doctor, or dentist may be an art collector or wish to become one. A dealer's friends or relatives may aspire to collect works of art. Artists who are also teachers are likely to discover that some of their colleagues, students, and members of students' families are art collectors. The circle broadens considerably when we consider the professional contacts, friends, and relatives of the dealer's or artist's own friends, acquaintances, relatives, and collectors.

In recent years, a great deal of time and money has been spent by various non–profit, government–funded arts agencies setting up artists' directories, slide files, index programs, and similar central listings. The advertised purpose of such com—pendiums is that collectors may consult them if they are looking for a particular kind of art or artist. In my own judgment, such activities are largely a waste of time because they are characteristically passive and do not reach out to collectors. Further, since the arts administrators who main—tain the slide files and indices are seldom able or willing to make subjective judgments, they do not discriminate in any way between artists of different persuasions or levels of competence. Here, as elsewhere, I must reiterate: artists and dealers cannot afford to wait for collectors to seek them out. They must find their own clients.

Just as soon as you begin to think in terms of entering the art market, a card file should be established with a card devoted to every potential client the artist or dealer actually meets. On each card, the contact's name should be noted as well as the spouse's name, residence and office address, telephone numbers, and any pertinent information the artist or dealer may have learned regarding the esthetic interests of that collector, plus any preferences which may have been expressed for particular artists and their works or for particular kinds of images.

Your contact file should grow steadily as your dealer's business matures or as your artist's career develops. It will be a useful asset to an artist even after that artist has acquired satisfactory dealer representation and a substantial following. Even negative information can be useful. It helps avoid wasting time on a non–prospect or curiosity seeker whom one has previously met, if a note on an index card suggests that this is not a legitimate prospect.

As indicated earlier, there are many potential clients who are total strangers to the dealer or artist. Finding their names and addresses, finding a way to interest them in examining art works is a matter of effort and energy. In the art market, the supply of untapped contacts is almost limitless. It must be cultivated by the artist or by the dealer. Every dealer and every artist who shows works which are for sale should keep a guest book of visitors who drop by to see an exhibition. The more interesting names and addresses collected in this book should be transferred to the contact card file. I have worked with an artist who regularly collects prospect infor–mation at street art festivals. He finds that such contacts can be very useful.

Once a contact file has been developed with at least a few hundred names, the artist or art dealer is ready to begin soliciting for sales. This first step often seems presumptuous and bothersome, even frightening, to the inexperienced sales person. It should not be any of these. The simple fact is that genuine art collectors and even many novices will usually welcome an opportunity to see an artist's work, especially if these have not previously been available to them and may contain surprising, interesting, or exciting features.

After all, it is only by viewing works for themselves that collectors can determine whether they are really interested in them. It is axiomatic that if an art work is worth owning, it is worthy of being offered to the view of a prospective art collector. As for novices who are just learning to collect, their needs are great since their prior opportunities to study con—temporary art have been necessarily more limited.

As suggested earlier, one simple technique for opening a sales campaign involves sending out personalized solicitation letters. These should be typed on your stationery. Generally, such letters indicate that the writer is an artist or a dealer who will be phoning within a few days to invite the collector (plus spouse) to a private presentation of original art works in the hope that one or more of the works shown might find their way into the collection of the potential clients.

The letter might begin with this type of opening paragraph:

When we met at the County Museum exhibition last Thursday, you commented that you were inter—ested in seeing some of my own original art works. As I remarked at the time, I work mainly in acrylics and oil although I occasionally also create small sculptures.

An alternate opening might read:

Our mutual friend, Mrs. John Wylie, recently suggested that you might be interested in seeing some of the art works which I have recently added to my gallery (studio) collection. As you may know, she owns two works which come from that collection.

A third alternative might begin:

You may not be familiar with my art works, but I believe you will find them both interesting and provocative — — perhaps even worthy of your own collection.

The letter could go on:

Although I am not currently represented by any of the major art dealers, my work has recently been exhibited at the Municipal Museum's New Artists Show. I was awarded a special purchase prize at the Spokane Art Association Show last fall. As a student, I worked with several of the best contemporary artists in this part of the country, including James Canto.

An alternate conclusion, from an art dealer, might say:

Since I understand that you are developing a collection which is meaningful to you, it would make me very happy to arrange a private presentation of some of my works at my own studio for an evening next week or for a Sunday morning, if that is more convenient. I will call you in a few days to make an appointment. Thank you for your interest and encouragement.

Very truly yours,

With your personalized letter, it will be very appropriate to enclose some sort of illustrative material to serve as a promotional sales aid. A suitable enclosure might be a fully labeled color photo. Another enclosure might be an interesting reprint. Of course, the best enclosure is a house brochure which contains several works in color. Do not expect people to return your enclosures.

Once the dealer or artist has developed the means and the habit of producing a constantly expanding contact list and has designed a few personalized solicitation letters, the task of systematically sending out individually addressed letters and then following them up with phone calls leading to appointments should become routine matters. As discussed earlier, a certain number of letters and phone calls will yield a certain number of private sales presentation opportunities. Continued effort will yield continued results. Improved letters and better prospect lists will yield even better results.

Some contacts will decline to visit the artist's studio or the dealer's gallery simply because they are truly disinterested. They may even be the majority of those contacted. Others will be interested, but simply unable to arrange a convenient date. These should be calendared and followed up at a later time. You will seldom wish to throw any contact cards away. A refusal or a postponement is not really the same as an outright rejection.

After all, these potential prospects have not seen the works. They may become more interested later after they have become more involved with art or after they have learned from others about the interesting works they have been passing up. If the file cards are destroyed, the dealer or artist might forget whether a party was previously contacted. Or one might forget when the contact was made or what the response was. A renewed or different approach at a later date may prove more fruitful. Even the contact who seems negative or diffident at first may turn out to be a devoted collector. I have never discussed this approach with an ex— perienced sales person who took a different view. Every really successful sales representative knows that the best clients often do not start out as friendly, receptive prospects.

88. Qualifying Your Prospects

When a prospect expresses interest in visiting the artist's studio or a dealer's gallery, it should be made clear that while the visit may well be educational and pleasant, it is aimed specifically at selling art works. When first meeting the prospect and again when making an appointment on the telephone, the dealer or artist should first make the serious—ness of the proposed visit quite clear and should then attempt to discover whether the prospect already owns any original art works.

The names of the artists represented in the prospect's collection and the type of art in which the prospect is most interested should also be ascertained. This line of inquiry might lead to an opportunity to indicate that the collector will be shown works which are equally "worthy" of a place in the prospect's collection. You might say, "I think you are going to agree that mine are equally fine works and deserve a place on your walls."

So, too, the solicitation letter may mention the fact that the artist or dealer hopes that some of these works will find their way into the prospect's home or office. If collectors do not clearly appreciate the business function of the im—pending visit, it might be necessary to expend a good deal of energy simply "educating" them on the importance of art collecting. This is a worthy and socially useful endeavor, but it is not the primary consideration.

The question which must be answered is *why* the prospect wants to visit the gallery or studio. Is this a fairly serious collector or just someone who is curious about how artists and art dealers spend their time? The latter type of person is not a very good prospect. In fact, non–collectors are generally poor prospects, unless they have decided to become collectors. This is usually a conscious decision. Artists and art dealers should devote a fair amount of time to finding and encour–aging non–collectors to join the ranks of the collectors. Such activity is good for art and for the novice collectors as well.

But a private sales presentation is not the right occasion for educating potential novices. This is a proper function of the lecture hall or of the publicly funded gallery. The private presentation is a formal sales situation. It should be accessible only to qualified prospects. When I have my choice, I do not even like to permit the prospect's friends to participate in such a presentation. Outsiders often spoil the mood of the occasion and interject irrelevant views and conflicting interests. Dear old Aunt Tillie always seems to know a talented high school student who does "better " work.

It is, of course, possible to sell art works under very for–mal circumstances to totally unqualified contacts. But only a relatively few works can be sold this way because the circumstances are all wrong for the prospect to study and react to the works, for determining what is really needed, for making a positive decision. The best justification for making private sales presentations is that they produce more con–sistent, more effective results for the artist, the dealer, and the collector.

In recent years, I have had good success in encouraging artists and art dealers to try to turn casual, informal contacts into more formal sales situations. For example, it is possible to encourage people at an exhibition opening to leave the party and join you in the private "viewing" room, so that a work in which they are interested may be considered "in a more intimate, home—like setting." There is no reason why an art seller cannot remove a work from a gallery or studio wall while a party is in progress, returning it later, perhaps with a red dot on it.

So, too, it is possible to turn a casual, drop—in visitor to the gallery or the studio into a qualified prospect by making the right comments and suggestions when interest is signifi—cant. However, the seller should generally avoid making a formal presentation when a spouse is absent. It is wiser, in such a case, to try to set up an appointment for a later time when both parties can be present.

89. Isn't This Approach Too "Aggressive"?

By this point, a number of my readers may be objecting that this rather formal, self—conscious sales approach is crass, commercial, brazen, or simply "pushy." I would like to submit that the alternate approach to selling art — — to let the works "speak" for themselves — — is not more polite. It is just less productive. The artist and the art dealer should certainly not be overly aggressive in presenting works or in asserting their virtues. Exaggerated claims, idle boasts, and puffed—up attitudes are out of order. A high—pressure sales person will often fail through insensitivity to the needs and sentiments of clients. But an easier way to fail is to avoid making any effort at all.

If art dealers or artists are to make any headway with a marketing, program, they must take an active rather than a passive approach to sales problems. Long ago most merchants discovered that the world does not beat a path to the door of the best mousetrap inventor without active stimulation, guidance, and encouragement. Certainly, in the field of art, clear pathways must be opened for collectors, or they will remain lost to the dealers and artists for all their *bona fide* interests and good intentions. Few artists are ever really "discovered." Few art works are ever really acquired by accident.

Every artist and art dealer who is seeking to develop a following — — who is more than a hobbyist — — must reach out to people in a friendly, helpful way. Collectors do not ordinarily "drop in" until they are habituated to do so by prior contact. And "casual " purchase decisions are seldom made in the art world.

Making Sales
Presentations

90. Setting the Scene

Whenever art collectors arrive for an appointment, after making them welcome, the dealer or artist would be well advised to "requalify" the prospects by clearly restating the purpose of their visit.

For example, one might say,

> *I feel sure that you will find these works inter—esting and unusual. I hope to be able to show you several which belong in your own collection.*

Alternatively, the artist or dealer might say,

> *I remember that you said you admired Joe Vivaldi's work. While his works differ a good deal from those I am about to show you, many collectors feel that they are comparable in several significant ways. In fact, I know a number of individuals who prefer certain of these works to any of his they have ever seen. I would like your judgment about that.*

Before the prospective clients arrive, the dealer or the artist should prepare a comfortable sofa or, preferably, two separate arm chairs in a specially dedicated room or a segre—gated area of the gallery or studio. The seating should be located at a suitable distance from the exhibition easel. The exhibition easel itself was discussed earlier in the Facility Planning portion of this *Handbook*.

Natural or artificial illumination should be directed at the easel—mounted works from the ceiling, well in front of and above the head of the prospective clients. In this position, lighting will be most useful, as neither the clients nor the sales person can cast a shadow on the work itself. Several of my clients have installed a rheostat in the light switch which controls the illumination on the display easel. This simple device can add a great deal to the drama of a sales presentation as it modulates the light on a work.

In presenting certain art works to a prospect, you should avoid having too many other works on casual display. Par—ticularly to be avoided are powerful or important works which are not for sale. They can prove to be an unwanted distraction. In general, distractions of all kinds should be avoided. A sales presentation should concentrate on the examination of par—ticular works which are available for sale.

The sales person should not present more than one or two works at a time and should keep the total number of works shown at any viewing well below twenty. Ten or fifteen good works, carefully considered, are really a large number for a sales presentation. Only experienced connossieurs are able to examine a larger number of art works without developing a good deal of confusion regarding the works which they have seen.

If the art works to be shown are three–dimensional or otherwise difficult to handle, they might be set on the floor on pedestals or on tables in various parts of the gallery or studio with pre–arranged lighting. They should be fully draped before the prospects arrive. This arrangement raises the viewers' anticipation and sharpens their attention. Of course, gracefully removing a drape from a sculpture can be difficult. It is a good idea to practice before the client arrives so that you do not seem clumsy in your handling of the work. A three–step ladder may be useful, too.

The greatest advantage of a private sales presentation over a gallery exhibition is one of focus. But the client's focus is diffused quickly if too many works are on view at the same time. In this connection, the Italian writer, Pavese, made an important observation regarding the role of the artist when he proposed that the primary task of the artist is to call attention to a work in such a way that the viewer is made to see the work as if it had just been discovered for the first time. We all seek the fresh, clean experience of discovery which has become almost unobtainable in many art galleries with their busy, over–filled walls.

91. Requalifying Prospects

Even with a client who has expressed great interest in a particular artist or work on the gallery floor a few minutes earlier, it is wise to remind your client as he or she is being seated regarding the purpose of entering the private viewing room. This is called "requalifying" the prospect.

You might say,

> *You remember, Mrs. Adams, that I told you I thought some of my works belong in your collection. I hope tonight to learn that I was correct.*

Or you might say,

> *The work you were looking at a few moments ago in the main gallery looks much warmer in these more intimate surroundings. I hope that I can give you a good idea of how it would look in your own home.*

In either case, you are making your mission clear to your prospects. If they do not understand and approve, you will probably be wasting your time.

Having requalified the prospect and carefully arranged the viewing circumstances, the seller is now ready to begin the next step of the selling routine. The clients are present on a clearly acknowledged business mission. It is now im—portant to see that they become personally involved with the works which are being examined. This involvement may or may not lead to a sale, depending on the qualities of the art, the perception of the clients, and the communication skills of the seller. But a sale cannot generally occur without it.

92. Showing Art Works
Focusing Attention & Heightening Interest

The first work is disclosed and mounted on the easel simultaneously. It should probably not be the most arresting or even the most effective work on hand. It will be useful in telling us something about the visual equipment and esthetic bias of the prospects. Before you put it on the easel, you might name the work or the artist. You might add a comment about the size or medium.

You can begin the focusing process by asking the clients to tell us what they "see" in a work. Remember that many inexperienced viewers look only for subject matter. They can be blind to color, form, composition, symbolism, tech- niques, reference, and other esthetic criteria that may be very important to understanding the work which has been shown. One should try to be patient with viewers whose esthetic and visual capabilities are not as well developed as they might be.

Encourage them when they recognize something signif- icant in a work. Guide them a little if they seem confused or need orientation. Sometimes a hint or a leading questior will be very useful. The title may be a clue. Most collectors will appreciate a little help. But, be careful. More sophisticated collectors will feel patronized if the seller is too helpful. Do not offer more information than the prospect seems to want.

Sometimes a client will ask an artist or an art dealer to "explain" a work. This is not a sales approach worthy of endorsement. In fact, it is easy to take offense at questions of this variety. After all, a work of art would not generally need explanation. Try to encourage clients to "see" for themselves what is happening in the work. This can often be accomplished by answering the customer's questions with appropriate counter questions.

For example, an artist might reply, in truth:

It is very difficult for artists to properly and fully explain their own works. Why don't you freely associate and tell me what you find here on the canvas? Perhaps then I will be able to tell you whether you see things the way I do or not.

Some dealers might prefer to say:

I am not sure I am always able to express my own views and reactions in works. I often have difficulty verbalizing a response to an art work. Perhaps that's why I am active in the visual arts. Why don't you tell me what you see? We may both gain a better insight this way.

Of course, an artist's image may contain political, religious, or historical references. It may include symbolic references to cultural developments or even to the imagery of other artists. Sometimes artists comment visually on society or on their own environment. If clients are astute enough to re— cognize such contextual references, they deserve credit and encouragement.

In some cases, however, if they are not able to recognize the subtler contextual implications of a work, they may really need a little advice or a little information. This could be given in a very general way, as when artists outline their basic purposes or motivating interests in doing a group of works. The seller cannot assume that every client possesses a full fund of knowledge, experience, and sensitivity of the type needed to appreciate a work. If they knew as much as the dealer, had as keen an insight as the artist, then they might not need the help of a sales person at all.

I was once helped considerably in my desire to better understand the work of a major abstract artist who took the trouble to show me some of the preparatory sketches which she had employed in developing a moving, but very complex, abstract work. As I examined these preparatory drawings, I gained enough insight into the artist's point of departure to get a grasp of the special symbolic language which she had developed as part of her esthetic idiom. It was all the aid I needed, and it involved me deeply in the artist's work. Her interests now became my interests, and I acquired the work.

As the prospective clients view the works, the seller should try to engage them in discussion, not simply regarding the merits of the work, but, more directly, regarding those relative values which could lead to discriminating choices — — to the acquisition of one or more of these particular works. For example, you might ask which of the first three works seem most interesting. Also, you might ask your clients to indicate the things they most dislike about these works or which of the three works they like* least and why. In this way, the seller can discover a good deal about a prospect's artistic in—terests, preferences, and biases. It might even be possible to tell some clients something about their own viewpoints which they had not fully comprehended.

*I do not recommend asking clients how they "like" a work. How they feel is more significant. What they dislike can mean even more.

It is always counter productive to assume that the art collector's interests and views are precisely congruent with one's own. Clients are developing individuals. They need to learn to express their own views and to understand their own preferences. Sellers who help a client to do this may find that they have made contact with a personality worthy of attention and respect. Collectors are constantly defining for themselves what they want from art as well as from a parti—cular artist's work. This is the primary clue to the sales person which determines the objective possibility of making a sale.

When clients indicate that they do not appreciate a work because they do not "understand" it, you should not hesitate to point out that many fine works are not fully comprehended at first sight, even by the most experienced collectors. The language of many contemporary artists is often intentionally abstruse or difficult. It may take considerable effort to master, but those collectors who take the trouble are generally very happy that they did. As collectors study a group of works, their involvement with them is likely to increase. However, work which produces a simple, immediate response may readily become boring.

Although much has been written in recent years about the power of visual materials to instantaneously involve and move people in a non—verbal way, we cannot accomplish anything with a work of art until we get someone to take the trouble to look carefully at it, to react to it, to reflect on it. Lasting reactions are seldom really instantaneous and sub—liminal. More often they require concentration, comparison, even discussion.

To go further, the seller might lead the clients in any of a number of valid esthetic directions by focusing their attention on colors, forms, surfaces, emotions, references, contexts, subjects, or objects, where it is appropriate. When collectors begin to grapple with a discussion of the symbols they find in a work, or when they register emotional responses to a surface treatment, their interest and their appreciation are likely to improve because attention has been directed into a meaningful channel.

As the encounter between the seller and the collector proceeds, the artist or dealer should remember that every experience with a finished work is necessarily quite different from the artist's earlier experience. The artist's involvement probably reached its own zenith during the creative process. A collector may be moved today by something which was moving to the artist long ago or even by something which interested the artist only rather incidentally. Some of the more honorable reasons for buying art works are matters of association. A work carries a collector back to an important memory or a vivid experience − − perhaps even to a recurrent dream image. Such associations may be much more meaning−ful to the collector than they are or were to the artist. But the finished work of art has now acquired a life of its own. Its ability to amuse or amaze the viewer may not specifically coincide with the artist's recollected intentions. The impor−tant thing is that the collector is involved, interested, and relating to the work in a legitimate way.

As you proceed to show, examine and discuss works, it should become clear that this particular client has certain very definable needs and interests. Throughout this *Handbook,* and elsewhere in the best treatments of selling, you will learn that the most successful sellers are those who can best identify their client's needs and then fill them adequately. This takes some knowledge and skill, plus an interest in other people. And it takes some respect for the collector's integrity as a developing personality.

Most art collectors do not know what they need or even what their options are. But art has many different functions. We can use an art work to stimulate or soothe us, to agitate or assuage, to amuse or amaze, to provoke or reassure. We may prefer earth tones or sky and water references, spring or fall color combinations, abrasive or smooth textures, etc.

The intelligent seller will try to identify the client's preferences, animosities, intended uses, and most important — needs. As you discover these criteria, it will be helpful if you tactfully point them out to the client so that you have a common basis of proceeding.

93. The Trial Close

By now, the seller should be ready to move to the next step in the selling process. Presuming that the clients have expressed greater preference or interest in certain works as compared with others they have seen, the dealer or artist may decide to initiate a "trial close." A trial close question may be any of a number of questions related to the subject at hand which may be answered either positively or negatively at an appropriate point in the sales presentation.

You might ask whether the collectors respond to this particular work as much as they can to a work they already own. You might ask whether the work being examined seems to have certain qualities of color, form, substance, or reference which the collectors find provocative or exciting. Essentially, we want to know whether the presentation is succeeding in its objective.

If the answer to the trial close question is negative, the sales person has created an opportunity to learn something about the buying problems which these particular collectors are facing. The prospects may have a difficulty, a point of confusion, or an objection which stands in the way of com—pleting the sale. If this problem can be identified and resolved, the chances of selling will be greatly improved.

For example, if the prospects have focused on one work as more exciting to them than three others they have seen, the seller might ask "can you visualize this work on the wall of your living room with your other art?" If the collectors answer affirmatively, the seller might move directly to a dis—cussion of how the work might be framed or even whether they would like to write a check for the price of the work.

If the clients answer negatively, then the matter must be pursued further. What prevents them from seeing the work on their wall? Perhaps they feel it is very interesting but "out of scale" for their living room. Perhaps they think the dominant colors of the work might be discordant with the decor of the room's furnishings or with certain other works they own. The explanation of this negative answer may tell the salesperson a great deal about where the clients stand with regard to buying this or, indeed, any other work.

In some cases, it will be possible to resolve the clients' objections by showing that the colors do not clash with their decor or that the scale of the work is indeed quite appropriate to the room size. In other cases, the seller may elect to show certain works which come closer to the clients' stated space or color limitations.

Shortly, we will consider a series of commonly repeated objections together with a variety of alternative responses. One of these replies will be logical and appropriate to the specific circumstances of your client's problem. Remember that collectors in discussing their difficulties openly with the sales representative are also developing their own specifications regarding what they want and why they want it. An intelligent purchase decision can be made only when both the prospects and the dealer or artist clearly understand the needs and pre—ferences of the clients and when these requirements can, in fact, be either modified or met by the works being shown.

It does nobody any particular service if clients go away from the sales presentation repeating the familiar litany, "I don't know anything about art . . . but, I know what I like." Intelligent collectors will want to know at least a little about the art they have been studying and a good deal more about what they need and why they need it. The seller should help collectors to answer these questions in terms of the work in the artist's studio or the dealer's gallery.

94. The Question of Price

Up to this point, price has not been introduced into our discussion of selling art at all. The exact price of a work of art should not be a primary consideration, even with a client of limited means. After all, the easiest way for the client to "save" money is to not buy any art. This is true of all dis—cretionary purchases. Once the so—called necessaries of life have been provided, it is possible for a customer to consider the really important things in life, purchases which are ne—cessary in an entirely different sense. We "need" art, not for economic, but for cultural reasons.*

The very fact that collectors are present in your studio or gallery considering the purchase of an art work indicates that these collectors are prepared to acquire something beyond the common requirements of life, ostensibly for the purpose of enhancing the environment in which they live and work. Economic considerations may be important, but they should always be secondary in such a situation.

When clients raise the question of price too early in a private sales presentation, they may be signaling their fear that they are "in over their heads." Try not to reply with a specific price, but offer general price categories instead. For example, when a client asks for the price of the very first work shown, you might indicate that the works which you are planning to show range in price from $250 through $1,500, depending on the size, complexity, and esthetic significance of each work.

* *The latest evidence overwhelmingly supports the theory that even the most primitive "cave" people of Cro—Magnon days "needed" art. In fact, art of remarkable variety and quality seems to appear in profusion long before the dawn of civilization.*

But suggest that it would be best to defer the question of a specific price until your clients have selected those works which interest them most. Then they can select from among their favorites, rather than from those which are simply cheapest. You might wish to go on to ask whether the range of prices just quoted is too wide. You could offer not to show those works where the price is beyond the client's price limits at this time.

Another section of this *Handbook* deals at length with the problems of establishing prices for art works. The most important thing to remember about the price of an art work is that it is not the most important thing about that work from anyone's viewpoint. Discussing specific prices in the abstract, independent of a client's genuine interest and in—volvement with a particular work, is usually a misleading line of conversation. Try first to stimulate interest, appreciation, and a desire to acquire specific works. Then discuss prices.

A discussion of prices becomes meaningful after the clients' commitment to a work has been rather clearly indicated. If a client is sincerely moved by a particular work which happens to cost a little more than another work which evokes no interest, the difference in price is really a trivial matter. Such works should not be competing with each other in terms of their relative price, but only in terms of their relative esthetic interest for the collector.

Once the prospect has shown a positive involvement in a work, and as part of the next step, it is appropriate to discuss price. At that point, the discussion is no longer dealing ab—stractly with prices. If necessary, look the price up in your records.* The seller should now freely and confidently quote the price of a work which the prospect is actively thinking about buying because it is an appropriate thing to do. The dealer or the artist might say, "You have selected a work which is very reasonably priced, considering its high quality." Or, "This work, which pleases you so, is only $600." Too often a premature emphasis on the prices of the art works being studied produces a counter productive situation and a misplaced focus.

* *I do not believe it is ever in order to put prices on the backs of works or on the wall alongside a work when it is on display. Clients should be encouraged to ask for a price when they feel it is appropriate.*

95. Handling Objections Commonly Raised by Collectors
Alternate Approaches

Art works vary widely in medium, quality, size, and imagery. The reactions which they provoke from individual collectors also differ greatly. But the objections which can be raised by collectors to the purchase of works are remarkably few in number. They may be categorized easily and alternative methods of handling them may be developed in advance. These methods will work best when a seller has thought them through carefully and is really prepared to offer an appropriate response.

However, before dealers and artists can begin to consider how to respond to a client's objection, they ought to deter— mine its legitimacy and its importance. If prospective clients have been previously qualified before viewing any works, if they have stated that they are genuinely interested in building a collection, acquiring a particular artist's work, or adding art works representative of a specific school or variety of images to their collection, then their objections may well be significant.

On the other hand, even some highly qualified prospective buyers, when they find themselves in an uncomfortable situation, are unwilling to embarrass themselves by telling the truth. Rather than admit that the works which they are view— ing simply arouse no interest or that they are too expensive, collectors may fall back to a false objection with which they are more at ease. In this case, they may hide their real objec— tion behind a false facade.

The sales person is faced with a minor dilemma whenever collectors raise an objection. It is necessary to determine whether this objection is legitimate and significant. Suppose, for example, the collectors have said that they think the work is too large for their living room wall. The seller must decide whether this is a serious objection or perhaps just a cover—up for a larger problem. Again, the clients' remark could be just a passing comment not requiring any attention at all. How is the dealer or artist to judge the reality and the importance of the collectors' objections?

A highly skilled sales person can often judge intuitively whether the objections being made are genuine and significant or bogus and unimportant. Lacking a fine tuned intuition, you will have to test your prospects. For example, in the case described here, you might say,

> *Suppose that I can resolve this problem that the work seems too big for you. Is the work otherwise interesting enough that you would want to have it in your collection?*

Alternatively, you might say,

> *I think that I just might be able to show you works with comparable esthetic qualities which are somewhat smaller in scale. Do you believe that such works would be more attractive for your collection?*

In each case, we are bringing the argument right back to a discussion of the collectors' fundamental esthetic interest and needs. If the interest is not actually there, then any proposed solution to the stated objection is trivial. But, if the collectors really appreciate the image and can offer no additional objections, a solution to this problem will usually lead to a sale. A good sales person welcomes a chance to discuss legitimate problems with clients because it is a sure route to sales.

We have said that qualified clients can only raise a few objections. So too, their objections can be dealt with in only a few ways. First, the seller may substantially ignore the objection if it seems to be trivial. Many customers feel obliged to grouse about prices whenever they get the opportunity. We all complain about inflation. This does not always mean anything significant. The artist or dealer may be well advised to ignore or treat rather lightly a complaint regarding a quoted price or any other apparently trivial objection.

Second, the collector may be voicing a problem which can be best resolved if the seller will only express a position more fully. If we decide that our meaning has not been completely grasped, we can go more deeply into our views, discussing the artist's symbolism or theory of color in greater detail. Sometimes a good restatement of the position of the artist or dealer can resolve a difficulty for the client. Thus, when a collector indicates that a work is rather expensive you might explain how your layaway plan works or you might offer to write up a sale on the collector's Mastercharge.

In other cases, the seller may elect to resolve the client's problem by accommodating to it. He may show a smaller art work, a more representational image, a less flamboyant combination of colors. Not every effort to accommodate to the needs of the client should be viewed as a "sell—out." Truth to tell, the artist or the art dealer may once have had special needs or limitations quite similar to those of the art collector. It may well be that the accommodation will open an avenue of development for the client which is not otherwise accessible.

Finally, in still other instances, the seller may attempt to overcome the collector's objections by showing that they are not valid. Artists are, after all, outstanding authorities on their own work. They also generally know a good deal about color, scale, esthetic values, etc., — — in the most professional sense. Therefore, their views should carry great weight with the collector if they express them cogently and with confi—dence. So, too, art dealers are often authorities in several art related fields and can afford to take issue with a client to show where an error has been made.

These, then, are the four alternative approaches which can be made to a legitimate objection: We may *ignore, explain, accommodate,* or *overcome* them. The best approach to take will depend upon the specific circumstances.

96. Different Kinds of Collector Problems and Objections

One of the most commonly encountered client objections might be called the "esthetic confusion" problem. Here, prospects are interested in and attracted to the work, but cannot convince themselves that the attraction is deep enough to warrant an acquisition. If you determine that the objection is legitimate, that the collector has no other underlying ob— jections, then the alternate lines of resolution are clear.

Your task is one of showing that while the work may seem unfamiliar, enigmatic, even strange, as it becomes more familiar, the viewer's interest will grow and appreciation will deepen. An artist might describe comparable experiences of other collectors with works from the same period to demon— strate this point. This is a good use of testimonials. A dealer might report personal experiences with this particular work. In either instance, the point is that the collector's appreciation, like fine wine, will improve with time.

In taking this line of approach, the seller is arguing that the objection will be overcome as the art work grows more familiar. One might, alternatively, accommodate to the client's objection simply by offering another work which, hopefully, will not prove as confusing esthetically. Which approach will work best depends on the nature of the work and the needs of the collector. Some collectors are not ready for enigmatic or profound experiences. Some works require a more dedicated, more sophisticated collector.

A variant of the "esthetic confusion" problem is one in which the prospective buyer indicates an attraction to the work, but a lack of "understanding." Here, the collector may be expressing an insecurity or an immaturity of taste. Many collectors, even some who have been buying art works for many years, are unsteady regarding the quality of their own taste. When clients say that they do not "understand" a work, it does not necessarily follow that they do not like it or that they are unwilling to buy it. A good response to this objection involves asking the clients to try to indicate what they do understand about the work, or more to the point, how they feel about it.

This approach should stimulate an involvement by the clients in a study of the art work. It will give the seller an opportunity to guide or encourage the clients to a better sense of security with regard to their own appreciation of it. Occasionally, when one is familiar with the clients' collection, this knowledge may be used as an aid in handling this type of objection. For example, we might say, "Did you fully understand Canto's work when you first acquired it?" or "Hasn't your appreciation of Frescobaldi's imagery deepened since you made it part of your collection?" Here we are trying to get the collector to "explain" the problem away.

Still another type of objection commonly raised by the prospective collectors might be called "the sociological insecurity" problem. A prospect may say, "I like this work very much, but I am afraid that my friends will laugh at me (or frown on me) if I hang it in my home." One logical approach to this objection, again providing that the collector's comment seems to be legitimate, is that art works of this quality are generally considered "peculiar" only by those friends who understand little about art. However, we might add, the collector's more sophisticated acquaintances will recognize the value of the work under discussion, and others will follow in time.

A dealer I know once answered this type of objection by indicating that he fully expected the client's friends to follow that collector in acquiring this artist's work, as soon as their appreciation ripened. Here, the objection was turned into an advantage. The collector was being encouraged to join the tastemakers and cultural leaders, rather than the followers. The dealer patiently disagreed with the viewpoint expressed by the client and 'attempted to overcome it by showing why it was wrong–headed.

Sometimes art collectors are unfamiliar with the prices currently asked for works of a given caliber by artists of a given reputation. They may demonstate this lack of infor–mation by expressing concern over whether the art work is over–priced. As suggested earlier, this objection should not be treated seriously unless the client has clearly indicated that it is a real problem. That is, if the price were "right," the client would like to acquire the work. Many good sales are lost; many fine artists are hurt because a dealer "caves in" on the price question before first testing the legitimacy of the collector's objection.

Some clients habitually ask for a lower price before making a purchase. Instead of enhancing the collector's regard for a work, an eagerness to discount or otherwise reduce prices can have the effect of convincing the collector that the work is really not worth very much in the first place. To overcome the objection of a collector who is legitimately concerned that a work may be improperly priced, the seller can indicate that other collectors regularly pay such prices and more for works of comparable size and quality by this particular artist. One might also suggest that careful study of the recent sales of the works of other artists with comparable reputations indicates that this work is, in fact, quite fairly priced.

In certain cases, we may be able to state honestly that these prices have been gradually rising over a period of time and that we have reason to believe that works of comparable size and quality will appreciate even more over the next few years as the artist becomes better established in the market. From this point of view, the present price may turn out to be quite reasonable. Such a reply may have serious ramifications which are discussed later in this *Handbook*. It should only be used if it is actually true and then with some caution as it may permanently prejudice the collector against an artist if it turns out that prices have not been rising significantly. Again, in this case, the seller is attempting to overcome the collector's objections. Alternatively, we could also accom—modate to the objection by offering other works in a lower price range, but this approach is very often unjustified.

Another objection, closely related to the over pricing problem, is the "confidence" problem. Almost everyone is aware that unscrupulous artists and art dealers have misrep—resented their works and otherwise defrauded collectors from time to time. The prospective buyers may indicate that they are worried about the physical stability of the work which they are thinking of buying. They may be afraid that they are being otherwise shortchanged or cheated in some way.

The best reply anyone can make to this concern, always providing that the objection is not simply a cover—up for another problem, is that the artist or dealer has been and intends to remain active in the art world for many years. A responsible person can ill afford to produce shoddy work or to misrepresent its true value. The collector should be made to appreciate that the dealer's and the artist's professional reputation for integrity are just as important as if they were doctors or attorneys. Every artist or art dealer should offer clients a written warranty regarding the quality of the work. A sample limited warranty is given in the discussion of sales invoices.

The seller might also suggest that a long and happy business relationship with the collector would be impossible if that collector were mistreated in any way. It is, of course, neither practical nor proper for anyone to wear integrity pinned to a sleeve, but artists and dealers must guard and cultivate their reputations for honesty and ethical business practices carefully. In a world where so much cheating occurs, they should not be surprised to encounter wary clients. They should be happy to explain their positions on this issue patiently and tolerantly.

Another common objection is raised by house—proud collectors who are worried about clashing colors, conflicting styles, and "overwhelming" objects. The dealer or artist may be displeased to learn that a collector is unwilling to accept a work simply because its colors clash with those employed by a decorator in the client's living room. To overcome this problem, you might indicate that many art collectors recognize that the colors of the work of art need not stand in absolute harmony to the decor of a home. Or you might demonstrate that the colors of this work are really compatible with those in the collector's home.

You might also point out that the decor of a modern home is rather transitory and more apt to pall on its occupants than the color values of a fine work of art. In any case, the artist's or dealer's authority, as one who works with color and form professionally, should be asserted and employed to help resolve the problem. A decor objection may be explained away or it may be overcome. It could occasionally be treated with accommodation as when the dealer elects to offer a work with different, more compatible colors.

Probably the most difficult type of objection arises from the collector who is by nature weak—willed or dilatory in making decisions. Clients may indicate that they do not want to move "too fast." I recently encountered a collector who simply could not decide between four works by the same artist. Since we cannot readily change the personality of the buyer, we may decide that we have no choice but to accommodate to such objections by agreeing to wait while the art collector thinks things over or "looks around."

It would be wise, however, if before leaving the private sales presentation without a sale, the seller at least narrows down the collector's field of choice. You might ask, for example, "If you were to select one work from all you have seen this evening, which would it be?" or "From which two would you make your selection, and why?"

In some cases, an artist or dealer might elect to encourage the dilatory buyer to take a few works home to see how they "work." This is generally a dangerous procedure, especially with a new client, since one cannot be sure of the integrity of the prospective buyer or even of the client's ability to properly care for these works. Further, the artist's or dealer's insurance coverage is probably void when the work is removed from its normal storage or display place.

When a collector asks to take home a work on trial, the seller might reply, "Yes, you may take this work home on the basis of a thirty—day free exchange privilege. I'll need a one—third deposit, of course." Thus, the work is not being "loaned." It is actually being purchased, with the provision that it may be exchanged within a month if the prospective client decides in favor of a different work. Now, the client is being asked to match the dealer's or artist's desire for a sale by indicating a comparable seriousness of purpose. If this level of cooperation is not available, the seller might be better off passing up the sale.

An alternative approach would be to offer to bring the work to a client's home to see how it fits into the surrounding ambiance. This approach is often quite effective. Still another approach to narrowing down the decision—making process involves reviewing the key elements you have discovered about the client's needs in terms of the specific works under consideration. Sometimes the seller must do the winnowing and the decision making for the art buyer. I did this recently for one of my client's customers, mentioned above. She was very appreciative of the help I gave her since it relieved her anxiety.

The foregoing discussion shows a variety of common objections and possible approches to handling each of them. The reader may wish to employ the appended check—list to review these objections. In each case, the collector's problem is either explained, accommodated, or overcome. On the other hand, the specific approaches suggested are not the only ones which could have been utilized. An alternative approach might have actually been more appropriate in a particular instance.

Finally, the novice sales person must remember that not every qualified prospect will buy, no matter how well one handles the presentation. To be sure, every artist and dealer should be prepared for a variety of objections. They should try to learn to distinquish a real problem from a contrived excuse. They should also appreciate that not all collectors will buy the works which are available. But an artist or dealer only needs a fair share of the market to succeed. This is accessible if collectors are handled with reasonable care and consideration.

Handling Objections Which Collectors
Commonly Raise To Buying Works Of Art

Type of Objection	Customers' Typical Catch-Phrases	Alternative Approaches: Ignore*, Explain, Accommodate, Overcome
1. Esthetic confusion	"I'm not sure I like it." "I'm not sure why I am attracted to it."	a) "Others did not appreciate it at first, but now they do." b) "This work will grow more meaningful in time."
2. Esthetic confusion (variant)	"I'm not sure I understand it."	a) "What is it that you do understand about it?" b) "Your undertanding will improve in time."
3. Sociological Insecurity	"I like it, but I'm afraid my friends will think me foolish."	a) "Your most knowledgeable friends will admire it." b) "Let others follow you."
4. Economic Insecurity	"That price seems rather high."	a) "It is not high for a work of this quality." b) "Actually, this price may prove to be very reasonable in the long view."** c) "Perhaps you might like to see something less expensive."
5. The Scoundrel Syndrome	"How do I know I'm not being cheated or fooled?"	a) "My integrity as a professional is your best warranty."
6. The Decor Problem	"The colors will clash." "The scale is too large for my home."	a) "Colors need not harmonize." b) "Try a smaller work." c) "Art is long. Decor is brief."
7. Dilatory Behavior	"I simply cannot make up my mind today."	a) "But, which works do you feel attracted to at this time?" b) "What do you most enjoy about these works?"

*One possible approach, if an objection seems trivial or unreal, is to avoid answering it.
**Use only when almost certainly true, and then with caution.

97. Closing the Sale

Once the clients' legitimate objections have been explained away, accommodated, or overcome, and they have responded agreeably to a new trial close question, the seller is ready to move to the final step in the formal selling process. This is known as "the close." Closing a sale is sometimes considered the most difficult task in selling because it involves a certain finesse which can only be acquired after some practice. But closing, like everything else related to selling, can be learned by anyone who takes the trouble to acquire the skill.

Sellers should never attempt to close a sale unless the client has indicated a specific interest in the possiblility of owning one or more of the works which have been shown. Premature closing efforts can confuse and offend the client. They are a mark of the novice sales person's insensitivity to the level of interest of the prospective collector. When a positive reaction has been indicated and the clients' desires are clear, the artist or dealer may employ any of a number of standard closing techniques.

For instance, if the client is unable to decide between two art works which are equally attractive, the seller might suggest that it is possible to arrange for the client to acquire both works since they are complementary and will enhance any collection as a pair. Or it might be suggested, on the basis of prior discussion, that one of the two works is the best one for the client at this time and that the other might still be acquired at a later date.

In either case, the sales person is helping the client to better define or narrow the field of choice, a task which should be much easier for the seller than it is for the collector, who may be viewing the works for the first time. A failure to decide on a particular choice can result in the collector's leaving the presentation having made no choice at all. This would be most unfortuante. For all their good intentions, only a handful of collectors will be able to recollect the different works well enough to sort out their feelings once they have left the private sales presentation.

Related to the choice—narrowing close, is the assumed sale close, probably the most widely used of all closing techniques. Here the seller, recognizing the genuine, if somewhat hesitant interest of the collector, simply assumes that a sale has been made and promptly moves on to questions of delivery, framing, method of payment, etc. In most cases, collectors will quickly recognize this ploy. They may restrain the artist or dealer without difficulty if they choose to do so, or they may simply proceed with the transaction.

To help with this approach, the sales person may pick up a sales invoice form and carefully complete it, noting the customer's name and address, the date, description and dim—ensions of the work, the price, method of delivery, etc. The form should then be offered to the collector to check and initial. Few collectors will be offended if this approach is employed gracefully and intelligently. It simply formalizes and finalizes a business transaction that was clearly being consummated anyhow.

There are a number of other closing techniques which may be utilized when they are appropriate. One widely used method of consummating the sale of an art work is the so—called time—value close. Here, a seller points out that the work under consideration is indeed an excellent work by a popular artist and it can, therefore, be expected to be off the market in a short time. As every merchant and attorney knows, time is the essence of most business activities.

The client, in this case, is urged to make a positive decision before the purchase opportunity is lost. This closing device is particularly appropriate when the artist's market is, in fact, fairly active. However, in other cases, it is a reckless sales person who misrepresents the actual circumstances of the case. It could be embarrassing many months later to have to admit that the work is still available.

A more consistently valid variant of the time—value close involves a recognition that certain kinds of purchasing oppor—tunities have a way of not recurring. The seller might point out that it may be some time before the collector will be able to come in again. It might be added, if it is true, that the work will be offered to another collector if it is not sold on the present occasion. Perhaps the collector would like to make a modest deposit to "hold" the work.

I know a major contemporary art dealer who employs the time—value close with great success when he is visiting cities distant from his home base. This is the "visiting fireman" approach discussed earlier in the *Handbook*. In this case, the collector, indeed, has a limited time available to view and buy this dealer's works because the dealer is expecting to return to his home city shortly. The dealer tells me that he generally gets faster and better response from qualified prospects in a distant city by employing this approach than he can expect from regular home—based clients.

Still another commonly used closing technique is the negotiated or "fairy godmother" close, in which the seller helps an uncertain or undecided client to reach a conclusion by granting a "boon" of some sort. For example, you might say,

> If it will encourage you, I am willing to super-vise the framing of this work, and I will help you hang it in your home so that you can be assured it will make the best impression and be ready for the reception you are planning next week.

Or, you might say,

> To help you reach a decision, I will sell you all three of these fine works. But, instead of requiring full cash payment, which is my usual custom, I will take one—third down and the balance within ninety days, at no additional charge.

Such negotiated concessions or "boons" sometimes give a collector a significant added impetus in the direction of making a positive purchase decision at the time of the private sales presentation. A boon which should never be offered is an unearned discount as this impairs the artist's pricing structure. The issue of discounts is discussed more fully in the section on pricing.

As suggested earlier, many art dealers, and not a few artists, employ a closing technique which might be called the investment appreciation close. They may indicate, as an in-ducement, and often without foundation, that the works under consideration are likely to appreciate considerably in market value within a short time. Some even "guarantee" a given rate of appreciation. Approaches of this kind can actually harm the long—term interests of the artist or dealer, if they turn out to be false.

Certainly, some art works have appreciated significantly in market value, sometimes because of a prodigious growth of interest in the artist's work and sometimes due to intense and artificial promotion. Also, some art works may have been underpriced in the first place. But not every artist's works will appreciate significantly in value, and appreciation is very unlikely to continue indefinitely in most cases where it does occur. The whole idea has been wildly exaggerated. As suggested earlier, it can generate an unfortunate disaffection for collecting art. We will return to this issue in some detail in the section on Business Ethics.

When an art collector asks, regarding a work by a relatively unknown artist, if investment appreciation can be expected, you might honestly reply in this way:

Sir, investments vary in terms of their apprecia—tion potential. Blue chip stocks may be high in cost and relatively slow to appreciate, but they often pay dividends regularly. Growth stocks can be relatively expensive, measured in terms of earnings per share, but they may have a reassuring growth history to justify their high price. This work by a relatively unknown artist might be compared to a new stock issue.

It may indeed improve in value over the years. I hope it will. On the other hand, this is a gamble because the market price of the work may not change at all or might even deteriorate. Since this artist is not well known, his works are rather reasonably priced. If you enjoy them well enough to own them, then they are indeed a bargain, quite aside from any possible investment appreciation. This artist's best collectors do not plan to sell his works or donate them to institutions to reap a tax benefit. Please think of the appreciation potential as a risk which might pay significant returns, but which is strictly a secondary reason for buying the work.

This approach brings the closing argument back where it belongs, to the context of the intrinsic, esthetic merits of the work and the interest which the work provokes in the collector. The best closing argument and the best reason for buying any work is its esthetic interest or the impact which it can generate on the collector's psyche or environment.

As a client becomes more personally involved in an artist's work, the opportunity to appreciate it grows. The artist's and dealer's job is one of encouraging collectors to follow the logic of their own convictions. In the last analysis, the only valid reason for buying an art work is its merit as recognized by the collector. Without interest, any collector's acquisitions are built on sand – – no matter how famous the artist, no matter how glib the sales person.

Contrary to the popular view of the collector as one who has little concern other than the crass need for prestige, the good opinion of friends, or the economic appreciation poten— tial of a work, every real art collector realizes, even if only subconsciously, that what counts most is the quality of the selections. If the collector's prestige grows, it may be because good taste was exercised. If the art works increase in value, perhaps here, too, it is because the art collector has selected really good works. Intrinsic values are more important than secondary interests because they are their own justification.

Commonly Used Closing Techniques

Method	Seller's Typical Key Phrase
1. Esthetic Appreciation Close	"Buy this work because if you do, it will still be interesting and stimulating long afterward."
2. Ask For The Order	"May I take your order for this work?"
3. Choice—Narrowing Close	"As I see it, you really seem to prefer this work to all the others, because . . ."
4. Assumed Sale Close	"I think you are making a very wise choice. How would you like to pay me for it?"
5. Time—Value Close	"While this very unusual work is still available, I think you would be wise to give me a modest deposit so that I can hold it for you."
6. Negotiated Close — The Fairy Godmother's Boon	"To solve the dilemma, why not take both works?" "I'll be glad to help by waiting 90 days for final payment."
7. Investment Appreciation Close	"This work may well improve in value." (N. B. *Such an assertion can be harmful if it proves untrue.*)

Follow—up
What To Do
After The Sale

98. Recording the Sales Transaction

Once a sale is made, a sales invoice should be prepared. Multi—part form books for this purpose may be purchased in most stationery stores. Many small business operators prefer to design their own invoice forms. A useful sample is appended at the end of this section. All sales invoices should be pre—numbered and used consecutively so that every form may be audited and accounted for. Such a closed system is a fair guarantee against loss of funds and art works. Even when a form is spoiled, a voided copy should be held in the audit file.

As discussed in detail in the section on accounting, the sales invoice should be prepared in several copies, with one copy retained by the art dealer and another going to the artist, if the art work which is sold was the property of that artist. Another may be inserted in the client's file, and still another can be retained in a numberical sequence file for audit, costing, and sales analysis. A simple method of printing multi—part forms involves the use of No—Carbon—Required colored papers. This is particularly useful for forms where many thousands cannot be ordered at one time. Many "instant" printers can supply "NCR" papers.

In addition to the standard letterhead materials, the form should show the date of sale, the name and address of the client, the name of the artist, a description of the works sold, including title, dimensions, medium, and date of execution of the work. The price for the work, cash or volume discount, if any, sales tax, if applicable, and the freight and insurance liability, should be recorded. The down payment and balance due, if any, should also be shown. On the back of the cus—tomer's copy of custom—printed sales invoice forms, it is wise to print the seller's terms and conditions of sale, after refer—encing them on the face of the invoice. The sample form shown here has been adapted by a number of artists and art dealers with minor modifications to suit special interests and tastes.

Technically and practically, a sales transaction is a contract between a buyer (the collector or an intermediate agent) and a seller (the artist or the dealer, often acting as the artist's agent.) Like all business transactions of importance, it should be set down in writing. This is the most significant function of the Sales Invoice. It acts as a written agreement. Without it, you may have difficulty setting forth your policy regarding such important matters as: limitations on the right to return work, your recommendations for preventing flaws in the work, and your responsibility for them if they occur, limitations on the right to reproduce the work, etc. While you can take a number of different attitudes regarding such questions, any failure to indicate your policy simply means that you are willing to trust the judgment of the courts in the event of difficulties and differences with your customer.

It is a good idea to ask the client to sign the seller's copy of the invoice to indicate that the work has been received in good condition. It is also wise to get a signature when money is still outstanding on the purchase after a work has been delivered. I like to complete a Sales Invoice whenever an art work leaves the artist's studio or the dealer's gallery, even if the work is only out on temporary loan. It is a record of what is gone, where it went, how much it's worth, and who has it.

Your sales invoices will be useful for many purposes, including income tax and sales tax preparation and collection of outstanding balances due. The most important function of the invoice is that it tells what has been sold, to whom, when, and at what price and terms. Such records will be very important in future marketing efforts. Copies should be filed systematically in a safe place.

SALES INVOIC

Terms: Net 30 days

Ship To	Bill To	Purchase Ord No.
		Date
		Via

Item No.	Description: Medium, Title, Dimensions (Width × Height)	Price

All sales subject to terms and conditions on reverse of this invoice.

Terms and Conditions of Sale

Payment for all works shall be in United States currency, net, upon presentation of this invoice. Where pre-payment has been made, shipping charges will be absorbed by Seller. Except for pre-paid purchases, all shipments are F. O. B. Seller's facility and subject to Seller's regular schedule of shipping and handling charges.

Unless otherwise specifically indicated, all works described herein are originals, created, executed, and signed by Artist. These works are cer—tified to be free from all defects due to faulty craftsmanship or faulty materials for a period of 12 months from the date of sale. If flaws should occur during this period due to such causes, said works shall be subject to repair or to replacement with a work of comparable value by Seller at the option of the Seller. The Buyer is cautioned, however, that the Seller cannot be responsible for fading or other damage to these works caused by careless or improvident exposure to direct sunlight and weather or caused by improper handling once the works leave the possession of the Seller.

Provided only that these works arrive in new condition, the Buyer may return any work acquired herein within thirty days from the date of receipt for full credit against the purchase of any other works available at that time.

All shipments are insured by Seller against loss or damage. If a work is received in other than new condition, the Buyer should notify Carrier within 48 hours of receipt.

The original works described herein are individually copyrighted by the artist. Sale of such copyrighted work does not include sale of rights to reproduction, in any form, unless specifically granted by the artist in writing.

99. Cultivating Collectors for Repeat Business

Fairly well established artists often find that their newer works are readily sold to collectors who already own one or more of their earlier works. If an artist has a good deal to say, or a variety of interpretations of a certain image, that artist is probably worthy of being collected "in depth." Every artist and dealer should try to cultivate a number of collectors who are interested in developing a broadly representative collection of an artist's various periods and modes of expression. This is the artist's "following" and constitutes a most significant measure of success.

Whenever collectors acquire a work by an artist, they should be elevated to a special status in that artist's future marketing efforts. So, too, a dealer should learn to deal with a client in a wholly different way from the treatment normally offered to a non–client. The clients' index card should be specially coded in the Contact File. They should not only receive a Christmas card annually, they should also be invited to studio parties, exhibition openings, lecture–demonstrations, and any other special events which might interest them further in the artist's career and future output or in the dealer's activities. They should receive reprints of reviews when it is appropriate. My client, Florence Putterman, has adopted the excellent practice of sending out a newsletter periodically to her collectors. It outlines the more interesting recent develop–ments in her career.

In some cases, an artist or dealer may wish to encourage collectors to lend works for special museum and other exhibitions or to illustrate art magazine articles. In other cases, they may encourage collectors to bring their friends to the studio or to the gallery for special activities such as a Sunday morning brunch or a special exhibition and sale. The artist's collectors should come to feel that they are really important to the artist − − as indeed they are. The dealer's clients should feel that they are members of an exclusive club with special privileges and rights.

Old, established customers are almost always the best source of new business, either in terms of their own needs or as expressed in the interests of their friends. Developing such clients out of more casual buyers is a time consuming, but ultimately a very rewarding task. To be sure, occasionally collectors abuse their privileges and make extraordinary demands on the artist's or dealer's time. Care should be taken to avoid this level of entanglement.

But the artist's and dealer's economic security depends, in most cases, directly on their collectors' continuing and deepening interest. Occasionally a collector will lose interest in an artist's image as it develops, or clients will find it necessary to give up collecting for economic or other reasons. In most cases such people should not be discarded. Their interest may return, and their economic capacities may be revived. Just about every former client is a prospect for further sales if proper follow−up is maintained. I like to think that selling art is a very circular process. When it works best, one sale leads rather directly to another.

A Summary Of Steps To Follow
In Selling Art Through Private Sales Presentations

Step	Seller's Typical Key Phrase:
1. Locate and qualify your prospect.* Arrange a formal presentation.	"I think I shall be able to show you that some of these works belong in your collection."
2. Requalify the prospect just prior to presentation.	"You remember, I said I hoped that some of these works would be just right for your collection."
3. Formally present selected works under restricted viewing conditions.	"Why do you like this work better than the other?"
4. Forcus attention and heighten interest in the works shown.	"From what you tell me, it seems clear that you need something with a very subtle imagery."
5. Attempt a trial close.	"Can you see how this work might enhance your collection?"
6. Identify and handle valid objections and problems.	"I believe that your appreciation of this work will deepen as you live with it."
7. Close the sale.	"May I help you select the framing for this work?"
8. Prepare a sales invoice for your client.	"Will you please initial this invoice for me?"
9. Follow–up on you client. Old customers are the most reliable supporters.	"When I first saw these new works, I thought of you at once."

*Well established artists and dealers will already have a number of collectors, some of whom are a regular source of repeat sales and referrals. Even so, they should always be interested in locating and developing new prospective collectors.

Pricing
Original
Art Works

100. Why Some Art Prices Have Been Rising
Faster Than Most Non–Art Prices

Unlike many commodities which have a more utilitarian nature original art is not "consumed" by the buyer. It is partly for this reason that we call art buyers "collectors" rather than "consumers." Given proper care, a work of art will not wear out nor lose its power to excite, please, and otherwise interest its owner. Since they possess these unusual attributes, art works can enrich the lives of collectors in many ways and over long periods of time. Further, art – like love – may be shared.

An art collection often represents the best expression of the personal taste of its owners. When collectors lose interest in specific works, they may find someone else to buy them or they may donate them to a museum or college where others can enjoy them. They seldom abandon them. The growing recognition of these lasting qualities serves to buttress the price of art works just as it reinforces the price of diamonds,

Since the end of World War II, contemporary artists in the United States have witnessed a substantial climb in the prices which may be commanded for their works. These increases apply not only to the works of famous masters, but also to the efforts of artists who are not as well known or as widely collected. I have discussed this question with literally hundreds of professional artists. They have all experienced significant price increases, providing their works have some sort of market. When I encounter artists whose prices have not been rising, it is usually because no one has been cultivating a market for their works.

One reason for the sharp upward trend in art prices is the generally inflationary character of our economy. Money simply buys less today. Thus, if a work of art were to be offered at the same price this year as it might have brought in 1970, then its real price would have declined considerably. During the past few decades, prices have risen in general, reflecting the inflation with which every merchant and every customer must contend. In terms of other goods and services that money can purchase, the retail price of an art work should have increased by a factor of fifty to one hundred percent over the past ten years just to keep up with inflation.

The prices of many original art works have been climbing at a rate considerably faster than can be explained solely in terms of inflationary factors. As the discretionary income available to the growing American middle—class has expanded, as its members have acquired more leisure, better education, and higher aspirations, the funds devoted to cultural pursuits have also grown. For a variety of reasons, the thirst for cul—ture in its many ramifications has increased.

Our art museums are generally the best attended public facilities in every major city. Enrollment in art courses rivals or exceeds that in other varieties of part time adult education across the country. Expensive, illustrated art books enjoy substantial sales in most book stores. Business institutions seem particularly anxious to find ways of associating them—selves with the works of artists as collectors, exhibitors, and sponsors.

Art dealers and artists thus find themselves in contact with thousands of new collectors — men and women whose par—ents, in most cases, owned little or no original art. Some of these novice collectors have only a rudimentary acquaintance with the history of art. Most are conscious of the need for further development of their taste and appreciation. But they want to own original, contemporary art works. Further, they are buying regularly and to the best of their ability. This increased interest and its attendant market activity exert an upward pressure on art prices at all levels of the art market. Even many works which might have generated little interest in other periods have a market today. Thus, the often mass – produced prints of Parrish and Icart which were widely sold for modest sums in the late twenties are today commanding substantial prices, having lain virtually unnoticed for several decades.

Further, the old masters of earlier generations have been getting scarcer and dearer. Those which have not left the market by entering public collections have naturally increased in economic value. When an important private collection containing significant masterworks does come to the market these days, it is almost a matter of course that new price records will be set, often without regard to the intrinsic quality of the works in the collection. The structure of our

tax laws and their impetus on philanthropy makes it difficult
for wealthy collectors and their heirs to retain such works,
once they have appreciated significantly over their acquisition
cost. Of course, as the major masterworks enter the public
domain, disappearing from the marketplace, they leave con—
temporary works relatively free to vie for the art collector's
primary attention.

A careful examination of the buying habits and motiva—
tions of different kinds of art collectors will show that the
collectors seek to extend their own taste and experience when
acquiring works. In significant ways, their collecting often
parallels the creative experiences and viewpoints of specific
artists. Further, like the artist's urge to create, the urge to
collect art is self—reinforcing and self—justifying. Thus, the
art collectors find the activity absorbing, exhilarating, and
important — worth the time and the money.

For all of these reasons, the art market is not primarily a
"price" market, where bargains are sought by clients over
other considerations. Even for the collector of modest means,
prices are not the primary determinant of purchasing decisions.
I regularly encounter the "hard—headed" budget—conscious
institutional buyers who first set tight budgets for art and then
disregard their own restriction when they find work which
has real meaning to them. The collector's needs and interests
determine his willingness to buy and place limits on the price
which will be paid.

101. Three Criteria for Pricing Art Works

The retail price a collector may be asked to pay for an original work of art depends upon a number of different, sometimes conflicting, sets of factors. Some considerations, such as the scale of the work, are fairly easy to quantify. Determining the relative importance of others is a matter of judgment and experience. Their significance will change, depending upon the level of development of the artist, the motivations of particular collectors, and on the shifting levels of interest to be found in our culture.

For convenience, we may divide the elements which influence the pricing of an artist's work into three main groups:

o factors related to the *intrinsic* qualities of the work of art, the esthetic and technical merits of a work.

o factors related to *recovering the costs* associated with producing and marketing the works, and

o factors related to *extrinsic* issues, such as the artist's reputation, the demand for or the scarcity of an artist's work, the reputation of the dealer, etc.

Each set of factors is worthy of separate consideration.

102. Intrinsic Qualities —— The Basis of Value in Art

The well known collector, Mr. Richard H. Rush, in his useful study, *Art As An Investment,** points out:

> *Quality is the essence of art value. For a painting to be worth anything, it must have quality ... a successful collector of art must be a person who appreciates the quality in art. He buys because the quality is there, and he arrives at his conclusion as to the quality through his native taste, through an intense enthusiasm for art and for collecting.*

But quality in art is not as self—evident an absolute for some collectors as it is for others. Even so, knowledgeable collectors tell us that there are certain works within the *oeuvre* of particular artists which have greater appeal, more significance, and deeper interest for them than other works by the same artist or by other artists with similar images or viewpoints. The fully eclectic collector who appreciates everything equally, but nothing especially, is not a major factor in the art market. Such clients lack the capacity for discrimination on which choice must be founded. They seldom buy any significant amount of art.

Whether art collectors apply a set of critical standards peculiar to their own tastes or shared with a large number of reputable art experts has little direct effect on the price such collectors will pay. They are, in either case, looking for certain qualities inherent in the work. Without these essential qualities and the interest which they provoke, there will be little demand for an artist's work. All questions regarding the recovery of production costs, the artist's repu—tation, and their relationship to prices, would be trivial. Two examples of the importance of quality may be useful.

In the early twenties, when Dr. Barnes, then assembling his now world famous collection, was making his annual inspection of the Paris art scene, he discovered the works of Chaim Soutine, at the time a totally unknown artist, in the gallery of a very unimportant dealer. The works were without any recognizable pedigree. That is, no one had made any significant effort to exhibit the works or publicize the artist's views. Soutine literally had no market.

But Barnes, who had decided to devote his rather consid—erable fortune almost exclusively to his passion for collecting art, was not much interested in the opinions of others. He knew major art when he saw it, and he proceeded, over a period of two days, to buy fifty Soutines. Barnes bought the lot for three thousand francs — about six hundred dollars, equal in purchasing power today of approximately six thou—sand dollars. To both Soutine and his dealer the sale seemed astronomical. But I am personally convinced from my own study of the market prices of Soutine's work and those of his contemporaries that these works were really underpriced. I am further convinced that Barnes — ever the careful con—noisseur — would have paid two to three times as much for this same collection without hesitation. In fact, he spent a good deal more time and money framing, shipping, and publicizing his new treasures than he spent acquiring them.

Ironically, Soutine later decided that Barnes had somehow gotten the better of him although no one had haggled over the quoted price. Barnes bought these works, as almost always, purely in terms of intrinsic merit. It is for this reason, that, as James Johnson Sweeney once noted, Barnes' selections were seldom made at record—breaking prices, but were always top quality works. He had developed a fine eye to match his keen appetite.

Another instructive example of the importance of quality in determining the price of art works comes from an exam—ination of the performance of buyers at major auctions such as the 1978 von Hirsch Collection auction in London. *The ART Newsletter* (July 11, 1978) reporting on this historic sale notes with some dismay, "many bidders showed a notable lack of discernment: many minor items, which would have fetched much less at an ordinary auction or at a dealer's gallery, went for prices beyond the wildest dreams of Sotheby's, von Hirsch's heirs, and many knowledgeable experts." They go on to quote New York art dealer David Tunick to the effect that "these prices could not be reached the next day, except at a sale like the von Hirsch." Beyond the promotion—caused excitement, about the only valid explanation of the record prices was that the buyers, including those representing major institutions, were "celebrating the taste of this discriminating collector."

But, the remarkable, and apparently unrecognized thing about the von Hirsch Collection is that while it was dispersed at record prices, it was acquired at relatively modest cost. Von Hirsch made himself an expert in many kinds of art. He sought outstanding examples of the various fields in which he was interested, and he worked hard at developing reliable sources, but he seldom bought any work which was at the top of the prevailing market at the time he bought it. Art collectors with less discernment or less confidence in their own taste are forced to rely on the judgment of others and, therefore, tend to pay higher prices for lesser works. In my own experience with famous art collectors such as Joseph Hirshhorn and Fred Grunwald, I was also struck by the interest of such "advanced" collectors in finding fine examples of lesser known artists and their relative lack of interest in buying high—priced works by "famous" artists.

Some artists inbue their work with a disirable quality by creatively employing certain mechanical, structural, or manipulative techniques. The sculptor who applies an attractive patina to the surface of a work is seeking a particular visual effect through a technical process. The artist who employs motors, lights, plastics, or reflective surfaces, like the artist who employs a specialized technology, is seeking to utilize these materials, devices, and methods toward an esthetic end.

A kinetic artist like Fletcher Benton employs his considerable skill as a metal worker and his extensive knowledge of optics to create color blending mechanisms and moire patterns which are very important in developing the works for which he has become so well known. So, too, an artist like Yaacov Agam utilizes his extensive command of color theory, and his years of study and experimentation in the field of optics to make his own kind of kinetic objects. In both cases, part of the price is associated with unusual technological qualities.

Other artists may be less concerned with objects which can be generated by special techniques and materials. They consciously avoid the use of unusual artifices. Instead, they seek to generate an esthetic experience much more directly by relying primarily on their artistic ability to evoke an image which has a meaningful impact on the viewer. They use their skills in drawing, painting, designing, shaping, carving, and abstracting to achieve this result.

In any case, the artist is striving to produce a work which has certain desirable esthetic as well as technical qualities. When an artist succeeds, the work has intrinsic value, at least to the artist. Often it also has value to a collector as well, although the nature of their experiences may differ. From these fundamental esthetic and technical values, practically all of the work's economic value must ultimately be derived. Esthetic quality should form the foundation of every artist's pricing policy.

Does the art work induce a pleasurable response? Is it exciting or stimulating? Is it evocative of certain emotions? Does it intimate certain significant concepts? Do the colors, lines, forms, surfaces, attract the viewer, do they provoke or disturb? Is the work interesting? "Value," as Ralph Barton Perry pointed out, "is the object of any interest." Unless a work arouses interest, it is fundamentally without value, economic or otherwise.

The intrinsic quality of an art work can refer not only to esthetic matters, but also to fabrication issues and their solu— tion. The knowledge, skill, and integrity of an artist contribute significantly to the longevity and stability of a work. An improperly stretched canvas, a poor choice of paper or ink, a careless application of plastic, an improperly designed or hastily executed armature may obliterate a work's esthetic qualities in a relatively short time, making it subsequently undesirable and unsalable.

When an artist is not particularly concerned with the "lasting" qualities of a work, this may create no esthetic problem. Certainly, the artist is not bound by the dictum that art is, or should be, "long." But, for the collector, this issue is often a significant one. The price which an artist's works command is sure to be affected by its intrinsic structural, as well as its intrinsic esthetic, qualities.

Incidentally, most artists are very conscious of the fact that their esthetic success varies from work to work. Van Gogh speaks in his letters to his brother of the vast quantities of "paste" he had to generate in order to create "a few diamonds." And yet, I find many artists hesitate to express their own relative sense of achievement with differentiated prices. Often all works of comparable size, medium, and image carry iden— tical prices. This suggests a puzzling unwillingness to indicate the artist's or even the dealer's personal preferences. When such a judgment is made, however, it can reinforce the artist's pricing structure substantially. I am always pleased to find this theory confirmed by experience. Better works sell more readily when their quality is underlined by an artist's or dealer's readiness to differentiate qualities in terms of price. Whenever I am asked to assist an artist or a dealer in pricing a collection, I start by selecting the most outstanding works. These should bring the best prices.

103. Recovering the Costs of Creating & Selling Work

I am still a little shocked at the suprisingly large number of artists and dealers who are not aware of the importance of recovering their costs from the sale of their works. They do not seem to realize that if they do not recover their costs, they are actually subsidizing their collectors. Many serious, professional artists with whom I have discussed the question have never even bothered to calculate the actual cost of their works. This is most unfortunate. No artist or dealer should ever sell art works below cost.

To be sure, there may be times when an artist is in dire financial straits and may feel impelled to "sacrifice" works at a price which is below actual cost. I have been told by many artists that they felt they had no alternative. At the depth of the Depression, Arshile Gorky found it necessary to part with some of his best works at very low prices. However, jobs are relatively plentiful today, even if they are sometimes distracting or annoying. Self—respecting artists have little excuse for demeaning their own works and for hurting their future market, to say nothing of the market of other artists, by selling works below cost. Despite the high pressure pro—motions seen on television in recent years, there are really no "starving artists."

There is one circumstance where my insistence upon recovering costs might possibly be disregarded or mitigated. When new artists are seeking to improve or extend their reputations by placing certain art works in important public collections, they might adopt a policy which temporarily includes judicious gifts to worthy institutions. Many fine museums have miniscule acquisition budgets and simply cannot acquire all the works their directors and curators would like. Accordingly, they often depend upon gifts from generous collectors and artists for a good portion of their acquisitions.

Occasionally, an official of such an institution may abuse this practice by insisting on donations even when the museum can well afford to pay for a work. By using this power as a taste—maker, an official may also insist upon unwarranted discounts. Nevertheless, an artist may find that representation in certain prestigious collections is important enough to justify what amounts to a "free sample" or a "special promotion" policy.

In my opinion, it is wiser for an artist who is trying to build a reputation to occasionally donate a work to a museum than to reduce prices through excessive discounting. Too often, the volunteer workers around the museum will learn of an artist's willingness to discount and will presume that they too are entitled to privileges similar to those granted to the museum. Discounted prices quickly displace list prices.

Of course, the federal tax laws are very discriminatory in their treatment of any artist who donates works to a tax—free institution. Where collectors may deduct the market value of donated art works, the artist may deduct only the undeclared portion of material costs. Hopefully, this unfair provision will be repealed or proven unconstitutional. Meantime, I still believe that an occasional promotional gift to an institution might be warranted, but only for a brief period in the artist's career. In all other cases, I advise my own artist—clients and their dealers to avoid making gifts and, more particularly, to avoid discounts unless they are specifically warranted by the situations discussed later in this section of the *Handbook.*

Certain aspects of the cost of producing a work of art are easily identified while others are relatively hard to quantify. In most art media, the cost of the primary materials employed in making a work is rather easy to determine. Metal costs so much per pound, a canvas of a given weight and quality has a certain cost per square foot. The cost of clay, wood, and other materials employed by artists in their work can be calculated simply and often ascribed to specific works.

When the artist buys certain materials for use exclusively on a particular work or series of works, costing can be quite simple. However, readily measureable quantities of materials are not always used to make a single art work. In such cases, their cost must be distributed over several works. Where these materials are relatively low in cost, their relationship to indi—vidual works need not be too precisely determined. For example, a sculptor who uses several boxes of welding rod in producing a number of welded works may attribute such costs to the works by roughly estimating the approximate portion of the cost of the rods going into each work. So too, it can be a matter of a simple estimate for an artist to determine that a particular painting required an approximate expenditure for paint and varnish.

The basic task of good cost accounting is to find a simple and equitable method of accumulating and distributing those costs which cannot be directly applied to a particular work. The artist may accumulate the cost of all those materials which cannot easily be directly ascribed to individual works over a period of months. Then, an approximate cost can be developed for all such materials on the basis of a certain rate per average hour worked or per average art work produced. Such cost—of—materials rates tend to be fairly stable for an artist within a particular medium. Cost estimates derived by accumulating direct material costs and then adding a factor for other incidental materials used, based on the number of hours worked and a previously determined rate per hour worked, may not be precise, but they are generally adequate measures of material costs.

I have found that labor costs are often the most significant part of the cost of an art work. To determine the cost of labor, artists should keep a bound diary, obtainable in any stationery store, in which they may record the approximate amount of labor which they have expended on a given project each day that it is under construction. If they also contain a tentative title or work number, a start date, a finish date, plus information regarding the help of outsiders, such a diary can be very useful to curators in later years, for precisely dating an artist's work and for many other purposes.

But, it has a more immediate function for identifying and quantifying labor cost elements. If any technical or artistic assistants are employed on a project, the cost of their labor should be noted, together with the record of the artist's own labor. Even if labor is volunteered by someone who is anxious to help, the hours donated should be accumulated and eval— uated. Their worth should not be passed on to the collector, just because they were contributed to the artist. Before long, an artist who keeps labor records and studies them occasionally can learn to accurately estimate the approximate number of working hours needed to produce a work of a given magnitude or to accomplish a given task in preparing such a work. This capability can be very useful in scheduling art projects, in budgeting, and in pricing art works.

Once all the labor has been accumulated for a particular work, a dollar value should be assigned to the total hours ex—pended, whether any cash has been paid out for all or part of the labor or not. Failure to evaluate all the labor that has been devoted to creating an art work, because most of this labor was provided by the artist and friends "without cost," tends to understate the economic value of the work itself. It can lead to improper pricing. Of course, only actual expen—ditures may be reported for tax purposes, but a non—cash investment is real, even when it is not deductible.

To determine the actual cost of an art work, one must not stop after accumulating the direct cost, which is the sum of the value of labor and materials which were employed in making a work. The proceeds of the sale of an art work should also return some appropriate part of the cost of studio rent, utilities, insurance, advertising, business entertainment, etc. These are the "overhead" or operating expenses. Without finding a way to recover these, no one can remain in business for long.

Like the cost of incidental materials, overhead costs are not easily attributed directly to specific works. Still, an artist who keeps adequate records will discover that there is a certain relatively stable average monthly expense associated with business operations. This expense can be recovered only through the income produced by the sale of art works. Therefore, in addition to recovering direct costs, labor and materials, the artist should identify and recover indirect or overhead costs.

To develop an appropriate overhead cost for any work, we may begin by accumulating all such costs for a given period and then distributing them equitably to the individual works which were produced during that time. For example, if the total overhead or indirect operating costs averaged $800 per month over the course of a year, and if the artist expects to sell forty—five or fifty works per year, then about one—quarter of a month's operating expenses must be recovered from the sale of each work.

In this case, the artist needs to recover an average of $200 per work to pay for overhead expenses. If an artist adopts this simple recovery scheme, during a month in which the artist sells fewer works, all of the overhead expenses will not be recovered. In a month in which more than four works are sold, more than the cost of such expenses for that month will be recovered. Thus, income can be balanced out to at least return the artist's costs of doing business through the year. Operating expenses vary from one artist to another, depending on the scope and tempo of activities, but they should always be recovered as a part of any artist's pricing policy.

An alternate method of allocating operating costs func—tions the same way as described earlier for the distribution of incidental materials costs. If, in the example above, the artist spends an average of one hundred and sixty working hours each month making an art work, then five dollars per hour must be recovered to accumulate the necessary $800 from the sale of art. To calculate an overhead rate per hour, the artist simply divides the average number of hours devoted to making art during any period into the average operating costs for that period.

Several other costs which should be recovered from the sale of an art work remain to be considered. One of these is the cost of the investment which an artist makes in inventory. When an artist works exclusively on commissions and the work essentially is sold before it is finished, there is often no significant investment. More regularly, however, the artist produces a work, holds it in inventory for some time, and subsequently sells it to a dealer or a collector who previously had no investment in the work. If the work is lent to a dealer on consignment, the artist's investment continues until a collector is found for it. This process can require a substantial and continuing outlay on the part of the artist.

When a depositor makes an investment by placing funds in a savings account, that depositor can expect to receive interest as well as federal protection for the funds so employed. If an artist has invested $500 in creating a work and has held this work in inventory for two years, then the cost of this investment should be considered in any determination of that artist's prices.

If, for example, this artist expects a modest six percent return on the investment, then the $500 initial investment should grow in actual value to $562 over a two–year period. This entire imputed growth in value should be recovered from the sale of the work. Obviously, the longer a work stays in inventory, the more costly the investment becomes. Assuming that the work is salable and that a real investment has been made, then that investment should "pay its own way."

A rather ephemeral cost element, but one which should not be overlooked, is the cost of the artist's education. Like any other professional, an artist must spend a significant period attaining sufficient technical mastery, insight, and esthetic maturity to produce meaningful works. Renewing these capacities periodically is also a costly feature of the artist's routine development. Such expenditures represent a long–term investment, often costing the artist, or the artist's family and society, thousands of dollars. Educational costs can best be recovered out of the income which the artist receives from the sale of works.

Once a work has been produced, the artist should antici–pate a significant expense associated with locating a collector and selling the work. Even when an art work is specially commissioned, there is almost always a good deal of time and energy required to visit proposed sites, prepare models and proposals, discuss alternatives, and write orders. Like other costs, the cost of distribution has its own justification and most be recovered from the selling price. Showroom space, advertising, and the time devoted to sales efforts can be costly. If the artist, or a spouse, functions as an art dealer, the time spent making contacts, cultivating clients, arranging private sales presentations, exhibiting works, and otherwise engaging in marketing activities embodies a sizable expenditure which should be recognized and evaluated. Perhaps it would be useful if the artist remembers that this same time could be spent creating valuable art works. Marketing work has an identifiable cost, regardless of who does the job.

When an art dealer undertakes to acquire works, hold them in inventory, exhibit them, advertise them, find clients, encourage these clients to buy, arrange credit, furnish framing and crating, deliver the works to the collectors, exchange them (in some cases) and perform all the other activities in which an art dealer must engage, a useful service has been performed for the artist and for the collector.

In the view of any modern economist, such marketing services add value to the work. To omit these values from consideration when the retail price of a work is established, is an unfortunate failure to provide for the recovery of an important part of the total cost of that work. Marketing costs can vary, depending partly on the complexity of the channels of distribution which are employed, but they should not be ignored. Sometimes when marketing costs are a fixed sum or a percentage of the selling price, they are easy to define. Otherwise, they must be estimated and allocated as were the overhead costs or the costs of incidental materials in the foregoing discussion.

I have had many opportunities, over the past two decades, to examine the financial records of a wide variety of different artists and art dealers. I find that these days it is not really possible for an artist who sells modestly priced art works directly to collectors to do so at an average selling cost of much less than fifty dollars per work, if we attribute even a modest value to the artist's or artist's spouse's marketing effort. An art dealer who carries on any sort of marketing activity will incur a good deal of expense. Seldom will this amount to much less than twenty five percent of that dealer's annual sales volume. Often, the dealer will spend much more, and when the value of the dealer's own contributed effort is considered the figure will go even higher.

It is for these reasons that I have little patience with artists who, in defiance of their own self—interest, are willing to sell art works to collectors at prices lower than those which they expect dealers to demand. Such policies are self—defeating, but they are also terribly confusing to collectors and dealers. If I can buy direct from an artist at one price, why should I be willing to pay a higher price to an art dealer? The costs of selling must be recovered from the retail price, regardless of who sells the work.

In summary, before all of the costs can be recovered, we must determine direct costs for labor and materials, as well as an appropriate portion of overhead and operating costs asso—ciated with the artist's studio. After these costs are established, we should provide for interest on investment and for some recovery of the cost of the artist's education.

We should then determine the cost of selling the work to a collector, either directly or through a dealer, and the cost of handling the work as well. Even when all these elements have been included in the price, no profit has been provided, nor has provision been made for the value of the creative image which the work represents. To recover all of the costs mentioned above, for all of the works produced by an artist during the course of a year, is only to break even during that period. But, an artist who does not study costs carefully may not even be breaking even. Near the end of this *Handbook,* a more complete discussion of break—even analysis will be given.

From time to time, I encounter an artist's work where the price cannot, for one reason or another, yield enough to recover costs. When this happens, I may recommend one of a variety of courses of action, depending on the circumstances. First, the artist may work on a variety of activities aimed at increasing the prices to a more equitable level. Second, there may be ways of reducing the artist's costs. Third, it might be wise to simply withhold works from the market until better conditions prevail.

104. Extrinsic Factors — Demand, Supply, Reputation of Artist and Dealer, etc.

The most significant considerations for determining how far above cost a price should be set are the factors associated with the general interest in and demand for an artist's work. Critics and connoisseurs may consider that an art work is moving or otherwise possesses significant esthetic quality, but unless collectors are actively interested in acquiring that work, any question of appropriate pricing is simply an academic exercise.

Generally, interest promotes price. Reversing this logic, a dangerous exercise, an artist or a dealer might feel impelled, if there is little demand for a work, to reduce the price in order to promote greater interest. But collector interest may be weak for reasons which have nothing to do with the artist's pricing policy. A badly executed work cannot become more desirable if its price is reduced. More to the point, a properly promoted artist will find that the interest of collectors in art works can increase simultaneously with an increase in the level of prices for these works.

Art dealers generally recognize their obligation to generate demand for works of the artists they represent. Accordingly, as suggested earlier, they should encourage the artist to enter juried exhibitions and competitions. It is toward this end, too, that dealers produce and advertise their own privately spon—sored exhibitions of the artist's work. The basic assumption here is that if the work has quality, as the artist and dealer suppose it has, then its systematic exposure to a cultivated public will stimulate demand. Such activity serves as a strong support to the artist's pricing structure.

In certain cases, this assumption does not hold. Works are exhibited and may even receive critical acclaim, but they do not always get comparable collector support. This may be due to the art dealer's inability to attract the right group of collectors, or it may be due to a certain lassitude in connecting general promotion efforts with more concrete sales activities. On the whole, however, there does seem to be a correlation between the exposure of works of significant quality and their acceptance by the collecting public. Exposure stimulates interest and demand. Demand strengthens prices.

While the interest of art collectors is a primary factor in establishing the price of a work, the artist's own reputation may be cited as an important reinforcing factor in influencing price because the growing reputation of any artist can improve the demand for that artist's work. Where an artist is relatively unknown, a dealer might have difficulty engendering collector interest. Extra effort is necessary to stimulate adequate de—mand. On the other hand, dealers have found that, with an artist of well established reputation, one has an easier time developing interest on the part of collectors, even in a new or unusual image. We shall return to the issue of reputation in a moment.

105. The Inelastic Effect of Price on Demand for Art

When price increases significantly diminish the demand for a product or a service, economists say that such a demand is "elastic" with respect to price. In cases of this kind, the price cannot be significantly stretched without doing serious damage to market support. But when shifts in price do not appreciably alter the demand, such a demand may be considered "inelastic." Characteristically, the demand for vegetable produce is very elastic. Each year as the price of tomatoes rises in the off–season, our housewives tend to buy fewer tomatoes. As the price drops, they buy more.

However, the demand for gasoline has proven relatively inelastic, as ex–President's Fords' advisors discovered to their own embarrassment a few years ago. Automobile and truck drivers do not curtail their driving activities too significantly because the price of fuel increases by a few pennies per gallon. Also, when motoring is a bit less expensive, they do not engage in more driving. While housewives can readily adjust their interest in salad vegetables to changing prices, most motorists cannot as quickly adjust their needs for transportation to price fluctuations.

I have observed that collectors of art do not tend to buy more works because prices are down or less frequently when prices rise. Instead, they often behave like stock speculators, buying avidly when prices are rising and losing interest when prices fall or sometimes even when prices are not advancing steadily enough. The artist would do well to think of the price structure for art works as relatively inelastic in relation to demand. Reducing art prices does not improve demand. Moreover, increasing prices, within reasonable limits, will not reduce demand significantly.

In fact, as the artist's career matures and gains broader acceptance, prices should be expected to increase steadily. In the case of valid work, this process will continue, hopefully, even after the artist is no longer living. Certainly not all artists, most of whom work in art because they are artists and not primarily because they are seeking fame or wealth, can expect to achieve such reknown that their prices will attain stratospheric proportions. But serious artists should recognize that the increasing price of their own works is, in some sense, a measure of continued or growing acceptance by a significant number of art collectors.

On a number of occasions, I have encountered art dealers who, very much against my recommendations, embark upon a widely advertised "sale" or "clearance" of some sort. I once worked with a very reputable dealer in Honolulu who decided to reduce her inventory in this way. As I had predicted, this kind of sales activity did not produce measurable positive results. In fact, I believe that many regular clients began to lose confidence in a dealer who had obviously made many bad acquisition blunders. They seemed to think that the lower prices were a sign of poor judgment. Of course, many of those who had bought works from this dealer before prices were reduced felt that they had been misled.

As suggested above, however, there are legitimate and effective ways of using price to stimulate demand. For example, if an artist or art dealer is producing an edition of multiple originals, it may be in order to offer the work at a "pre—publication" price for a limited time. Recently, four original lithographs by Wade Reynolds were offered for a period of three months at three hundred and twenty five dollars. At the end of this time, the price was advanced to three hundred and seventy five. The pre—publication offer was particularly attractive to Reynolds' regular collectors who bought a good portion of the edition. Western sculptor Harry Jackson has long pursued a similar policy with his own limited edition bronzes. In his case, the price escalates as the edition reaches any of several stages so that the last work in the edition sells for considerably more than the first. Of course, such a policy presumes that the artist's work enjoys a fairly active market.

An alternative approach for using price as a stimulus to demand involves a special pre—exhibition offer. The artist or dealer may arrange that available works will be increased in price at the time they are put on exhibition. However, these works may be available at the old, lower price schedule until the day before the exhibition or studio sale. This is a par—ticularly useful device where an extra effort is being made to "pre—sell" a show. Of course, buyers are asked to permit their works to remain on view during the exhibition. A number of red "sold" dots on art works seen at an art opening can have an exhilarating effect on viewers.

106. Testing the Market for *le prix juste*

As discussed earlier, it is possible to identify and allocate the costs of producing a work of art with some precision. But, the creative talent which lies behind that work, determining its esthetic merits, cannot have a fixed economic value. It is thus not possible to determine, with any objectivity, the ultimate economic worth of an original and creative artist's images. Nevertheless, in setting the price of a work of art, we must try to measure the relative, if not the objective, dollar value of the artist's creative effort at a particular point in time. One way to do this involves periodically increasing the prices of the art works, as collector interest increases, carefully avoiding drastic or capricious price in-creases, which might anger or confuse the artist's following, and giving particular emphasis to the best works available for sale.

Artists should not think of their prices as fixed, but as based in good part on the growing demand for their works. Some artists and dealers might hesitate to embark upon a systematic program of price modification, partly because they fear that it might result in lost sales and partly because they find that regular price adjustment reviews can be bother-some. Nevertheless, if the artist's work really has significant intrinsic qualities, and if clients are increasingly more attracted to these qualities, then, as the artist's reputation and market grow, prices should be periodically increased. Any other course of action is unfair to both the artist and the dealer.

In the last analysis, it is even harmful to the interests of the artist's more discerning collectors, who stand to gain as the economic value of their earlier selections increases, vin— dicating their good judgment and taste. Only when prices are increased pecipitously and without apparent justification can this process harm the interests of the artist, art dealer, and collector. As suggested earlier, the proper starting point for testing an artist's prices is always with the best works. The prices for these works should be advanced ahead of all others.

107. Scarcity and Prices

One important ingredient of pricing, which is quite extrinsic to the quality of the work itself, is the relative availability of works by a particular artist or of works from a particular period by that artist. While Rembrandt's works have been widely recognized as masterpieces for many gen— erations, the primary force causing the price of his works to skyrocket in the last few decades has been their increasing scarcity. To put the matter a little differently, late twentieth century collectors pay more for a Rembrandt not because they value the work more highly than their nineteenth century forebears, but because far fewer works are available to today's buyers. Many major museums lack even one Rembrandt. These institutions and affluent collectors bid the prices up.

Even certain contemporary artists, whose output has been for one reason or another generally low, can command a better price for their works than is possible for other artists with a similar interest but a broader supply of works. Thus, the works of Gorky and of Soutine, in short supply for many years, generally fetch a higher price than one might expect to pay for a work of comparable scale and interest by one of their more prolific contemporaries such as Hoffman or Chagall.

So, too, the experiences of many artists in the original graphics field indicate that, all other factors being approx—imately equal, an impression from a smaller edition can command a better price than one from a larger edition. A few short—sighted artists, sometimes urged on by avaricious publishers, have produced unusually large graphic editions, only to find to their dismay that astute collectors question the legitimacy and the technical quality of such works and hesitate to buy them, even at bargain prices. "Art for the multitude" has been a recurrent slogan for many years, but it is usually associated with low standards of quality along with low prices. I seldom recommend editions of original prints much larger than one hundred and never larger than two hundred. I like to see editions of bronzes not larger than forty.

In summary, scarcity is an important determinant of the price of an artist's work. Artists and their dealers occasionally ignore this relationship and exhibit more works than their own markets can comfortably absorb. For every artist's work, there is a balance between supply and demand which is appropriate at a certain point in that artist's career. A prolific artist might, therefore, be well advised to hold certain works off the market until the demand has become sufficient to justify their release. I get the impression that Picasso under—stood this very well since he withheld many of his best works from the market until after his death.

Art dealers are sometimes alert to such supply—price relationships and intentionally withhold a portion of an artist's *oeuvre* for sale at a more mature price. The artist seldom shares in this gain, however. As indicated in the section of this *Handbook* which discusses artist—dealer relations, there is substantial interest in the development of a marketing system which will permit the artist to participate in such price increases. Ideally, the artist would receive a residual payment or royalty whenever a work of his changed hands, just as performing artists receive a payment when a record, film, or tape is sold, broadcast, or reissued.

108. The Relationship of Reputation to Prices

When making selections for their collections, some art collectors rely not on their own reaction to the quality of an image, not on their appreciation of the techniques, not on their knowledge of the relative merit of different works which are available from different artists. Instead, they may depend on the reputation of the artist as an index of quality. Such collectors are, of course, courting serious problems. They may not always buy that artist's best works. Nevertheless, reputation is a significant factor in determining prices. I have long campaigned and lectured against the proposition that a famous autograph or pedigree determines the value of a work.

But even art collectors who consider many of the other factors cited here in making their art purchase decisions are influenced, if to a lesser degree, by the artist's reputation. We seek the approval of others for our decisions in a wide variety of fields. Clearly, an artist whose reputation is vouch-safed by other collectors and by curators and critics as well must have an image worthy of respect and attention. Given two art works of comparable quality, image, and scale, the collector will generally pay more for the work created by the better known artist.

So, too, we are influenced by the reputations of certain art dealers who are well known for their leadership in various schools of art. The fact that an artist's work is carried by such a dealer may enhance the collector's willingness to buy and strengthen the price which will be paid.

109. Price Ranges for Groups of Collectors

Works by artists of a given reputation, medium, subject matter, or level of interest are often lumped together mentally by certain collectors who regularly buy within a fairly narrow price range. A collector may be accustomed to paying from $500 to $750 for an oil of a particular size by a contemporary artist who has a certain modest reputation in the art world. When such a collector is shown an interesting work by just such an artist at a price well below this range, it may be rejected. Perhaps the collector will suspect that the work is a fake or defective or simply that "something must be wrong."

If, on the other hand, the same collector is shown just such a work, and the price quoted is considerably above customary expectations, another work may be selected which is more in keeping with familiar buying habits and which seems just as attractive. Or, the collector may put off a buying decision entirely. The narrow price range is used as a gauge within which certain purchasers' decisions can be made.

Thus, certain collectors will impose a degree of constraint through exercising a notion of a range within which prices are "appropriate" for various classes of work by particular groups of artists. This constraint works two ways. It tends to reject works which are priced "too low," as well as those which are priced "too high." Years later, the collector may sigh over some important but lost purchase opportunity. But the habit of buying within the narrow price range persists.

I once met a very wealthy, otherwise astute, collector who confided that it was his policy to never pay more than $1,000 for an art work, no matter whose. While he had a good collection, because his tastes were sound, he had missed the chance to buy many great works, including some which he sorely regretted passing up. I understand that James Johnson Sweeney once advised an intermediate collector to always try to buy works which were "a little more expensive" than he could afford. This wise dictum stretches the collec—tor's aspirations and purse as well. But not all collectors are able to utilize such advice.

110. "Competitive" Prices

In setting their prices, some artists rely rather heavily on the guidance offered by prevailing prices asked for the works of other artists. As indicated above, there is a certain degree of logic to this. Collectors within a community may have accustomed themselves to certain price range limitations regarding works of an assigned character. However, artists and their works are seldom in direct competition with each other. If the works are truly the expressions of individuals, then they are not strictly comparable.

Occasionally, artists will indeed compete for a commission, but seldom is one artist granted a commission over another simply because a price was a bit lower.* On the other hand, art collectors seldom think of their avocation as an inexpensive or money saving activity. I can think of no case where col—lectors have ever described themselves as "price comparison" art buyers.

*However, the artist who enters a bid for a commission in competition with other artists would be well advised to try to base the price, at least in part, on what other artists are expected to ask. If not, he might find the price far beyond the client's budget or far too modest.

The importance of "meeting" competition in establishing the price of an art work is probably overstated. Collectors do not buy works simply because they are available at competitive prices. Prices asked by other artists are useful, then, primarily as a starting point for establishing a price structure for an artist's own works. They may also serve as limits on a dealer whose clients have adjusted themselves to a preconceived notion of that dealer's prices. But the prices for the works of two artists are seldom really competitive even in the same gallery.

I recently had an unusual experience with an art dealer who specializes in wild life art. When we started working together, she assured me that her clients would buy only rather inexpensive works. We found out, much to her pleasure, that this judgment was incorrect. Her clients have gradually learned the value of buying better works at higher prices and, of course, she has attracted new clients who never knew that she once sold only rather inexpensive art works.

111. Discounting Art Sales

From time to time, artists and art dealers who are clients of mine have raised the question of the propriety of such well known merchandising activities as price cutting and discounting in the field of art. I can think of no case where an unearned discount serves to enhance the long–term interests of an artist. Certainly, an art dealer who performs a valuable marketing function for an artist is entitled to receive a trade discount from the artist or from another dealer. These are established discounts, below the retail price. From this discount, the purchasing dealer must recoup marketing costs and support a retail establishment.

But the policy some artists and dealers follow of giving discounts to friends, collectors, and institutions is harmful to the interests of the artist since it undermines the regular price structure. It sets up two categories of customers: insiders, who can buy at "wholesale" rates, and outsiders, who must pay the full price. Later on, the outsider may become justifiably angry when it is discovered that friends have received preferential price treatment.

Wholesale rates should be reserved for wholesale transactions. Why an institution or a well connected individual should expect preferential price treatment by virtue of no special economic consideration is beyond me. In fact, considering that the cost of making such a sale is generally greater than the cost of a sale to an ordinary art collector, some arts institutions should probably pay more.

There is one condition under which a special pricing policy is indeed justified by the nature of the transaction. The merits of special pricing treatment in this case are recog— nized in the Robinson—Patman Act, the Federal legislation which is designed to prevent unfair price discrimination. A collector who buys many works at a time may be entitled to a better price per work than a collector who buys only a single work at a time.

This is fair because serving the client who buys in large volume generally creates a lower cost of sales per work than serving a client who buys only one or two works at a time. Some artists and dealers reduce their prices by as much as ten percent when the total value of a single transaction exceeds a given sum, say five thousand dollars. For the same reason, original graphics artists often set the price of their suites at ten percent below their prices for single impressions of com— parable quality and interest.

Another case where discounting is economically justifiable is related to terms of payment. Many merchants will allow a client to take ten days to pay a bill; some will give as much as ninety days no—interest credit, after a minimum down payment, without charge. Such merchants will often offer a one percent cash discount for bills which are paid on presen— tation or within ten days.

But all other discounting practices which seek to give special consideration to certain classes of customers, without regard to relative selling costs, are probably illegal. They are certainly unwise because they materially reduce the possiblility that the artist and the dealer can be supported by the sale of works. They are essentially a form of subsidy to favored collectors.

One final and really rather curious discounting practice should be mentioned. Several large firms which sell pictures of rather consistently poor quality on a nationwide basis, often imported from Asia, have adopted what is called the "gimmick discount." A large price tag attached to the work shows a "list" price which has been lined out and replaced by a "special sale price," usually exactly half of the other figure. Clients are advised that an appraisal is available, attesting to the higher value (for insurance purpose). This old dodge derives from the cheap furniture business and apparantly still works on quite a few unsuspecting yokels. I have been pleased to learn that the Consumer Affairs Division of several govern— mental agencies in various states have successfully prosecuted false representation cases against certain of these scoundrels.

112. Pricing the Artist's Services

Artists are regularly engaged by a client to create a work of art or to desgn and supervise the creation of a work under circumstances in which the client undertakes to pay all ma— terial and incidental costs as they are incurred. The artist's relationship to the client, from the point of view of pricing, is, in this case, radically different from that of the artist who produces self—financed works for subsequent display and sale. Where one is only selling creative talent and personal labor, and all other expenses are to be paid by the client, the artist's profit opportunity may be considerably reduced. But invest— ment and risk have also been reduced.

Often, such arrangements are negotiated on a fixed—price basis. Occasionally, they may also be made on some sort of time—oriented or percentage—over—cost basis. If the artist accepts a fixed—price assignment, all the time required to do the work should be carefully estimated, and the intrinsic value of the creative activity should be carefully established. Comparing the price to the fee which might be earned during this period by an art teacher or by a skilled laborer is improper and irrelevant.

One way to determine an appropriate price for the artist's services is to develop a price which would be logical if such a work were being sold to a collector after its completion. From this amount, the artist can subtract the estimated cost of materials, assistance labor, overhead, and other elements which are to be furnished by the client. The remainder is a good guide to an appropriate price for the artist's services.

When the artist is paid by the hour, week, or month, it should be remembered that during this time a creative func- tion is being performed as well as a supervisorial and labor function. Since the artist is not simply a mechanic, following a blueprint which has been prepared by someone else, the higher value of creative activities must be taken into account. Again, in order to test the validity of the artist's pricing policy, the artist should compare the anticipated price with the net income, after all expenses are recovered, which would be generated from the sale of finished works which might be produced during this same time period.

When the artist's dealer arranges work of this kind, certain marketing costs are incurred. These costs include the com- mission earned by the sales person, a portion of the dealer's overhead, certain specific travel and legal costs, etc. In addi- tion, the dealer is entitled to a profit on the transaction. All of these factors should be considered in establishing a price.

113. Pricing Under the French Point System

Many European art dealers, and a few in the United States, price the works of their artists on the basis of the *French Point System.* Each work is assigned a certain number of points, based primarily on its scale. An 11" x 14" work is evaluated at five points while a larger work gets a greater number of points. One measuring 32" x 40" is worth 40 points and a 50" x 64" is worth 100 points. For each artist represented by a gallery, a dollar or franc value is assigned to one point. The price of an individual work then becomes a matter of simple arithmethic.

This system has the virtue of being internally consistent. Using a standard table, any clerk can determine the correct number of points for a given work and can then calculate the price. But the system does not give recognition to the vast differences in quality which occur within an artist's *oeuvre,* even within a particular period. Since these differences are not considered, the system can produce prices which are not accurate reflections of intrinsic or extrinsic merit.

However, even if this problem were resolved, the point system still cannot avoid a number of significant difficulties. Not the least of these is the task of determining the value of the point. For this, we must fall back upon the considerations discussed earlier. How are we to establish the value of a point for a particular artist without considering the extrinsic and intrinsic factors discussed earlier in this section? How can we avoid the issue of cost recovery? But, when we have considered these issues carefully, what added purpose does the point system serve? As Bertrand Russell suggested, consistency is a virtue of small minds. Scale is indeed a factor in determining the price of an art work, but it is only one of many factors, and not always the most important one.

114. The Effect of Credit on Pricing

In the modern credit economy which has developed in our culture over the past eight decades, it is curious that the artist and the art dealer often have no clear—cut credit practices. Art works are often too expensive even for quite affluent collectors, if they are asked to pay cash for them.

A fairly large number of art dealers proudly offer very "flexible" credit terms to their collectors at no cost, neglecting to note that the works so distributed are generally not their own property, but are consigned to them by their artists. I feel that offering "free," uncontrolled credit is almost always a dubious practice. Offering works which are not the dealer's own property to collectors, without adequate protection for the artist, can be an outrageous assault on modern business ethics and can be ruinous to both artist and dealer.

Every modern consumer understands that credit is an expensive privilege, not easily obtained and almost never rendered without cost. A collector who is not required to pay appropriate interest charges for the credit rendered by a dealer has little reason to believe that the price of the art work does not already include a certain charge for credit. Since the passage of truth—in—lending legislation, the major merchandising firms have found that the addition of clearly—stated credit charges does not diminish their business, as some had thought it might. It works the other way around, en—couraging many customers to buy merchandise they could not otherwise afford.

If a concern is too small to develop and install a credit system, it is useful to affiliate with any of a number of widely—held credit card systems such as Mastercharge, Carte Blanche, American Express, and Visa. These agencies pay the merchant, often at a discounted rate, and then collect directly from the client, charging no interest for prompt payment. The plans vary, but they work no great hardship on artist and dealer. I find that those art dealers who offer such credit facilities to their collectors meet no appreciable resistance when they withdraw their earlier "free credit" terms. I see no reason why an individual artist cannot offer similar credit accom—modations.

An alternative to giving credit involves putting works on lay—away for collectors. Many art lovers are willing to make a small deposit and pay regularly until the day comes when they can afford to take ownership of a work. I think that this is an excellent, no risk sales technique, but I advise my clients not to permit lay—away purchases whenever the buyer is unwilling to complete the transaction in four months.

115. Prices for Framed and Unframed Works

Quite regularly, I find myself working with artists and dealers who do not fully understand the importance of suitable framing or, in the case of artists who work in three dimensions, proper mounting. I have been able to prove, experimentally, that good framing is often vital to the selling of art works. On many occasions, I have found that a carefully selected frame will cause an art work to sell which had previously engendered only negative or indifferent response when it was shown. So too, proper bases for sculptural works can be a significant matter.

Good frames and bases can be expensive. The cost of properly preparing any solo exhibition can readily exceed a thousand dollars; but failure to present work properly to the public can ruin an artist's economic opportunities. Someone must make an appropriate investment and this investment can and should receive proper compensation.

When the artist incurs the costs of framing or mounting, or when a master dealer supplies a framed work to a secondary art dealer, a rather strange mark—up problem occurs. For example, if the artist makes an investment of fifty dollars in a frame and expects a profit of twenty five dollars on the investment, a not unreasonable fifty percent mark—up has been placed on the frame. This yields a gross profit of only one third of the selling price, which is indeed a modest return.

Now, if the retailer wishes to make an additional profit on the sale of this frame, a second mark—up will be necessary. Thus, the seventy five dollar frame might be offered to the collector for one hundred and twenty five dollars. This would give the dealer a forty percent gross profit on the transaction, but it also makes the retail price of the frame rather dispro—portionate to its original cost. Further, if the artist consigns a frame to a wholesaler, who then consigns it, in turn, to a secondary retailer, the price of this frame can easily make the work being offered quite uncompetitve.

This problem is particularly acute where the unframed work is modestly priced in the first place. It is not unusual to find an original print offered for sale where the selling price of the framed work is more than half attributed to the price of the frame.

Where it is at all practical, retailer sellers should do their own framing, eliminating the need of multiple mark—ups. Where this is not possible, I feel that the mark—up of frames and mountings should proceed at a fairly modest rate to avoid embarassing or excessively expensive framing and mounting prices.

116. Recovering Crating and Shipping Costs

If an artist or dealer sells work to tourists or others who are visiting the community where the work is sold, it will become necessary to recover the cost of crating and shipping the work to the client. Where such costs are modest, say fifty dollars or less, and in cases where the crating and shipping cost is a small fraction of the selling price, say five percent or less, I prefer making these costs a part of the general cost recovery problem. That is, I think that relatively insignificant shipping and crating costs should be included in the selling price and not added as an extra to the client's bill. But more significant costs should be billed directly to the client, and the estimated cost of crating and shipping art works should be reported in advance to the collector.

When the art dealer undertakes such costs with respect to a consigned work, it is not appropriate to split this portion of the proceeds of the sales invoice with the artist. The same principle applies to the proceeds of selling a frame which was furnished by the dealer for an artist—owned work. To avoid confusion, a consignment sheet should always indicate whether the stated and mutually agreeable prices include framing and mounting, as they would when the artist furnishes them or do not include framing, mounting, crating, and shipping, as is the case when the dealer furnishes them.

117. Checklist of Factors Related to Pricing Policies for Art Works

The problem of pricing art works is one of recognizing values under rather subjective circumstances. This, too, is an art which must be cultivated before it can be practiced successfully. Prices for art work should recover costs, measure intrinsic merit, and test the demand for the artist's image and reputation as well as for the available supply of works. Since these are dynamic forces, the prices to which they give rise must be reviewed and modified frequently.

The appended checklist is not inclusive of every pricing problem, nor is it a "formula" for establishing prices. But it can act as a series of unweighted reminders which the artist and dealer should discuss and consider regularly when they establish and review prices for art works. At various times and circumstances, different elements of this checklist will become relatively more or less significant in determining the appropriate price of a particular work or the proper range of prices within a collection. For example, an artist's reputation will become a more significant factor as that artist's career prospers. At the same time, cost recovery can become less important.

I Intrinsic Qualities

A. Esthetic Factors*   Check One

(1) Collectors with a particular esthetic interest or bias will appreciate these works. ——

(2) These works are good examples of an art movement or school which has attracted the interest of a significant number of art collectors. ——

(3) These art works are representative of the *oeuvre* of a well known artist. ——

(4) These works are the best examples available by a moderately well established artist. ——

(5) These are among the best available works by a very well known artist. ——

B. Technological Factors   Check One

(1) The structural quality of these works is sound. Materials employed are standard or better and methods used are acceptable. ——

(2) These art works are well constructed and properly mounted or framed. Materials are of high quality. ——

(3) These works are attractively mounted or framed and are composed of very high quality materials. ——

(4) The artist employed unusually fine, pain-staking or difficult techniques in executing the concepts. ——

* With any group of works, always begin by selecting the best works for the highest prices.

II Cost Recovery

Yes No

(1) The cost of all the materials directly em—
ployed in making these works has been carefully
calculated. — —

(2) The artist's labor and any labor furnished
by assistants or volunteers have been eval—
uated at established hourly rates. — —

(3) An allowance has been made to recover an
appropriate share of the artist's studio rent,
utilities, insurance, and similar overhead
costs. — —

(4) The cost of carrying the works in inventory
have been calculated. — —

(5) The cost of the artist's education has been
considered. — —

(6) The anticipated cost of promoting and selling
these works has been distributed equitably to
the estimated total cost of each art work. This
includes provision for the salesman's commis—
sion, if any, and for a fair share of the gallery's
operating expenses. — —

(7) The cost of handling these art works, including
crating, framing, and shipping in and out has
been identified and included.* — —

** If not included, a special charge should be added to the
invoice price.*

III Extrinsic Factors

A. Artist's Reputation   *Check One*

(1) The artist has no significant following among
collectors.   —

(2) The artist has a small but loyal following of
collectors, each of whom owns two or more
works.   —

(3) The artist has a rapidly increasing reputation
through awards, acceptance in juried shows,
critical reviews of solo shows, and sales to
collectors.   —

(4) The artist's reputation has been well estab—
lished for some time among a significant
group of collectors, critics, and curators.   —

(5) The artist is a leading force in contemporary
art.   —

B. Demand: Collector Interest   *Check One*

(1) These works were not created by a well
established artist.   They currently generate
sporadic collector interest.   —

(2) These works are not by a well established
artist.   They currently arouse modest, but
fairly consistent collector interest.   —

(3) These works are by a fairly well established
artist.   Nevertheless, collector interest in
them has been rather modest.   —

(4) These works are by a well established artist.
Collector interest is fairly strong.   —

(5) These works are by a well established artist.
Collector demand often exceeds the avail—
able supply of this artist's works.   —

C. Scarcity *Check One*

(1) The artist's works are generally available in a quantity which significantly exceeds the current demand by collectors. —

(2) The artist's works are readily available in a variety of images and moods, but demand for the better works can be expected to closely approach supply over the next few years. —

(3) Demand for the artist's works is growing faster than the supply of new and pre–existing works. —

(4) The artist's works have historically been in short supply. Collector demand is great. —

D. Dealer's Reputation *Check One*

(1) The dealer is not well enough established to significantly stimulate interest in the artist's works. —

(2) The dealer is fairly well respected as a source for works of considerable esthetic interest. —

(3) The dealer is able to add significantly to collector interest in the artist's works be– cause of a broad reputation for taste and integrity and because of good contacts. —

(4) The dealer can place the artist's works in important collections without too much difficulty. —

(5) The dealer's reputation and affiliations are such that all the valid works the artist can deliver will be readily sold. —

E. Competitive Price   *Check One*

(1) The art works are comparable in scale and quality to those of other artists within a particular gallery.   —

(2) The art works are comparable in scale and quality to those of certain artists within a particular community or school of art.   —

(3) The art works are not really comparable for pricing purposes with other works available in this area, except perhaps in terms of the relative reputation of the artist.   —

F. Discount and Credit Policy   *Yes   No*

(1) A wholesale discount policy has been estab— lished for trading with dealers.   —   —

(2) A volume discount policy for purchasers of several works already exists.   —   —

(3) Special—interest discounts are prohibited or strictly curtailed.   —   —

(4) A credit or lay—away policy exists.   —   —

IV Framing, Crating, and Shipping

Check One

(1) No framing, crating, or shipping is included in the price.   —

(2) The artist has furnished framed, ready—to—hang works. No significant crating and shipping is anticipated.   —

(3) The dealer has furnished frames or mountings for the work. Crating and shipping costs are included in the price. Income from none of these is to be shared with the artist.   —

(4) The master dealer has furnished frames or mountings with work supplied to a secondary dealer. The retail price provides for no sharing of the income from the sale of the frame or mounting with the artist or the secondary dealer. —

(5) The secondary dealer will provide framing, crating, and shipping. The income from these elements of the sale are not shared with the artist or the master dealer. —

V Periodic Price Review And Revision

Yes No

(1) Prices have been systematically adjusted to reflect inflationary shifts in the value of money and changes in the cost of living. — —

(2) Prices currently asked for the artist's works have recently been compared with and adjusted to prices for the works of other artists whose works provoke comparable interest and demand. — —

(3) Prices currently asked for the artist's works have recently been adjusted to reflect a measurable increase in demand for the artist's work. — —

(4) Prices for certain particularly interesting or important works have been adjusted upward to "test the market," by determining whether collector resistance will be met at newly selec— ted price levels. — —

(5) Prices have been increased to reflect a shift in the balance between growing demand and diminishing supply. — —

Scheduling

118. Scheduling Simple & Complex Activities

Almost every artist or art dealer, like other busy people, is faced with the problem of accomplishing a variety of tasks. Sometimes these tasks are related to larger assignments and associated with specific time—related commitments. Other tasks stand alone and do not intrude on the consciousness except by an act of will. Only rarely is the artist or dealer so unencumbered with responsibilities and interests and so well supported with assistants and colleagues that there are no significant scheduling problems. If you have little to do, or if you can depend on others to help you get your work done, then you probably do not need to pay too much attention to this section of the *Handbook*. But learning to schedule can be very useful to most active people.

Many business people have already discovered the value of identifying and listing specific tasks which need to be accomplished. The housewife may resort to a simple, written shopping list, coupled with an occasional written reminder regarding appointments and commitments: "Deliver Johnny to the dentist on Thursday at 2 P.M." or "Find a substitute driver for the Wednesday car pool."

Such simple lists of tasks are rather straightforward. They start with an identification of activities which need to be performed and proceed to an ordering of these tasks into some system of priorities. As a task is accomplished, it may be crossed off the list. Periodically, a new reminder list may be prepared and its contents given priorities.

However, if the demands on an artist's or dealer's time are more complex, as they often are, the scheduling activity should be more sophisticated. Every artist and art dealer needs a good calendar, preferably a bound book, in which specific assignments, commitments, and allocations of time may be recorded. Such printed calendars are simple but effective, scheduling devices. They help us to reserve our time and tell us how it is to be deployed, or they indicate certain firm commitments around which other activities and responsibilities may be planned.

I use two calendars. One is a desk calendar on which my appointments with clients can be recorded. This calendar presents an entire month on each page and provides room for a number of entries on each day. The other is a pocket cal—endar with a whole page devoted to each day for a month, plus back-up pages for future months. Both types of calendars are available from stationery stores.

To these, I add a two part listing on a single sheet of lined paper. The left hand column carries a list of tasks which can be accomplished with dispatch: "Call Jimmy Canto." "Write to Mary F." "Evaluate Mary's new brochure design." The right hand column lists those activities which require more than a half hour for their accomplishment: "Plan promotional campaign for the XYZ gallery." "Review Canto's prices."

A listing of tasks awaiting completion, coupled with a bound calendar showing appointments and deadlines, will generally accommodate day—to—day scheduling problems. This will not suffice, however, when time is less available or when the elements of a project are too complex and inter—related to be identified in terms of a simple listing or date assignment. The planning and execution of a major art pro—ject or the accomplishment of an exhibition and sales program presents two typical recurring scheduling problems. Of course, the same scheduling principles and methods discussed here for such projects could be employed to deal with other kinds of complex art activities.

To begin, we must divide the project or program into its logical components. The following is a typical list of subsidiary tasks into which a major art project, such as planning and execution of a wall mural, might be divided. Individual artists will want to revise this list to suit their own needs and meth—ods. Of course the list could be subdivided as well.
1. Planning conference and work session to determine physical and financial limitations of the assignment. (What are the dimensions of the available space? What materials will be employed? How much con—trol will the artist exercise over the work? How is the work to be installed and supported? What illumi—nation will be provided during and after installation? Are footings required? Are scaffolding and assistants needed for installation? Will a permit be necessary? What budget is available? How will funds be made available?)
2. Preparation of preliminary sketches, estimate of costs and price, preparation of proposal.
3. Sales conference to present preliminary proposal and sketches to client.
4. Development of working drawings, material lists, sources, final budget and contract.

5. Conference to finalize plans, approve working drawings, discuss and sign contract.
6. Preparation of work area.
7. Execution of the project — may be divided into several segments: surface supports and braces, surface preparation, rough block—outs and renderings, paint—ing, finishing, etc.
8. Installation, preceded by crating and shipping, if execution has not been performed on site.
9. Finishing and clean—up. Inspection may be required as well.
10. Release of work by artist to client and final billing.

In the case of scheduling a solo or group exhibition and the related promotion and sales program, the subsidiary tasks are different, but also rather clearly identifiable. They will probably include the following:

1. Initial conference between artist and art dealer to establish exhibition opening and closing dates. Ap—proximately how much work will be shown? Which media are to be included? Will the exhibition have a theme: display an attitude, technique, or specific range of interest? How will the exhibition be publi—cized and advertised? Who is responsible for promo—tion? Will the artist participate prior to the opening? Afterwards? What sales activities are to be employed?
2. Preparation of works.
3. Preparation of promotional campaign and promotional budget.
4. Selection of specific works for the exhibition.
5. Preparation of brochure — rough layout and planning.
6. Brochure copywriting.
7. Special photography for brochure and for publicity.
8. Final design of brochure & opening invitation.
9. Final pricing of brochure and invitation printing.

10. Shipment of works to the framer.
11. Mounting and framing of works.
12. Special additions to gallery mailing list.
13. Updating of mailing list.
14. Letting brochure production contract — review of "brownlines" — review of color proofs.
15. Shipment of brochures to mailing agency.
16. Mailing brochures, timed to arrive two weeks prior to opening.
17. Preparation of advance press release on exhibition, with illustrations.
18. Preparation of press kit.
19. Preparation of feature story with illustration.
20. Placement of feature story.
21. Mailing press release.
22. Shipment of works to the gallery.
23. Pre—hanging, decoration, and lighting of gallery.
24. Special previews for critics and established clients.
25. Hanging of exhibition.
26. Telephone invitations to opening.
27. Pre—opening party.
28. Opening.
29. Follow—up of prospects.
30. Release of follow—up publicity.
31. Closing of exhibition.
32. Debriefing conference between artist and gallery staff on results of exhibition: prospects, failures, opportunities, future plans.
33. Storage or return of works to artist.

Inspection of these lists will indicate that some items can be accomplished through a relatively brief meeting or some similar activity at a certain point in time. Other tasks require an expenditure of effort over a longer period. Particularly, when an activity will require more than a few hour's effort or more than one person's involvement, the scheduler should carefully estimate the time required and indicate the persons who must participate. Each item, event, or activity should be identified at the bottom line of an individual index card. The cards may be 3" x 5" or 5" x 8." They are mounted along the left–hand edge of a 48" or 60" wide bulletin board with tape, thumb tacks, or pushpins, and they form an easily modified vertical file of tasks to be scheduled.

Next, the remainder of the bulletin board can be sub–divided into an appropriate number of spaces along the top or bottom to represent twenty–six calendar weeks. This permits planning exhibitions or special art projects six months ahead. Each week should be numbered. The first square might represent week one or week twenty–seven of the cal–endar year. The second square would represent week two or twenty–eight. To begin scheduling, the firmest dates, which are generally called "demand" dates, should be scheduled first. The exhibition opening date can be scheduled on the board, opposite its card, Item 27, by placing a marker at the appropriate week. If the opening is scheduled for the first week in December, the marker will be placed at week 48. So, too, the targeted completion or installation date of a major work may be indicated. Other dates are logical consequences of these demand dates and the time required to accomplish each activity. We should send out a brochure mailing so that it arrives two weeks before the scheduled exhibition opening. We should install the special project far enough ahead of the scheduled completion date to allow adequate time for finishing and clean–up between these two events.

It should be apparent that certain sets of activities are sequential. That is, one depends on the other. We cannot mail the brochure until it has been completed by the printer. We should not begin fabrication of the mural until the working drawings are completed and approved. Other sets of activities may be performed more or less simultaneously. Someone can expand and correct the gallery mailing list while someone else prepares a feature article for a newspaper or magazine.

Someone can erect the scaffolding while someone else locates and purchases the materials which are needed. Whenever activities can safely be scheduled in parallel, it is possible to reduce the total calendar time needed to complete a project or program. This valuable principle can only be realized fully when the schedule is carefully prepared and faithfully main—tained.

Activities which require any significant amount of time should be indicated on the schedule board as a line extending the length of the estimated time span. For example, the execution of an art project may be shown as a line several weeks wide. If specific elements of a schedule go awry, certain of the subsequent tasks can be rescheduled by re—locating the cards on which the time for these scheduled events is represented. If previously unscheduled tasks are identified, new cards can be prepared and inserted in the schedule.

By carefully identifying tasks, estimating the time each requires, the manpower which is needed, and arranging these tasks in appropriate sequential or parallel relationships, we can quickly determine the practicality of any schedule. If the time available does not seem to rationalize with the esti—mated time required, a series of remedies is available which may be employed early in the history of the project.

We might reschedule the critical demand target date, if that is still possible, or we might schedule an early added effort (Sunday work, extra hours) to meet the date, if re—scheduling this date is not permissible. We might reassign certain duties or find a helper for specific kinds of tasks. Alternatively, we might wish to change the scope of a project to meet our scheduling limitations. For example, if the artist cannot execute 35 new works in time for the exhibition, it might be possible to consider showing 20 new works and 15 earlier works. If the client cannot wait three months for delivery of a certain material which is needed in a mural, perhaps the design of the mural can be satisfactorily modified to accommodate more readily available materials.

Where the artist or the art dealer wishes to schedule more than one project at a time, the schedule board may be readily utilized toward this end. A dealer might wish to schedule four or five different exhibition programs on the same board — even combining certain recurrent activities, such as brochure planning or mailing list maintenance to effect economies of time and money. An artist might wish to schedule the fabrication of several major art projects on the same board.

In these cases, the listing on the left hand edge of the board would probably remain as it is proposed for scheduling a single program or project, but the rest of the board may be used to display more than one exhibition opening date, brochure mailing date, etc. To avoid confusion, colored cards might be employed, with blue signaling those activities related to one exhibition or art project, while yellow cards signal a similar set of activities in a different time pattern for another program.

Once an activity has been completed, the target date cards or time line segments may be removed from the board, leaving it free for new scheduling activities. The twenty—six weeks which occupy the bulk of the board do double duty, representing week number one, the first week in January, or week number 27, the first week in July, at different times of the year. The board can be used continuously on a year—round basis, because new space becomes available for scheduling as each week passes. We can always schedule six months in advance with this simple scheduling board.

As an alternative to the bulletin board, many other kinds of scheduling boards may be built or purchased. Remington Rand distributes an excellent board called Sched—u—Graph which consists of a series of 48" wide Kardex visible file pockets in which tasks may be described and events may be represented graphically with time lines. Other enterprising entrepreneurs have built boards with channels which hold and display tasks and time lines.

Even more sophisticated scheduling concepts, such as PERT and CPM, are simply extensions of the concepts dis—cussed here. They were developed for projects in which more precise quantification of results is important, and the volume of detail to be scheduled is great. Fundamentally, however, all scheduling is based on the simplest of concepts: identifi—cation of sub tasks, determination of critical delivery or demand dates, estimates of the time needed to achieve each individual task, graphic deployment of available forces and capacities to meet specific targets, division of tasks into sequential and parallel series, a simple graphic scheme for plotting and monitoring anticipated versus actual performance, and provisions for re—scheduling when things go wrong.

A final word about scheduling. Once a schedule has been developed for any particular project, the experienced artist or art dealer would be wise to do a little "disaster planning." All activities of mankind are apparently calamity prone. The delay that might result in a small organization as a result of illness or injury can be very significant. So, too, the delay which results from strikes, the failure of a supplier or shipper; a siege of inclement weather, etc., can be costly and embar—rassing.

But calamities are not absolutely random events. While their nature and occurrence cannot be predicted precisely, many specific failures can be anticipated and counter—measures can be planned and in readiness when they do occur. An artist might anticipate the possiblility of late shipment by scheduling shipping a few days earlier than necessary. So, too, one might anticipate the possibility of damage to a work in transit by bringing a kit containing certain appropriate art materials and tools to an installation site to make minor repairs and restorations if they are needed.

When illness or bad weather forces a delay in certain activities, a good scheduler may have prepared certain "work—around" tasks which can be accomplished whenever time is available. Every calamity cannot be anticipated and remedied, but disasters should be expected. The proper counter—measures should be planned and scheduled just as rigorously as any other activities in the artist's or dealer's life.

Business Ethics

119. The Fakers, Finagler's & "Con" Artists Arrive

My own work in the arts began with several studies I made of the economic potentialities for original prints. In 1959, when I first began advising artists who were working at the Tamarind Lithography Workshop, I was taken aback at the often absurdly low prices at which original prints were available. Major artists were, in many cases, asking retail prices of $35 to $50. These sums were seldom sufficient to permit the recovery of the artist's costs plus the selling cost. When I spoke about the need for more realistic print prices to permit cost recovery plus reasonable profit, I found many artists who insisted that their dealers would not tolerate significant price increases. At the same time, dealers told me that collectors would be unwilling to pay more than a few dollars for an original lithograph or intaglio print, regardless of its esthetic merit. Some major dealers even refused to exhibit the best original prints of their own artists.

Much to my dismay, I discovered that much of the disfavor into which the print medium had fallen in the thirties and forties in this country was a direct result of a major marketing miscalculation, springing from the social—realist school of art. These artists and their dealers thought of the print as "art for the masses." As such, they made large editions, often of very poor quality, produced to sell at low prices. As a direct result of this misguided policy, they soon found these works competing with cheap reproductions, and as the Depression deepened, the original print medium all but died in the United States.

During the sixties, the original print enjoyed a renaissance in the United States. Many artists of varying esthetic interests were attracted to the medium for its unique characteristics. They made remarkable works which were acquired by novice, intermediate, and advanced collectors at appropriate and profitable prices. *Ateliers* were founded to work with artists, and several became well established business institutions. Dealers became more deeply involved in the sale of original prints. Some specialized exclusively in original prints. Others added large, successful print departments.

And then came the fakers and forgers, the charlatans and "confidence" operators. It seems inevitable that whenever a segment of the marketplace succeeds in legitimately correcting a business problem by finding and satisfying a significant in—terest, a counter force will come forward which negates that healthy development through misrepresentation and skull—duggery. The problem of false and misleading sales activities involves a socio—ethical issue. It touches every aspect of the art world — artists as well as dealers, collectors as well as publishers. A few actual examples are given here to illustrate specific aspects of the new disease which is afflicting the field of the multiple original. Unfortunately, many other cases could be added, as the disease has spread significantly.

120. Just How "Original" Is This Print?

A merchant I know has for many years been a broker representing home furnishing manufacturers to the retail trade. He told me some years ago that he had read about the "boom" in original graphics in *Fortune, Time, The Wall Street Journal,* and *Business Week*, and that he has decided to "cash in."   First, he hired a talented young lady to make a few drawings in color. Next, he retained a printer who is competent in the photo—offset printing process. This is a process which is derived from the basic principles of lithography, but also differs greatly from the technology first developed by Senefelder in that it employs photo—sensitized plates, plus machine fed papers and inks, and optical systems of separating the colors of the painting into four half tone plates. Only rarely is an artist's image simple enough that it can be faithfully reproduced with this commercial process.

For a start, he told me he planned to produce ten editions of one hundred and fifty "works" apiece by sending the color drawings to his printer who would then reproduce them on a "pebbly—grained" paper.   His artist would then sign and number each work in pencil, after which he would frame and distribute them to department stores as signed, limited edition lithographs.

The merchant planned to invest about a dollar apiece with the printer and another dollar with the artist. He said he would invest an additional few dollars in a simple frame. He expected to sell the works for twenty—five dollars to major department stores, which would retail them to customers for around fifty dollars.

My acquaintance was startled when I suggested that there were many in the art world who would consider that these works could not be called original graphics. He protested,

but the edition is limited, numbered, and signed. And the works are going to be beautiful. The artist will make $1,500 on the deal. That's a lot of money for a few pictures and her signature . . . I'm taking all the risks — doing all the work.

I replied that the works may indeed be interesting, even pleasant and colorful, but they are simply mass—produced, photo—offset reproductions — possibly worth a bit more than the two to five dollars one might pay for a good reproduction of an art work at a museum gift shop, but certainly not worth fifty dollars, solely because they carry a few personal—izing pencil marks at their bottoms. When I checked into the "pebbly—grained" paper, it turned out to be a cheap, machine—finished, pulp product which quickly yellows and deteriorates, just as most nitrocellulose decomposes.

This loquacious, fast—dealing fellow really does not think he is cheating anyone, and, if we stretch the doctrine of *caveat emptor* to mean that any customer who buys without know—ing the nature of what is offered or what it is worth, deserves to be shortchanged, I guess he might well be legally within the letter of the law.

I cannot personally go along with this view. In these days of massive promotions, when a handful of clever scoundrel—communicators can twist simple facts to suit their own needs or fancies, the customer seldom has adequate information available to properly judge the quality of the things being offered for sale or even the integrity of the merchant with whom he deals. As a result, more and more consumer affairs organizations are adopting the position that customers of all kinds must be protected against their own lack of information.

The practice of misrepresenting reproductions as original art works has become so widespread that the legislatures in California, Illinois, and New York have taken steps to regulate the use of the word "original" as it applies to art. Whether these measures can succeed in correcting the situation remains to be seen. I generally have insisted that, while there is no real harm in a legislative effort of this sort, many regulations are easily circumvented. Artists, dealers, and collectors should learn to handle such problems on their own.

Sometimes I find myself thinking that artists and their dealers often take a perverse pleasure in confusing an already badly confused problem. How else can we explain an art dealer who sells original prints, but cannot explain the difference between a signed reproduction and a hand—pulled original intaglio?

What are we to think of an artist who consistently refers to his own paintings as original art works when he means they are unique (one—of—a—kind) but does not really believe that his own hand—pulled lithographs are mutliple originals? Perhaps this would be a good point for a few words on the semantics of the art world.

First, not all one—of—a—kind art works are "originals." When an art student copies a painting, and when a production artist in Taiwan or on Long Island copies a sample, each result can be called unique, at least in certain respects. But no self—respecting art critic or connoisseur would call these works original. That would require a level of creative effort and energy which is clearly not present. The student exercise and the production painting are simply "copies." On the other hand, when Soutine produced a painting of a veal carcass, he was clearly paying homage to Rembrandt's "Flayed Ox," but his work is distinctly original. So, too, when Toulouse—Lautrec

made his lithographs, the conceptions, expressions, and ren—
derings were distinctly his own creative efforts. They are
originals in every sense, without regard to the well known
fact that this fine artist worked at an *atelier* where specialists
helped him in many ways to achieve his ends. To go a step
further, if anyone wishes to photo—mechanically reproduce
the original work of Soutine or Toulouse—Lautrec, the result
cannot be considered an original, no matter how successfully
the technicians copy that work.

It seems clear that art cannot, by its nature, be mass re—
produced in mutiple limited editions. This clear line can, of
course, be muddled very easily. For example, a workshop in
New York has for some years been making editions of original
lithographs based on the illustrative paintings of Norman
Rockwell. This workshop uses *chromistes* to make the
Rockwell plates. These are relatively unknown artists who
work from the Rockwell paintings, by hand, sometimes with
the aid of optical separations.

The technique may seem repugnant to certain knowl—
edgeable collectors who prefer to buy works which have been
made more directly by the artist, but it differs little from
the nineteenth century and earlier practices where engravers
and *"schnitters"* were employed to make graphic works for
artists like Gustave Dore and Albrech Durer. The difference
between an art work which was created by an artist who had
helpers and one who works alone is not so much a matter of
multiple graphics versus unique oils. DaVinci and Durer both
used assistants. If Rockwell did not, he would not be a greater
or even a more honest artist. The key, as we shall see, has
a great deal to do with how the work is represented to the
public. But of this we can be certain. When an artist or dealer
hires a printer to photo—mechanically reproduce an already
existing art work the result is not an original of any sort,
but a reproduction.

121. When Does An Original Become A Reproduction?

It is easy enough to criticize the disreputable importers of production paintings with their phoney "mark—downs," but not every strange or unsavory deal is quite so obvious. Consider the curious dealings of one of our "better" dealers. It is not hard to understand how an impression from "an edition of 200 original, hand—signed, and numbered litho—graphs or serigraphs on Rives, Arches, and other fine papers" differs from an impression of "an edition of 4,000 original (sic) lithographs signed in the stone or serigraphs signed in screen on heavy papers," even when the image is basically identical in each case.

But it is much harder to appreciate how an impression from the latter set of works can differ from an impression of "an unlimited edition of offset posters." These terms were employed recently to differentiate three different offerings by a reputable dealer in the art trade magazines. If an edition of 4,000 is limited, when does an edition become "unlimited"? How does a massive run of photo—offset prints on "heavy" paper differ from a poster? The dealer's advertisement con—tains no clues regarding the differences.

This much is clear about the art dealer's three—way ad offer: the images are the same in all three sets of offerings. They are all the same size, colors, etc. The works on "special" papers are hand—signed. Perhaps there are significant tech—nological differences. Certainly, the paper employed in the smaller editions is more costly — perhaps five to eight times as costly. And better papers will last longer.

We know that machine—processed papers are usually made of cellulose, a wood product which has been reduced to paper chemically with acids. Such papers discolor and decompose rather quickly while the finer textile fibre papers are relatively stable because they contain fewer harsh reducing chemicals. But the difference in paper cost is of the order of a few cents per page for the common "heavy" papers versus a few dollars per page for the fine, hand—made papers.

Also, the inks in the smaller edition might be finer inks. The advertisement does not indicate whether the ink was laid down by hand in the smaller edition nor whether the colors were registered meticulously by hand. These things can make a print more costly. For example, a hand—inked, hand—pulled, multi—color original print can readily cost thirty dollars or more per impression just for workshop labor, materials, and overhead.

In some small editions, where the difficulties of pulling consistent, high—quality impressions elevates the labor costs, or where unusual materials are employed, workshop costs can amount to as much as a hundred dollars per impression. But we have not been told whether these particular impressions were hand—registered, hand—inked, or hand—pulled. They may have been run off on one of the four big, machine—fed, machine—inked commercial presses which are operated in the workshop where these particular prints seem to have been produced.

To further explore the quality of these works, I thought it might be useful to test the inks which were employed in printing them. Like some superior paints, some inks contain pigments which are relatively light—fast, that is, they do not fade significantly when exposed to the ambient artifical and natural light of a living room, office, or gallery. Some other pigmented inks fade quickly. If an independent research laboratory ran standard tests on color fastness — tests used to evaluate the suitability of inks for use in hand lithography — the results would probably be dismaying. The higher priced works from the smaller limited editions would fade just as quickly as the low priced works from the massive editions.

The works so tested might not stand up. Did the publisher check this, or did he simply not care? In either case, is the collector buying a work of art, which he hopes will yield many years of interest, only to discover that the yellow, blues, and reds will pale and perhaps disappear in a few years? How would such evidence square with the oft repeated claim that these particular graphic works represent a "good investment" — even a hedge against inflation?

I have come to believe that in this particular case the impressions of the smaller edition differ from those of the larger one in only two significant respects. First, the papers employed in the more expensive works are definitely superior to those used in the smaller edition. That makes these impressions more valuable, but not by much.

Second the smaller edition impressions carry what appear to be authentic, original pencil autographs and numbers. These were not only done by hand, by the artist, but also (unlike certain mass produced French prints) these signatures were probably applied after the print was executed. How much does a genuine autograph by a famous artist add to the value of a work?

Some of the greatest masterworks in the history of art are unsigned, but indubitably, a signature adds something to the worth of a work, as every art dealer (and every art forger) would agree. But how much does it add? Well we can buy a real signature from a dealer who specializes in autographs from the pen of a famous statesman or poet for $25 to $1,000.00. Some autographs are more valuable than others. How much, then, is a particular artist's original pencil auto—graph worth? Would the same autograph bring the same price at the bottom of a work from the larger edition? at the bottom of a poster with the same image? at the bottom of a laundry bill? One artist has made an original print edition of photo—graphically enlarged laundry bills.

The story has gone around for some years of a famous man who always paid small obligations by check. He discovered that his checks for less than ten dollars were seldom cashed, but retained by merchants as mementos of the great man. Of course, he changed laundries and liquor stores with regu—larity. Incidentally, his checks for twenty—five dollars or more were regularly cashed.

I have concluded from my own study of the case which I have just summarized that the three "different" editions are basically quite similar but that the many collectors bought higher priced works because they felt that they were much more "original" than the lower priced works. The images contained in all three editions were indeed rather unique examples of the artist's work, but the methods employed in generating each of the three kinds of editions lead me to the conclusion that the two larger editions in each case are hardly "originals." This casts suspicion on the smallest edition as well. To top this strange performance, a major art magazine pressed the issue by offering "works" from a "limited edition" of 60,000! Of course these promoters did not suggest that their prints were in any sense originals.

122. Does the Business Press Understand?

"What is an original print?" asks free lance writer Elizabeth Stevens at the opening of a feature on the editorial page of the *Wall Street Journal.* She then devotes three columns of copy to answering her own question, starting by observing that the simple definitions of the Print Council of American are "conservative, widely quoted, and less widely followed." She continues, citing a variety of other sources which discuss the question in detail, including some of my own studies for Tamarind Lithography Workshop, and then digresses into the interesting experiences of a few major print collectors and exhibitors, none of whom were actually bothered with the task of answering her question in the article.

Finally, after meandering into a discussion of collecting photographs, which has no apparent relation to the announced topic, she restates her opening question and answers, "Future answers may well come from the artists themselves." While this conclusion cannot be denied, it merely suggests that the author might well have waited to write her article until more conclusive material was available.

Actually, many artists have already answered the question although none were quoted. Some artists have been careful to avoid large–scale, machine–made reproductions because it interferred with the quality of their work. More have insisted on registering their own control over their works by demanding cancellation proofs at the conclusion of an edition, by co–signing documentation sheets with their master printers, and by withholding their signatures from works which they felt did not measure up to their own standards of originality. Of course, not all artists are saints. Several have cooperated in the production of editions which are clearly reproductions rather than originals.

123. The Need for Full Disclosure

I suspect that circular discussions like Miss Stevens' report are, at least objectively, obfuscating. The issue is a simple one which has been long understood by almost everyone who has taken the time to read the literature in the field. An original print is a work generated by any of a variety of printing pro—cesses in which the artist's creative imagination and labor have been directly involved. How directly? This has always been a matter of choice depending on the artist's technological skills and interests, the nature of the artist's expression, and the milieu in which the work is produced.

If an artist wished to employ assistants, advisors, techni—cians, photo—mechanical devices, computers, or even laser beams, to create unique or mulitple works, including prints, that is the artist's inalienable right, whether Miss Stevens or the Print Council grants it or not. But if the artist or the distributor conspire to withhold, misrepresent, or significantly distort important information regarding their processes or their working relationships from the public, then someone might well be cheated.

A rather remarkable image was shown to me recently. I asked what it was. The dealer replied, "It is a limited edition, photo—offset lithograph, hand—signed and numbered on BFK Rives paper." I asked for the edition documentation and was told that none had been prepared. My interest waned.

I wanted to see the documentation in order to learn the type and manufacturer of the inks; whether the inking of the stone or plate was accomplished by hand or mechanically; whether the paper was laid on the press, registered, and pulled by hand; the name, location, and reputation of the printer; whether the artist and printer had guaranteed the limited size of the edition; whether any significant number of works existed outside the edition; and a few other important ques—tions which a good documentation could have revealed.

Always a cautious customer, I need detailed information when I buy an automobile. Although I would grant the auto manufacturer's right not to furnish it, when I cannot obtain satisfactory data, I will seldom buy — even if I like the looks of the car. I am much more cautious about multiple original art works. My advice to art collectors who have not learned to be this careful is as follows:

> *Learn to insist on documentation. Learn to interpret the significance of omitted information. You might be buying a work worth considerably less than the asking price. There might be more of these works than are advertised on the face of the impression. The paper may be a machine—made, pulp product, in which case, it has probably already started to change color. The inks may be fugitive or brittle. The pro— cess of reproduction may look expensive when it was truly cheap. One might be able to buy an authentic autograph and a fair photo—reproduction of the same artist's image for less.*

Should the unwary collector give up collecting original prints? Certainly not. But we must learn to distinguish real art from imitations. It is not hard to do, and it will prove rewarding — esthetically, if not economically. We should insist on full, reliable information: *Where? When? Who? How many? With what? Who said?*

To assist any artist or art dealer who may find the con— struction of a documentation sheet somewhat difficult or confusing, I have included good examples of actual docu— mentation sheets for two art works at pages 189 & 190 in the *Handbook.* The Martin Green is a unique work — a monotype which was created specially for a client in Southern California where Green works. The Florence Putterman documentation is for an edition of original prints produced by this Pennsylvania artist at the Ernest de Soto workshop in San Francisco. In addition, I have included two forms — one for multiple originals and the other for unique works. These forms are in many ways similar to those which I developed a few years ago for Artists Equity Association, the national organization of professional artists.

124. An Old Confidence Game

Some of the better established, more prestigious art merchants join with their less respectable confreres to play an even more convoluted role in deceiving collectors. Like most "confidence" games, they rely partly on the cupidity of the "mark" — the willingness of the customer to partici-pate in a slightly shady or at least somewhat unethical deal in the hope of enjoying quick and fabulous profits.

Ignorant of the most fundamental facts of the unique art and original graphics fields, many wealthy non—collectors and novices have been encouraged, sometimes by well established art dealers, to buy art on the premise that the works will inexorably increase in market value much faster than money drops in value because of inflation. In truth, certain contemporary art works have enjoyed remarkable advances in market price over the past few years as large numbers of new collectors entered the field and as certain artists and their images gained wider recognition. The claim that good art works can increase in market value is not entirely without merit.

But, before we can afford to speculate in art, we should know how broad the market is for the particular works being examined. How much unregulated, behind—the—scene manipulation has gone into the quoted price advances? How readily can the work be transformed into cash? What com—mission rates would a collector need to pay if it became necessary to liquidate a collection? Will the current market values of these works continue to climb at the same pheno—menal rates enjoyed by other similar works? Why? Is there reason to believe that these works will even retain their current high values?

The answers to these questions are matters of esthetics more than economics. Aside from promotion or manipulation, an art work will only appreciate in value economically if it appreciates in value esthetically — that is, if its appreciative audience grows. Thus, a good impression of Picasso's *Le Repas Frugal* has indeed improved in price over the years, primarily because it is an outstanding example of a seminal work by a great modern master, an example which is, inci—dentally, in great demand by connoisseurs and museum curators who consider it a remarkeably successful art work, characteristic of the best of Picasso during the period in which it was made.

A similar statement might be made about some of Sam Francis' works which were produced in the sixties at Tamarind. They are generally recognized by the authorities on this major contemporary artist's work to represent a high point in the development of his images during that period. Remarkably successful action works in very small editions, they were sold out in a short time and have not since reappeared on the market in any great number.

Since then, Francis has gone on to other images, but his works from that era are in ever greater demand. I happen to be fortunate enough to own one of these works, but it is not now on the market, nor is it likely to be. I bought the work because I was able to relate to it, not because it was "underpriced." I do not like it less, now that it has gone up in market value. I would not be interested in "cashing in" my investment at a profit, even if it were easy and inexpen—sive to do so. But I would feel the same way about this work if it had not gone up in market value. The attitude of a collector towards an art portfolio is necessarily different from the attitude of an investor towards a portfolio of stocks and bonds. Perhaps the words of my friend, the libertarian economist and writer John Pugsley, himself a fine critical student of investment practices, will exhibit more fully my own views:

> *Artists and art dealers have played very heavily on the idea that art is a great hedge against inflation, and should be part of everyone's portfolio. It's true that works of fine art, done by artists of widely established reputation, have appreciated dramatically in value during periods of inflation. Unfortunately most of the dramatic price rises that you hear about are for great works by world renowned and usually dead artists. These works are passing through the hands of extremely knowledgeable and dedicated art connoisseurs. The unknowledgeable investor will be buying less well known works by less well known artists, and will be paying retail prices through art galleries.*

> *The idea that the average person can select art works of new and promising artists, buy them, and hold them for long term appreciation is lunacy. There is no doubt that a few of the unknown artists who are today toiling behind hot paint brushes in dimlit garages around the world will someday be discovered, and their early works will command prices hundreds of times what they sell for today. The sheer quantity of new art being produced makes finding the budding Picasso a task far more difficult than finding the proverbial needle in the haystack. Even the super—pros of the art world; those presti— gious dealers who comb the art fairs, galleries, and*

studios around the world; who have thousands of sources constantly supplying them with examples of fresh new talent and who really know talent when they see it; even they are rarely lucky enough to come across the diamond in the raw. Your chances of buying a work from an artist at the Laguna Art Festival, or any of the thousands of galleries in New York, Chicago, or Los Angeles, and having it ever appreciate enough to be worth what you paid for it are about zero. It can be done. But it's just about as reasonable an amibition as rolling five consecutive sevens on the crap table at Las Vegas.

If you want to make money at new art, become a dealer. Don't become a collector. If you want to become a collector, do it for the sheer pleasure of the art itself, not for the money.*

*Pugsley, John, *Common Sense Economics,* The Common Sense Press (Costa Mesa, CA: 1976).

125. As Bernie Cornfeld Once Asked:
"Do You Sincerely Want to be Rich?"

The most successful schemes for encouraging novice "investors" to part with their money whether for undeveloped desert land speculations or for solid gold bricks are often built of a formula which includes, as one part, a sincerely stated true statement and, for at least two parts, an appeal to the avarice and culpability of the intended victims themselves. But we make a big mistake if we believe that every "funny money" scheme is perpetrated by a sleazy looking operative wearing suede shoes and a peculiar hat.

In our own materialistic society, obviously misleading propositions are regularly put forward by very respectable institutions to sell magazine subscriptions and encyclopedias or even political candidates. Within the art world, we can find an excellent example in a feature story which appeared in a Sunday magazine section of the *Los Angeles Times* in January of 1971. The author of the article, aimed at reviewing the role of the Gemini Workshop in the rebirth of original graphics, is a publicist named Robert Levinson. He begins by talking not about art but about money. Quoting Kenneth Tyler, one of this country's finest master printers, who was the director of Gemini at the time, he suggests that this workshop might indeed be some sort of long sought perpetual money machine. Tyler's remarks in this article are reported as follows:

> *Let's face it, we're printing banknotes . . . and you better well believe we're printing bank notes. That shop, that place back there, is a bank, and better than a Swiss bank, because we don't have to depend on the value of the dollar or the franc.*

The author of the article goes on to explain, rhapsodically:

Yet it is the individual buyer who achieves the greatest benefit, a certain aesthetic satisfaction be— cause the works are on his wall and in his collection, and the constantly verified knowledge of blossoming value. Mister Modest Buyer, granted opportunity to spend an average $1,000 on random selections each year, today might have his $5,000 stockpile of Gemini prints appraised for $15,000. The heavy collector with cash to match passion, could watch as acquisitions costing some $50,000 at retail soared upwards of $125,000 in the same period. Whatever the combinations of purchase used for illustration, the result is routinely the same, an investment yield of 250 percent and beyond.

Levinson goes on at a feverish pace to give examples of Rauschenberg, Stella, and Johns prints made at Gemini which opened on the market at modest prices and promptly moved up. A Stella started at $175 and moved to $1500 in three years. A series of Johns prints opened at $800 each and moved to $3500 each in less than a year.

But, Levinson continues, money is not the primary motivation of this workshop. In fact he gives an excellent short definition of the process of making an original print.

Take an image created for the medium, usually on a special stone, by an artist working hand—in-hand with a printer artisan. Consider a certain number of impressions drawn from that stone on a hand press, each matching the other, checked, numbered, and signed by the artist. Presume the stones to be de— faced, so that no more prints can be made. Presto! A primer paragraph defining the limited edition, original lithograph.

That definition is indeed good even if it is a little on the "primer" side. It is, nonetheless, valid. The author goes on quoting Tyler:

> *Fakes with forgeries abound in the field, and they increase as market demands expand . . . we document everything we do . . . We believe in the honesty of the act.*

We must all agree with the ethics of Tyler's position, but for all the welcome stress on frankness and full documentation, the story has made a rather fantastic claim. This is the assertion, made boldly and with lavish illustrations, that in five years, an investor of "$1,000 a year on random selections each year, today might have his $5,000 stockpile of . . . prints appraised in excess of $15,000."

Levinson calls this an example of an investment yield of "250% or more," which it is not, although it certainly is an impressive performance. If we measure yield as the annual rate of increase of a given investment, the illustration works out to an average rate of less than 100% per year. This is still pretty good, if one could do it consistently with "random" acquisitions from this *atelier's* output.

But, whose "random" selections might be expected to appreciate in this way? Does the *atelier* in question, for all its good taste and good fortune, never lose? The specific data given to support the feature writer's contention so overstates the case as to prove that something is amiss. In a special inset box, next to the article, eight internationally famous artists, surely not selected at random, are listed. The opening and the 1971 market prices for certain of their multiple original works are quoted. It turns out that if one bought these particular works, at the time of publication, they would have so appreciated in value as to precisely yield $15,000 for a $5,000 investment, providing they could be liquidated without cost.

The same *atelier* has, however, produced other works, many other works, some of which did not do nearly as well in the marketplace. I suspect that, if another, less friendly feature writer prepared a different article and selected different examples, he might show that $1,000 invested annually for five years on these works, produced considerably less financial appreciation. He might also show that the works cited in the original article did not continue to appreciate annually at the same rate indefinitely.

In fact, as it must to all highly promoted phenomena, the reports from the major auction houses have indicated a sharp and very notable resistance to certain of the finest Gemini works as their prices reached higher levels. Many such works have had to be "bought in" at public auction for lack of appropriate buyer interest. Just as Levinson was proclaiming a great investment discovery, art critics like Hilton Kramer were announcing "the death of the *avant garde.*" That is, the very popular artists of the sixties reached some sort of market apogee in the early seventies and demand for their works did not continue to increase astronomically. In some cases, it actually dropped off noticeably.

This should not have been wholly unexpected. Most of the Gemini artists of the sixties enjoyed the support of an immense promotional apparatus, a good part of which moved on to other interests in the early seventies. As new stars arise and new fads develop, older stars often fade. They may even disappear.

Levinson suggested that Gemini's owners had discovered a business which was "better than a Swiss bank." Just as claims regarding perpetual motion machines should be exam—ined skeptically, so too, claims implying guaranteed perpetual investment appreciation should be taken as hyperbole or worse.

Art Marketing Handbook

In these days of consumerism when truth in advertising has become a major issue, it is the duty of the artist, dealer, and publisher to be cautious, not to make immodest, puffed—up claims. The art market in the United States has enjoyed a prodigious growth over the past four decades. Many artists and dealers have gained a great deal, while many collectors have benefitted, too. It is unfortunate when greed, immaturity, and outright misrepresentation should threaten the health of a segment of our culture which we need so much.

126. Honest Representations

In sharp contrast to wilful misrepresentations and con—cealment of important information which occurs so often these days is the refreshingly frank and full disclosure of an announcement from the justly famous *Officina Bondoni* of Verona regarding its limited editions of two books illustrated by Durer.

It seems, according to the *London Times Literary Suple—ment* of February 4, 1972, that for one book — an illustrated Terence — the proprietor of this remarkable *atelier,* Giovanni Mardersteig has taken a group of drawings from the Basle Print Room which were made by the young Durer on wood for a publishing project which was abandoned in 1492. We are told:

> *These designs, which existed up to now only as drawings on the blocks, have now been copied on to pearwood and cut in accordance with 15th century technique by the master of engraving, Fritz Kredel of New York. The result is truly astonishing . . . (Durer) would have been delighted with such a skilled and sensitive* Formschneider *as Mr. Kredel proved to have been . . . The cuts are used to embellish a text, the printing of which is of the highest distinction. The specially made paper sets off beautifully the Dante type in which the text is set.*

The report goes on to carefully detail precisely how many impressions were pulled by hand, how many works exist outside of the official edition, how the inking was accom—plished, etc. Similar details are furnished on the other project, a republication of Durer's *The Little Passion.* The words "original print" are neither employed or needed since the collector has enough information to judge what is being offered on its own considerable merit. While the works are advertised at a modest price, no claims or suggestions are made regarding potential investment appreciation despite the fact that many of this workshop's better efforts have appreciated significantly in recent years.

The TLS reviewer closes on the following enlightened note:

> *The idea behind these editions, the thought and immense labor that must have gone into their pro—duction, are nothing short of miraculous. These limited editions are not to be classed among the many reprints with which publishers all too often try to cash in on a temporary fashion. They are a wholly original and valuable contribution to our knowledge of Durer, the whole in a guise worthy of the artist it celebrates and of the* Officina Bodoni.

The two Italian books of Durer's works discussed in this article were sold out shortly after they were released. If any of them should come on the market, they would, without doubt, fetch a better price than the one at which they were first offered. But very few of the owners expect to sell their precious acquisitions and there is a very minimal quantity of promotional "hype" required to maintain their value. Durer's works no longer need this kind of support.

So, too, more recently, the multiple original works of Piranesi have enjoyed a significant amount of attention for their esthetic — not for their economic — value. 1978 was the bicentenary of Piranesi's death and the *Times Literary Supplement's* reviewer was duly impressed by the exhibition assembled by the Arts Council of Great Britain. He notes, with characteristic restraint:

> *Piranesi sustains a major artistic reputation through prints alone. His choice of medium signals that prime requisite of greatness, which is to know instructively what one needs. For him, as for Durer, the sculptural act of making plates for printing transfigured a brilliant but otherwise constrained imagination.*

To further develop the point that the original print is not necessarily a cheap imitation or copy of something else, the TLS reviewer discusses how superior Piranesi's prints are when compared to his own drawings. He then quoted the artist:

> *Can't you see that if my drawing were finished my plate would become nothing more than a copy while, on the contrary, I create the impression straight on the copper making an original.*

I find it curious and refreshing that Piranesi's greatest master prints have remained readily available and modestly priced in spite of their acknowledged importance right through the nineteen sixties and seventies. Only recently have they begun to increase in price.

127. Other Ethical Problems

This *Handbook* has stressed two major ethical issues associated with the art market: faulty and inadequate repre—sentation of what is being offered for sale and puffed—up or misleading representations of investment appreciation opportunities. There are, of course, many other ethical problems in the art market. The right of artists to protect their works against unauthorized mutilatior or mistreatment, sometimes called the *droit de suite* as a good example. Our country has no laws and few practices designed to prevent the owner of an early David Smith sculpture from removing the paint and cleaning up the metal surface to make the work look like a later, more high—priced Smith. This has, in fact, been done. So, too, original Remington bronzes have been carefully copied by avaricious foundries and the results have been offered not as forged copies but as originals.

On an entirely different scale, we have art dealers who take works on consignment from artists and then "forget" to pay those artists when the works are sold, and we have artists who demand a certain price for a work sold through a dealer who is willing to sell similar works at lower prices direct to collectors in their own studios. The fact that such practices often lead to loss of reputation and the breakdown of im—portant business relationships does not seem to act as a deterrent to many artists and dealers. Such people seem to feel that business is necessarily "dirty" and they wallow in it. We shall return to several of these questions in the discussion of artist—dealer relations later in this *Handbook*.

Symbiotic Artist/Dealer Relationships

128. Who Needs Symbiosis?

The world of plants and animals affords thousands of illustrations of the principle that even the mighty and powerful are often quite dependent for their existence upon the support of others. In the art market, we regularly encounter organizations and individuals who conduct their affairs without regard to any notions of fairness or consideration. The artist who is unwilling to protect the interests of a dealer and the dealer who takes unfair advantage of an artist are excellent examples. I am pained but pleased to report that avaricious artists and dealers often suffer for their own short—sighted behavior towards each other. Sometimes they are aided in the development of their unfair policies by the advice of accountants who have no appreciation of long term issues and look only for immediate gains. In other cases, they may be encouraged by attorneys who have been trained by the adversary legal system to take advantage of the weakness of others. More often, the artist and the dealer simply assume that business is a dirty thing by nature and that they have no real choices.

In truth, many of the best and most successful merchants in the art market are artists and dealers who conscientiously recognize the proposition that a good business relationship must be fair for both sides or it will not work over the long term. Thus, an art dealer who pays artists promptly, who works hard to build a clientele, and who encourages relatively unknown creative talents can expect a good deal of loyalty and support from artists after they become well established. The internationally famous Jose Luis Cuevas once explained to me that he would never willingly terminate his relationship with a certain dealer even though others might be more pro— fitable for him because that dealer had been helpful and considerate when Cuevas was just getting started.   I often meet artists who have left their dealers precisely when they were in a position to help them most because of some unfair or thoughtless behavior by those dealers.

In a business where money is only one of many important considerations, it is generally unwise for the stronger party to press a bargaining position too far or to deal unfairly with others. The results can be quite counterproductive.

129. Sources — Art Works and Sales Representatives

Artists need a following for their work, and they should be willing to recognize the value to them of the sales organizations which help them to build such followings. Dealers need a reliable supply of art work accessible to them from established sources. It generally takes a fairly significant investment of time and money to build a following for an artist that is meaningful. The real benefits of such activities can only be measured after they have matured to a point where artists can depend on their dealers for meaningful results and these dealers can, in turn, depend on their artists.

In the beginning, a curious imbalance will usually exist in favor of the dealer because, as suggested earlier, an unfortunate disproportion exists in the United States today between the rather small number of art dealers capable of properly representing contemporary artists and the comparatively large number of artists worthy of such representation. Not every business which calls itself an art gallery is able or willing to represent the contemporary artist. Many might be more properly described as "picture stores" or "frame shops" since they specialize in the sale of low—cost, decorative pictures, reproductions, and frames. Another group of galleries is not primarily directed at representing contemporary United States artists, but has concentrated instead on trading the works of very well established master artists of this and earlier eras. Neither of these groups is willing to invest a great deal of effort or money in developing the careers of contemporary artists.

In the New York area, more than 1000 businesses describe themselves as art galleries. Fewer than half actually represent any significant number of contemporary United States artists. More than ten percent of these close their doors during their first year of operation. Since a gallery usually handles between ten and twenty artists at any time, it may be seen that only a few thousand living American artists are represented by the entire New York art—dealing community. Some of these in—stitutions are "vanity" galleries, cooperatives, or "alternative" exhibition spaces which do little or no selling but offer some sort of wall space and other services to artists.

The situation is even more difficult in other markets. Los Angeles and Chicago are among the largest art markets outside of the New York area. In each of these communities, fewer than 200 dealers actively represent contemporary artists. In communities such as Detroit, Dallas, Houston, Philadelphia, and San Francisco, the number of galleries devoting their attention to contemporary art is even smaller. As a rough approximation, it seems reasonable to conclude that not more than 20,000 artists are currently represented by art dealers. Many are poorly represented in that their works are seldom shown by their dealers and even less regularly sold.

On the other hand, by any measure, there are tens of thousands of artists who, for one reason or another, have no real gallery representation. Some find their way into the "picture stores." Others join cooperative associations where they can pool their resources with other artists to arrange for at least a little exhibition and sales opportunity. Some sell through relatively less prestigious marketing institutions like the street fairs, offering their works in a circus atmosphere.

Increasingly, effective methods of representation for contemporary artists are through the private art dealer. These enterprising art sales organizations generally sell works from a small office or in their own homes. They emphasize private sales presentations to individuals and to business institutions and avoid public exhibitions. This group appears to be growing in many communities and prospering as well. Their ranks are augmented by a group calling themselves artists' agents. These specialists sometimes sell works directly to collectors, but more often place works in galleries and other retail outlets.

Still, large numbers of artists simply have no sales repre—sentation at all, regardless of the quality of their image or the potential demand for their work. The opportunity for new galleries remains great if their founders can find a way to cultivate and satisfy the needs and interests of collectors through a combination of good taste, hard work, and adequate working capital. The greatest opportunity is to be found outside of the major metropolitan areas in high income com—munities of more moderate size.

For the present, however, relatively unknown artists must realize that they are looking for representation in a market where good dealers and qualified sales representatives are at a premium. If the artist's image is new, exciting, arresting, it may be possible to find representation in a gallery which devotes itself to promoting novel images. The artist whose image is somewhat more conventional, must compete with many other artists who are creating good but relatively familiar images.

Earlier in this **Handbook,** it was proposed that one very reasonable way of overcoming the competitive disadvantages which a new artist faces in seeking representation involves building a reputation and a clientele outside of the galleries. This approach can provide a good foundation for subsequently finding a reliable dealer. If a dealer is shown works and slides by an artist whose image reflects competence, style, and in—terest, that dealer may or may not be moved to accept the artist for representation, depending on the dealer's need, available capital, and time. But if, in addition, the dealer learns that the artist has already successfully entered important competitions, exhibited in significant juried shows, and has established a growing clientele in the dealer's own marketing area, then interest in representing such an artist should be increased significantly. Most dealers simply cannot afford to help an artist get started from the beginning in developing a clientele.

When an artist feels ready to look for a dealer within a particular art market, some market research should be inaug—urated. First, a list should be prepared of those dealers who presently represent artists with images and reputations which are generally compatible with the artist seeking a dealer. Clearly, an artist whose work involves kinetic effects or sur—realistic symbols will be wasting time by contacting a gallery owner whose main interest is in more conventional images.

To develop this list, the artist might review the listing in the local Yellow Pages directory or might consult the local art calendar, if one is published. *The Artist's Market* and the *Fine Arts Market Place* are fairly good directories, listing a large number of art dealers by geographic area together with some descriptive material on each gallery. Your preliminary listing should be culled by visiting the galleries to examine the works which they show or by writing for recent brochures. There is not much sense in making a presentation to a gallery which presents the works of very well established artists unless the artist seeking placement has a comparable claim. So, too, you should carefully evaluate the other artists represented by each gallery. Their images should be at least generally com—patible with those of the artist who is looking for a gallery.

Once an artist has compiled and edited a list of potential dealers, each qualified gallery should be sent a letter requesting an interview and enclosing a one or two page resume. This resume should contain the artist's name, age, address, tele—phone, and media. It should also contain a summary of art education, showing schools attended and the years in which the artist was at these schools, together with the names of any significant artist—teachers under whom the artist studied. A separate section should list significant exhibitions and competitions, together with dates and prizes. Another section should list the names of significant public and private collec-tions in which the artist's work may be found. A certain amount of promotional material should also be enclosed. This might be a house brochure illustrating the artist's work or some colored postcards. It might also be some carefully mounted color photographs of works.

The letter and resume should be followed by a telephone call to set up an appointment. As in the case of selling the artist's work, this call has the purpose of "qualifying" the prospect, in this case the art dealer. Some dealers are very courteous and may be willing to see the artist, even though they cannot possibly undertake to represent any new artists for the next few years. The artist should determine the cap-ability of the dealer for handling additional artists before finalizing the appointment. This can often save a good deal of wasted time.

At the appointment, the artist should show the works individually, remembering, however, that the dealer may know a good deal more about art than many collectors. If the dealer is interested in the work, the artist should discuss sales representation first and exhibition opportunities second. The dealer should be particularly interested in the number of collectors who already own more than one of the artist's works and who live in the dealer's marketing area. The artist should also show any significant critical notices which the work has received. These activites are designed to stimulate interest, add information, and strengthen the possibility of a mutually advantageous business relationship.

The artist should learn how the dealer works with other artists and whether an investment of time and money can be made in the artist's work. If the dealer is not interested in handling the work at this time, the artist might ask for suggestions regarding other art dealers who might react differently. If the dealer wishes to handle the work, the artist should offer to help contact collectors who might be interested in examining certain recent works in private sales presentations at the gallery.

The relationship between artist and dealer should always be formalized and reduced to writing at this point, even if it is only a trial agreement. As indicated more fully later, even the content of a casual consignment agreement covering only a few works deserves to be put into writing.

130. Sources for Art Dealers

If you are a new art dealer or a new private dealer offering works to business institutions, you may have difficulty finding suitable artists even though you live and work in a community where such artists are plentiful. Not all new art dealers are as readily visible as they need to be. Some have rather limited contact or the wrong kinds of contact with the art world.

You can, of course, buy art from wholesalers if you live in markets where they are available or if you are willing to travel to the major cities to do so. This approach involves two kinds of risks, however. First, you may acquire work which you will have difficulty selling. I once met a wealthy novice art dealer who had invested a sizeable sum in a number of art works by famous artists. She subsequently learned that these works would not sell readily at the prices she was asking and in the market area in which she was working. She would have had less risk and greater opportunity to survive if she had cultivated and worked with a few artists whose work was more appropriate to her own sales ability and development. Starting with famous names, she soon found herself in an untenable situation.

Any dealer who undertakes to sell an artist's works must plan to make a certain investment in introducing the artist to a new clientele. If only a few works are to be left on consign— ment and no exhibition is planned, it is often wise to set a short time limit, say three or four months, in which period the relationship will either deepen or terminate.

The minimum level at which a dealer can invest seriously in an artist's work includes some participation in the cost of framing and showing the work and a certain amount of direct mail and other advertising to encourage private viewings of the work. Some dealers ask their artists to share even in these costs, usually out of the first proceeds of sales arising from the exhibition. Such dealers should not expect to claim as large a share of the proceeds as those who pay all the expenses of sales.

Dealers in our principal art markets find that it costs them at least $1500 for a relatively modest solo exhibition held in their galleries. This includes the cost of properly hanging the exhibition and of operating the gallery in terms of rent, utilities, insurance, and manpower. Even a simple, three week exhibition in a dealer's gallery can lead to this expenditure. To undertake this investment, the dealer should have some expectation of sales between three and five thou— sand dollars.

Dealers should not undertake the representation of an artist unless they plan to invest considerably more than the cost of an exhibition. The latter is, after all, only a short term investment if it generates sufficient volume to cover its cost. Such dealers may also wish to purchase certain works outright from the artist, or they may guarantee a minimum sales volume or advance funds to the artist against anticipated earnings from the sales of the artist's work. In any case, such activities can improve the dealer's share in the proceeds of sales.

An astute dealer may go even further, placing the artists with whom involvement is greatest under some form of contract with guaranteed monthly payment or guaranteed annual sales. Again, in each of these cases, since the invest—ment level differs, the proportion of the sales dollar properly retained by the gallery may be fairly increased.

131. What is the Dealer's Fair Share?

Earlier in this **Handbook,** in the section on wholesaling, the issue of trade discounts was briefly introduced. Such discounts are, of course, not to be confused with the discounts sometimes given to collectors, which were also discussed earlier, in the sections on pricing. A trade discount is generally that portion of the retail selling price which the retailer is allowed to retain. It may also be a portion of the wholesale selling price which the wholesaler is allowed to retain. The size of the discount appropriate to any given transaction will vary significantly, depending on the knowledgeability of the artist and dealer, their relative bargaining position, and particularly on the relative importance of the contribution of each party to that transaction.

Where an art dealer makes a small investment and takes works only on consignment, the dealer's share in the proceeds of sales has historically amounted to one—third. However, a study of the financial records of a number of different art dealers shows that such an arrangement is seldom profitable for the dealer if from this share all of the gallery's costs must be recovered. The cost of operating a small or medium sized gallery (with volume under $100,000 per year) including rent, advertising, insurance, publicity, framing, crating, freight, etc., generally runs between twenty five and thirty percent of sales income, without providing any return to the dealer or even any compensation for the dealer's time.

In view of this, a number of dealers have concluded that they should retain forty percent of the income from the sale of consigned art works. This figure makes more sense, particularly if the artist's share is free of "charge—backs" for advertising, etc.* A few dealers even demand fifty percent discounts on consigned works, but this is usually a wholly unwarranted proportion, considering their low level of invest— ment. Where the dealer has actually made a substantial investment, either through outright purchase of works or through advances or guarantees to the artist, the dealer is generally justified in retaining fifty percent of the selling price because of the higher level of effort and risk.

Of course, there is a stronger incentive to sell the work of an artist when the dealer has a more significant investment in it. The artist should bear this in mind in negotiating with a dealer who handles some works which are owned outright and others which are held on consignment. It is very difficult for a dealer to be unbiased about works which have already been acquired and which will pay a better rate of margin. One solution which a number of well known artists have found to the problem is to insist that the dealer must maintain a certain minimum investment level in their works. This prac— tice is very common in other kinds of marketing where a merchant is required to maintain a minimum investment in the supplier's merchandise in order to qualify for the status of "dealer."

*I dislike the concept of "charge—back" since the artist seldom controls the level or quality of the dealer's efforts. Some dealers claim only one—third of the proceeds of the sale, but then charge the artist for all sorts of extras.

There are other factors which might easily justify the dealer's demand for a better than normal portion of the proceeds of a sale. A dealer who engages in expensive or risky promotional activities on the artist's behalf or a dealer who has an important and sizeable clientele might well fit into this category. Certainly, a dealer who engages in whole—saling as well as retailing is entitled to a wholesaler's discount, over and above the retailer's discount, which is passed along to the secondary dealer.

On the other hand, there are artists, including several with whom I have worked, who are willing to give no more than one—third of the retail price to their dealers. Several sculptors I know, who absorb all of their own mold, foundry, and shipping costs have adopted this practice and several high demand Western painters have followed it as well. I know one rather famous artist who furnishes many excellent pro—motional sales aids to his dealers, but permits a trade discount of even less than one—third. His dealers can, of course, only survive if their volume is much better than average for a mature gallery and if their operating costs are also much lower than average.

132. How Important is "Exposure" to the Artist?

When an artist has a strong bargaining position because of a well established reputation and an existing clientele, it is wise to insist upon a relatively substantial level of investment as the basis of a dealer representation agreement. The primary purpose of such a relationship is one of broadening and also deepening the artist's contact with collectors. This will ex—press itself best in plans and activities related to sales. Other issues should be secondary.

However, some artists tend to concentrate their attention on regular gallery exhibitions instead. While such gallery exhibitions can be helpful to an artist's career, they are not substitutes for sales. Nor are they equal in prestige with the artist's participation in important museum shows or national and regional competitions. A good monograph can also be more useful than another solo exhibition. Some dealers can even stimulate solo exhibitions at museums. But the dealer's most important function is to sell, not to show. The main attention of an artist—dealer agreement should focus on this issue.

In developing a viable artist—dealer relationship, both participants must be very cautious. Since money is not and should not be the primary consideration in the art market, it becomes rather easy to confuse priorities. Mere attention and publicity can prove to be an illusory if attractive goal. The artist's primary need is for the kind of activities that will produce a regular following. The dealer needs a growing clientele. Properly planned, an artist—dealer agreement should produce both sets of results. They are quite compatible.

133. Artist's Copyrights & Residual Rights

Many artists wish to retain certain rights often associated with the sale of art works. In some states including New York and California, artists automatically retain the right to control the reproduction of an image by others, even after the original work has been sold. Even where the law does not provide such protection, it may be obtained simply and inexpensively by registering a copyright claim with the Department of Copyright at the Library of Congress in Washington, and then by specifically excluding the transfer of the properly advertised copyright from the sale of the work.*

Copyrights are designed to protect creative artists, writers, composers, visual artists, and film makers against the un—authorized use or display of their creative efforts. A copyright must be "claimed" by an appropriate declaration on the work. This claim is a notice, consisting of a "c" in a circle, followed by the artist's name and the year of the work. The new copyright law, and the regulations appended to it, requires simply that the claim must be "in plain sight." This can be placed at the base of a three dimensional work or on the front or back of a two dimensional work.

To further protect the artist, forms are provided which can be completed and returned to the copyright office. These need not be filed at the same time that the claim is made. A fee must accompany each application to register a claim. However the key to a valid copyright claim is not the regis—tration but the claim on the work itself. This claim must be made before the work is publicly exhibited or offered for sale.

Exclusionary language is included in the Terms and Conditions listed on the back of the Sales Invoice shown earlier in the Handbook.

Artists may also seek to retain other property rights re—garding subsequent transfers of title of works. Ed Keinholz has done this in recent years. So, too, Seth Siegelaub and others have been urging artists to consider asking their collec—tors to sign an *Agreement for Transfer of Work of Art* (copies obtainable by writing to Post Office Box 350, New York 10013). This agreement was examined in detail in the April, 1971, issue of *Art News.*

The agreement provides for payment of a portion of the appreciated value of an art work to the artist whenever a transfer of title is made. A few firms have been organized to register the title of art works as one might register titles to real estate. This too, is an effort to lay the basis for allowing an artist to share in the appreciation of an art work.

Rueben Gurewitz, the accountant and business advisor for Robert Rauschenberg, for many years has campaigned for a state or federally—mandated law requiring art collectors to share with artists a portion of the increased value of the works which they sell to other collectors. Such a law was enacted in California in the mid—seventies and it has engen—dered a great deal of controversy but not, as of this writing, any visible benefits to artists.

It should be obvious that the payment of residual benefits requires a great deal of candor and cooperation regarding secondary sales of art works. If a collector plans to sell a work to another collector at an appreciated price, there is seldom any reason to publicize the financial facts of the case. Of course, even when these facts are known there is no easy method for compelling a collector to report and pay a residual which may involve hunting down the artist long after contact has been lost. I believe that the idea of residuals is an excel—lent one, but that it does not apply as well to the art market as it does to the entertainment world where it is very widely employed.

Of course, record sales, movie and television re-runs, and even broadcast music are quite susceptible to residual pay—ments because data can be readily assembled, and payments can be even more readily collected. The world of the visual arts is not as well organized or susceptible to controls.

It distresses me, however, that this single issue should receive such an inordinate amount of attention while other issues, including many of much broader importance, are virtually ignored. Thus, *Art News* devoted a special issue to "artist's rights" in 1977 without dealing with many signal and pervasive problems. These include the problem of the competitve exhibitions whose organizers treat artists unfairly by charging exorbitant entry fees so that refused artists essentially support the very organizations which have rejected their works. This abusive practice has been attacked by Artists Equity and by the National Endownment for the Arts, but not by the arts press. So, too, little attention has been paid to the paramount need for prompt payment when a consigned work is sold, and much remains to be done to restore the artist's right to tax deductions when an art work is contributed to a museum or college. These are, of course, less dramatic matters, but they are much more important than residuals in that they involve more artists and much can be done about them in a practical way.

134. Territories — Other Markets, Other Dealers

An artist who has become fairly well established in one market area should, of course, consider expanding into others. Again, the competition for representation in the better galleries is keen. But the fact that an artist is doing well in Chicago should be meaningful to a dealer in Cleveland or Baltimore.

One sure way to find acceptance involves first building up a clientele and a reputation in the new city. If the artist enters local competitions, meets collectors and curators, and generally builds a reputation and a following in that com—munity, it will, once again, be easier to find dealer acceptance. This generally means that the artist must travel to the city in question, perhaps in conjunction with exhibitions or museum shows.

The artist might also visit the city as an invited artist—in—residence at a local college. Whatever the occasion, advance letters should be sent to local collectors announcing the visit and seeking local publicity regarding the impending arrival. After establishing proper esthetic and marketing credentials in a community, the artist may seek gallery representation with greater assurance of success.

When a dealer has an appropriate exclusive agreement with an artist, this role of finding new markets and secondary dealers may be accomplished for the artist by the dealer. A well organized program of promotional support can make a dealer's artists attractive to other dealers because they can be assured of greater marketing success with smaller investment risks. Some dealers, such as Pace, have formalized their associations and distribute the works of a group of artists to a network of galleries under pre—arranged terms. This concept parallels a familiar distribution pattern which is generally called a system of "specially designated distributors" in other marketing fields.

Care should always be exercised to avoid conflicting market territories. Thus, if a New York dealer is representing an artist, the artist–dealer agreement may or may not cover that artist's clients in Connecticut, northern New Jersey, or Philadelphia. The limits of a dealer's selling or wholesaling territory should be defined at the outset and in writing.

A market has developed for a number of United States artists in Europe, Asia, and Latin America. Occasionally, the artist's most important United States dealer can help to estab–lish representation in foreign galleries. More often, however, the artist must make contacts independently, first by mail and later in person. In a few instances, foreign dealers have travelled to the United States to find artists and works. As important as it is in this country, it is even more important to keep agreements with foreign dealers in writing. To avoid misunderstandings and losses, the artist should do business only with well established business institutions.

135. Dealing with Dealers

Most artists in the United States maintain rather informal business relationships with their dealers. Few ever bother committing the agreements under which they distribute their works to writing. They seem to be unaware of the many different kinds of arrangements which are available, much less the underlying reasons for each of these approaches.

Lacking any other frame of reference for their dealings, artists often accept the first business proposal made to them by a dealer, disregarding its subtler or even its onerous impli–cations. In some cases, a greedy or thoughtless dealer can build many destructive elements into a one–sided agreement without realizing that this can hurt the dealer as deeply as it hurts the artist. As an artist's career develops, the relationship can become inappropriate or self–defeating because it was not well thought out in the first place.

When this happens, the artist has the difficult choice of trying to renegotiate better terms or of starting out all over again to find a new dealer. But disengagement from the old dealer can be a mutually damaging process. Collectors are not readily transferred from one dealer to another, and few artists acquire new collectors without considerable effort. This ill—conceived business relationship usually founders because it has proven unfair or failed to anticipate important issues in advance. A short term advantage for a dealer can lead to long term distrust and even hatred. Meaningful business relationships must be based on principles of fairness and equity.

The artist needs a dealer only in terms of the latter's ability to perform specific functions. And the dealer needs the artist for the works which can be created and for the business which these works can generate. Thus, there can be a fruitful and symbiotic business association between the artist and the dealer at many levels. But failure to set down the terms of the relationship clearly and fully so that possible misunderstandings are anticipated and minimized, often results in bruised feelings, anger, frustration, and lost opportunities. Many otherwise valid dealer—artist arrangements have gone awry because they were not worked out fully, fairly, and carefully, in advance and in writing.

136. What is the Dealer's Role?

The first question to be answered is: Which functions will the dealer perform? Many different tasks may be performed depending upon the dealer's abilities and interests, the qualities of the artist's work, the level of development of the gallery's clientele, the financial condition of the dealer, and the mission of the gallery. Fundamentally, of course, the dealer will be performing a sales function. That is, the artist's works will be offered for sale to private collectors and to institutions in a given market area.

To be sure, there are a few exceptions where the dealer's function is not primarily one of selling works, but of super—vising "happenings" or helping to create "environments." In this sense, however, the dealer is more a producer of en—tertainment of one kind or another, as the artist shifts from the graphic arts to the performing arts. But, despite the shifts of fashion, the graphic or plastic artist is primarily a creator of substantive works which may be viewed, appreciated, and, of course, purchased.*

Even the "conceptual" artist seems aware of this issue. I recently spent some time with a leading personality in this field, developing a project for producing limited editions of multiple originals which are to be based directly on the artist's conceptual perceptions.

In addition to the dealer's task of finding and cultivating collectors for the artist's works, the dealer may or may not also:

(1) Arrange and negotiate special—project commission agreements with architects and others, leading to the subsequent preparation of works specifically designed to fill a client's needs or interests.

In exchange for such services, the dealer receives a per—centage of the artist's fee. Rates for this service may be the same as are involved in the sale of existing works: sixty/forty or fifty/fifty. On the other hand, some artists and dealers prefer to split the net proceeds after certain costs of fabrication and sale have been deducted. Percentages here and elsewhere can be deceiving. A given percentage will yield much less after deductions than it will without deductions. By way of illustration, consider the case of a $60,000 sculpture which cost $20,000 to fabricate and install. An artist who pays these costs out of 60% of the gross price will be left with a net of only $16,000 while the art dealer will keep $24,000. On the other hand, if the net proceeds, after costs, are divided 60/40, the artist will receive a net of $24,000. This approach is obviously of great importance when fabrication and in—stallation costs are quite large.

(2) Coordinate the financing of a special—project commission by others, such as the client or some third party.

This function may be a regular part of the dealer's work as a sales agent or it may be needed only in special cases. Checking credit and putting together financing programs require special expertise and often good financial contacts, as well.

*(3) Arrange, install, and publicize gallery exhibi—
tions of the artist's work in group and in solo shows.*

For many dealers, as was pointed out earlier, this is the
most time consuming and most expensive activity involved
in operating a gallery. Artists and their dealers often over
expend their resources seeking public exposure in the gallery,
leaving relatively little time or money for other equally
important functions, such as cultivating potential clients
intensively or long range promotional activities.

*(4) Submit the artist's work to juried shows and
competitions.*

This function may be overlooked by the more compla—
cent dealer who is not always too alert to opportunities for
expanding the artist's area of public contact. But it is par—
ticularly important to the development of the career of a
relatively unknown aritst and can be readily accomplished by
the dealer.

*(5) Arrange and publicize museum and traveling
exhibitions where the artist's work can be featured
or where it is an integral component of a larger show.*

There are some dealers who eschew such efforts as outside
of their scope, but an artist who is exclusively represented by
a dealer should receive this type of assistance as it will build
sales opportunities of benefit to both artist and dealer. In
New York, the Andre Emmerich Gallery and the Associated
American Artists spend a great deal of time and money
packaging traveling exhibitions. They are excellent methods
for finding new clients.

(6) Promote the artist's reputation, views, and works through systematic advertising campaigns and publicity programs.

Carefully developed promotional campaigns are often the key to the success of a contemporary artist. The successful execution of good plans can be time consuming and sometimes expensive, but consistent effort to maintain the visibility of the artist and to promote active interest in specific works is essential to any artist's career. I find that an alert dealer can, for example, exploit the recent successes of an artist easily. A feature story showing work in a collector's home or in an institutional ambiance can be very beneficial in helping other collectors to understand the nature of an artist's work. The responsibility is primarily the dealer's.

(7) Produce promotional sales aids, including brochures, reprints, art books, films, and other publications regarding the artist's work.

Sometimes such activities can be partially self–supporting, and they can significantly enhance the career of an artist, making important images widely available to many who might otherwise have relatively little contact with them. While this activity does not always directly stimulate the sale of art works, it tends to increase their salability because it makes the artist's works more widely appreciated.

(8) Arrange for the rental or leasing of the artist's work for long or short terms.

This activity is of special significance for major works. As suggested earlier, some institutions prefer a long term lease–financing agreement to an outright purchase because they can in this way treat their lease payments as business expenses while outright purchases must be capitalized without any depreciation possibility. Short term rentals are an excel—lent device for attracting non—collectors, especially business institutions, to art and for generating income from the gallery's inventory.

(9) Arrange and finance collateral services such as crating, framing, delivery, insurance, and shipping for the artist's work.

The appropriate approach to such services should be discussed with the artist, but the costs must be passed on to the customer and the fundamental responsibility should rest with the dealer. Thus, the dealer may elect to build multi—purpose, returnable shipping crates or interchangeable frames which reduces costs.

(10) Extend credit to qualified collectors of the artist's works.

As indicated elsewhere, the costs and risks of this service should not be absorbed by the artist but, rather, passed on to the client by the dealer.

(11) Purchase specific works from the artist from time to time at an established discount rate.

In the case of an artist whose work is increasing in value, an astute dealer can earn substantial profits by buying works and holding certain of them until their value has increased. When an artist is not exclusively represented or receiving a guarantee from the dealer, the purchase of works is a good test of that dealer's interest, confidence, and financial strength.

(12) Issue periodic cash advances to the artist against future earnings or against an annual guaran—teed income level.

This function requires good capital resources and a great measure of confidence from the dealer, but it is a very desirable condition for the artist and should justify a higher discount rate for the dealer. I regularly advise both artists and dealers to try to find working relationships at this level. It is a healthier and more business—like arrangement than any other known to me.

137. A Few Problems of Consigning Art Works

All of these dealer activities, with the exception of the first two, involve the dealer in certain financial commitments. They also presume skill, taste, experience, and the proper utilization of time and contacts by the dealer. Generally, the first ten of these functions are less costly than the last two. These require regular cash outlays to the artist or outright purchases of the artist's works. Since there are few framers, job printers, insurance companies, or shipping firms willing to speculate regarding when or whether they are to be paid for their services, the first ten functions are generally con—ducted on a cash basis or on a short term credit arrangement.

To help reduce their operating cash problems, many dealers accept works from artists only, or primarily, on con—signment. As we have noted, this policy usually leads to a reduced discount for the dealer. But it creates conditions which the artist often finds self—defeating. When the dealer insists on a simple consignment of the artist's works, the ability of both artist and dealer to function properly is impaired.

The consigning artist is, in effect, financing the dealer's inventory. Such practices are seldom found in other mer—chandising fields. Thus, diamond merchants, jewelers, and antique dealers do not ask their suppliers to underwrite their inventories, although such firms are generally well capitalized and undoubtedly more capable of performing this financing function than most contemporary artists.

As suggested earlier, dealers tend to favor works which they have purchased over consigned works for reasons of their own economic interest. When a dealer sells a work from the gallery's own inventory, a gallery investment is liquidated and a profit is earned. When the artist's work is sold, a smaller profit is obtained and the artist's investment is liquidated.

But, further, the artist's control over works in the dealer's possession is relatively weak when they are being held on consignment. Adequate insurance coverage is hard to arrange. In many cases, the artist will remain unpaid for works that were actually sold months earlier. In the event of the dealer's death or bankruptcy, the ownership of the works may be contested by the dealer's heirs or creditors. A whole body of law has grown up in New York State in an effort to protect the unwary artist against the misuse and misappropriation of works and funds by the defunct or deceased dealer's creditors or heirs.

It is doubtful whether the difference in trade discount rates generally allowed for consigned works as compared to outright purchases is sufficient compensation for the artist's investment in the dealer. This difference usually amounts to between ten and thirteen percent. If a consigned work is held by a dealer for two years before it is sold, and if the artist then receives sixty percent of the selling price, compared to a fifty percent discount which the same artist might have allowed on a cash sale, we have a situation where the dealer is paying the artist less than five percent per year for the use of the artist's money.

Of course, savings institutions usually pay their clients more. A department store typically charges eighteen percent per year when it gives credit. But an artist who consigns a work with a selling price of $1,000 to a dealer receives $600 when it is sold instead of $500 which might have been allowed in an outright sale. Thus, the dealer has effectively been charged $100 for use of inventory. Over a two year period, this amounts to $50 per year. If the dealer borrowed $500 from a bank to buy the work and paid current bank rates, the dealer's costs, compounded, would have been more than double this rate.

These calculations do not even consider the possibility that the work may not be sold at all, in which case the artist's investment would be tied up indefinitely. Consignment selling is not, in the last analysis, a fruitful or mutually bene-ficial arrangement. It is neither wise nor productive for a little known artist in the long term, and it is unwarranted and unreasonable for an established artist whose works sell consistantly.

Nevertheless, where an artist is new to a gallery or other-wise untried, the art dealer may wish to be involved only minimally with a few selected works to see whether they can be sold. As the artist's clientele grows, the dealer may want to shift to a different kind of relationship, one in which the dealer's investment in the artist's work is greater or even one in which the artist is given some regular monthly guaranteed payment.

Such a payment may be an advance against the artist's future earnings, or it may be some other form of guaranteed income. In either case, the payment need not provide for transfer of ownership until a specific work has been sold. The dealer is then still acting as a sales agent for the artist.

Ownership actually transfers directly from the artist to the collector. If an annual guarantee has been provided, the dealer may wish to reserve the right to apply unearned ad—vances, if any, against the subsequent purchase of specific works when accounts are reconciled.

But in the case of a guarantee, the works which come into the dealer's care are seldom actually owned by the dealer. Whether the dealer has made cash payments or guarantees to the artist or not, clarifying the ownership of the works is a critical issue. In the absence of contrary agreements and properly executed and recorded legal notices, the dealer's creditors and heirs may still assume that any works which are exhibited and offered for sale in the gallery are the dealer's property. The burden is on the artist to prove otherwise.

Again, although the dealer does not own most of the works, it seems reasonable that the gallery should be respon—sible for the insurance of these works against damage, fire, and theft. While it is theoretically possible for the artist to carry a "floater" to protect works while they are outside the studio, such insurance is seldom practical or economical.

Finally, the artist needs a clear statement from the dealer regarding the issuance of credit to collectors and regarding the basis of periodic settlements between the artist and the dealer. I do not like to see long term credit being offered to collectors, especially where an artist's property is being given to someone who is unknown to that artist. Short term lay—aways are safer and more practical. Further, the perennial problems of promptness of payment need careful consider—ation. Dealers collect and hold money which "belongs" to the artist. Anything short of very prompt payment will almost certainly engender anger and distrust.

138. Why "Bother" to Commit the Artist/Dealer Agreement to Writing?

It is possible to have a valid business contract without reducing any understanding to writing. Essentially, a contract is nothing more than an accepted offer of a product or service which involves some valuable consideration. If I offer to supply an art work to you under certain terms and you then agree to these terms and subsequently sell the work and pay me my previously agreed share, we have effectively made and consummated a very satisfactory contractual relationship.

In short, an artist who does not have a written agreement with a dealer may, nevertheless, have entered into a legally binding contract without realizing it. The courts have generally held that whenever two or more parties engage in transactions where one or more are accomplishing certain specific, previously identified tasks or services, and where a substantial consideration is involved, a contract exists, objectively, until it is revoked. The basic elements of a contract, *viz:* an offer by one party to perform certain functions, an acceptance of that offer by another party, and a price or some other form of payment to bind the deal, need not be reduced to writing to constitute a valid contract.

Further, some artists have also, without realizing it, become business partners of gallery operators in "joint ventures." If the dealer participates in the cost of an art project and the artist agrees to share the proceeds of the sale, a partnership may exist, objectively. Again, a written partnership agreement is not a legal necessity, but it is certainly more useful than a series of verbal understandings which more often than not lead to serious misunderstandings. In the absence of a written document, the common law of partnerships will usually guide a judge in the settlement of a dispute between joint venturers.

Failure to consider fully and explicity all the terms and conditions of an agreement can lead to confusion, disagree—ment, and costly litigation. The artist and dealer who fail to insist upon a written agreement are simply increasing the chances of difficulty. They should seek the help of qualified attorneys in preparing a definitive agreement which conforms to the commercial code of the art dealer's state and which forms the basis of a sound and mutually beneficial business relationship.

139. What Elements Should the Artist/Dealer Agreement Provide?

Several years ago, I prepared a minimum artist—dealer agreement for distribution by Artists Equity. That agreement certainly does not cover all of the needs of every artist and is only pertinent in certain specific cases, but it is a reasonable guide and has the virtue of being even handed in its consi—deration of the interests of both artists and dealers. Significant portions of that agreement are included in the following discussion. To help identify these materials, they have been set in a sanserif italic typeface. Other materials, not included in the Artist Equity minimum agreement, are printed in serific italic type. These include both alternatives and additional materials.*

The full text of the Artists Equity Minimum Agreement is available from that organization's offices in Washington, D.C. at 3726 Albemarle Street, N.W.

A number of important contract elements, alternatives, and considerations are discussed below. While they are not a definitive treatment of the legal problems of the art market, they cover many of the key issues of artist/dealer relationships. They should be further examined and finalized with the aid of attorneys who are experienced in contracts and business law and who fairly represent the interests of the different parties to the agreement.

1. Who, Where, When?

Like any other contract, the Artist/Dealer Agreement should begin by identifying the parties and their respective roles in the agreement as well as the time and place at which the agreement is executed. It is important that this be done fully and accurately.

One might start with the following paragraph:

It is hereby agreed between. . . . ., the Artist, address:. . . . . and. . . . ., the Dealer, address: . . . . that the Dealer shall exhibit and offer for sale the Artist's work at the Dealer's premises under the following conditions:

2. What?

The next section should indicate precisely and completely which functions are to be performed by each party. Both the artist and dealer may have a wide variety of options and obligations. An option differs from an obligation. The former is a right which may or may not be exercised while the latter is a duty which must be exercised. Thus, a dealer may want the privilege of holding a solo exhibition of the artist's work or may promise that such a show will, in fact, take place within a certain time interval.

The Artists Equity agreement contains a very useful statement of the nature of the anticipated business relation—ship immediately after the opening statement. It warrants the nature, condition, and ownership of the art works and identifies their future ownership.

> *The works hereby consigned for exhibition and sale by the Dealer as agent for the Artist are enumerated, described, and priced at retail on the attached list. Such works are warranted by the Artist: to be free of inherent vice, to be his/her own original creations, and to be the unencumbered property of the Artist. They shall remain the property of the Artist unless and until they are purchased by collectors or by the Dealer.*

Since the Artists Equity agreement is primarily oriented towards use in connection with the consignment of works for public exhibition and sale, the scope of work of both artist and dealer is relatively simple. It reads as follows:

> *The works here listed shall be exhibited by the Dealer from . . . . (date) to and including . . . . (date). These works shall constitute a (solo/part of a group)* exhibition. Such exhibitions shall be held approximately every . . . . months.*

> *Approximately . . . . works on the attached list shall be hung during the exhibition period. The remainder shall be available for inspection by prospective purchasers. After the exhibition period, the Artist's consigned works may be re—tained by the Dealer for sale for a term of . . . . months. At the end of that period, they may be individually removed by the Artist providing five days prior written notice has been given. Other works may be supplied as additions or replace—ments for works sold or removed from time to time by mutual written agreement of Artist and Dealer. The term for retention of works may be thereafter extended annually by mutual written agreement.*

*Select one term or substitute another.

The Artist will assist the Dealer by: (select appropriate responsibilities/eliminate inappropriate items)
    a) crating and shipping works to the dealer,
    b) framing the works for exhibition,
    c) Furnishing advice, cooperation, and assistance in advertising and publicizing the artist's work,
    d) furnishing data regarding prospective and existing collectors.

On the other hand, there are many different activities in which the dealer and artist might engage to their mutual benefit. Thus:

In addition to offering existing, consigned works for sale to collectors, the Dealer (shall perform/shall have the right to perform)* certain other tasks in the Artist's behalf including, but not limited to:**

a) Negotiating special project commission agreements with clients or their representatives for the creation of works by the Artist.

b) Arranging and coordinating the financing of certain art works or art projects.

c) Arranging, installing, and publicizing exhibitions of the Artist's work in the Dealer's gallery (in group shows/in solo shows)* at convenient times, and at least once every . . . . . . months, during the term of this agreement.

d) Arranging, installing, and publicizing museum and tra—veling exhibitions which include or feature the Artist's works.

*Select one term or substitute another.
**These items may be divided into two separate groups, one listing options and the other describing duties.

e)   Promoting the Artist's works and reputation through the publication of announcements, invitations, and brochures and through advertising campaigns as well as through publicity programs, said activities to be performed (at the Dealer's sole expense/on the basis of a mutually acceptable budget, with the Dealer advancing all costs, and with both parties sharing the expenses equally out of the first proceeds of the sale of the Artist's work)*.

f)   Producing a (catalogue/monograph/an illustrated art book/ a 16mm. color–sound film)* within the next . . . . . months, illustrating and publicizing the Artist's work.

g)   Submitting the Artist's work to certain juried shows and competitive exhibitions regularly during the term of this Agreement, at the Dealer's sole expense. Proceeds from this activity shall be shared equally after direct costs have been recovered.

h)   Arranging all details associated with the rental or leasing of certain of the Artist's works.

i)   Financing and arranging the insuring, framing, crating, and shipping of the Artist's works, said expenses to be re– covered from the collector at time of purchase, where appropriate.

j)   (Extending credit to/arrange credit for)* the purchase of the Artist's works by collectors, except that no credit will be extended which does not conform to a mutually acceptable written credit policy.

*Select one term or substitute another.
**These items may be divided into two separate groups, one listing options and the other describing duties.

In return, the Artist (shall/may)**

a)   Make (all / all excepting certain/a specific group detailed in Exhibit "A" attached hereto)* works now in existence or herafter to be executed, available to the Dealer for display and subsequent sale.

b)   Cooperate with the Dealer in the development and execution of advertising and publicity programs.

c)   Pay all costs associated with maintaining the Artist's studio and with creating and executing art works, except as otherwise specifically provided herein.

d)   Make sufficient time available when requested, upon ninety days' advance notice, to execute to the best of the Artist's ability, certain major art project commissions which the Dealer may obtain, providing that said commissions are acceptable to the Artist.

e)   (Insure the works/Arrange for insurance by the Dealer)* prior to shipment to the Dealer.

f)   Supervise crating and shipment of works to the Dealer, said crating and shipping to be accomplished at the Dealer's expense and direction.

g)   (Refer all prospective clients within the Dealer's territory to the Dealer/Accomplish certain sales, but remitting a sales commission of . . . . % to the Dealer, in such cases).*

*Select one term or substitute another.
**These items may be divided into two separate groups, one listing options and the other describing duties.

3. How is the Artist to be Paid? When?

Every contract provides some consideration which binds the Agreement. Usually, this consideration is money, but, for example, the act of lending art works to a dealer which have not been purchased might be looked upon as a consideration, offered in advance, for certain services which that dealer has promised to perform. Also, the dealer may provide more than money in payment to the artist. Certain classes of the artist's expenses may be underwritten, certain services may be performed partially in exchange for works. Thus, barter can constitute a consideration.

Since the Artist Equity agreement provides primarily for consigned works, the matter of full, prompt payment is par—ticularly important, as are the related problems of credit for returned works and responsibility for collection of obligations due from clients.

> *a)   The Dealer will pay the Artist . . . . % of the retail sales price on any works sold. Notice of all sales, including the name and address of purchaser will be given to the Artist at the conclusion of each month and payment of all monies due shall be made not more than thirty days after the receipt of payment by the Dealer. The Dealer assumes full risk of non—payment by the purchaser. However, if a work is returned in good condition by a client for credit, the Dealer will make appropriate pro rata adjustments in future payments to the Artist.*

However, clauses treating the problem of payment by the dealer of expenses and of funds owing to the artist might be much more complex. They could read as follows:

a)   The Dealer will guarantee to purchase individual works from the list appended as Schedule "A" or from additions which may be made to said list by mutual consent, in the net amount of not less than $ . . . . per calendar year, based on a discount of . . . . . . % off the established retail prices of such works. Income from leasing or rental activities shall be lumped with income from regular sales for distribution purposes. Further, in the case of specially commissioned art projects, the Dealer will retain . . . . . .% of the net sum paid, after deducting the Artist's direct costs associated with crea— ting, fabricating, and installing such works and after deducting the Dealer's direct costs such as sales commissions, legal expenses, etc.

alternate a)   The Dealer will guarantee an earned income to the Artist of not less than $ . . . . per calendar year, based on a commission rate of . . . . % from the established retail prices on such works. Income from leasing or rental activities shall be lumped with income from regular sales for distribution purposes. Further, in the case of spe— cially commissioned art projects, the Dealer will retain . . % of the net sum paid, after deducting the Artist's direct costs associated with creating, fabricating, and installing such works and after deducting the Dealer's direct costs such as sales commissions, legal expenses, etc.

Said guaranteed sums shall be paid in (monthly/quar— terly)* installments, subject to adjustment twice each year, at the end of June and at the end of December, at which time additional earnings, if any, shall be paid or, if sales have not equaled the guaranteed sum, the Dealer shall purchase sufficient works to make up the deficit.

*Select one term or substitute another.

b)   In any case, the Dealer will furnish the Artist, at the conclusion of each (month/quarter), * with a copy of the sales invoices of all works sold, showing prices paid, the names and addresses of collectors and dates of sales.   The Dealer will also, on request, make available financial books and records and inventory records, as well as physical inventory, for in— spection by the Artist's financial representative to verify the accuracy, timeliness, and completeness of said reports.

c)   Except as expressly otherwise provided herein, the Dealer will authorize and bear the full costs of framing, crating, and shipping works consigned to the gallery or sold to clients, as well as the full authorized cost of travel, promotion, adver— tising, mailing, entertainment, entry fees, credit extension, and credit losses related to exhibiting and offering the Artist's works for sale.

alternate c)   The Dealer will authorize and bear the full cost of framing, crating, shipping, promoting, advertising, etc., for art works consigned by the Artist to the gallery, or sold to clients, except that when and if previously budgeted costs which were mutually accepted are incurred in relation to promotion, advertising, mailing, entry fees, and entertainment costs associated with exhibiting and offering the Artist's works for sale, such costs shall be borne equally by the Dealer and the Artist and shall be adjusted twice annually in the post—June and post—December accounting periods indicated herein.

*Select one term or substitute another.

4. Who Owns The Works?

Whenever the dealer has actually purchased specific works, it is important to indicate that ownership of these particular works resides with the gallery. This may be accomplished with a properly prepared and executed Sales Invoice issued by the artist. But when the dealer has paid or promised advances against guaranteed sales, thus enjoying an advantage over other dealers since a much broader selection of the artist's works can be shown, the ownership of the works should reside with the artist. This should be acknow— ledged in writing. The artist's right to remove this property from the dealer's premises, without cause, after proper notice, should be protected. One might also wish to require that permission be requested by the dealer before such works are removed from the gallery, for whatever reason.

In states which have adopted the Uniform Commercial Code, and in several other states, it will be necessary to record a legal notice with the appropriate state agency indicating the existence of a consignment agreement or a conditional sales agreement between the artist and the dealer. Such notices are generally advertised in legal publications to help establish the ownership of the works and to put the dealer's present and future creditors, assignees, and heirs on notice regarding the artist's prior claim to these works. Forms for recording and advertising such claims (U.C.C. Form 1) can be obtained at the state agency which handles the registration of sales financing agreements and at the offices of many newspapers which deal in legal notices.

Finally, the agreement should specifically enjoin the dealer from any action under the terms of which the artist's works may be assigned or pledged to some third party as collateral for a loan.

Unless specifically indicated otherwise in writing, all the works consigned herein are the property of the Artist and shall so remain unless and until they are individually or severally acquired by the Dealer or sold to a collector by the Dealer acting as the Artist's agent.

Sales shall be made only on the following conditions:

1) All sales shall be either for cash or, if for credit, only through a valid, properly endorsed, nationally recognized credit card.

2) No works shall be removed from the Dealer's custody except on the specific written permission of the Artist or on the occasion of their outright purchase, rental, or lease.

3) The Artist shall have the right, at any and all times, to enter upon the Dealer's premises to inventory, audit, and examine these works. The Artist reserves the right to remove works which have been consigned to the Dealer for a period of more than six months. In such case, either an appropriate replacement will be made or an appropriate adjustment will be made in the Dealer's financial obligations.

4) The Dealer holds the Artist's works herein in trust. The Dealer has the right to sell the same for the account of the Artist at previously established prices, but the title to any such works shall always remain with the Artist until fully paid for. Partial payment in any form shall be deemed col—lateral security only.

5) The Dealer shall not pledge, hypothecate, nor otherwise encumber the works herein while they are in the Dealer's custody.

6) Where required by the Uniform Commercial Code, the Artist shall prepare and the Dealer shall execute an appro—priate financing form indicating the Artist's property rights in the works herein and said form shall be duly recorded and advertised at the Artist's expense.

5. Sales Territory.

As the market for an artist's work expands, the dealer's normal area of activity may become too limited for the artist's needs and opportunities. Anticipating this difficulty, the agreement should specify the limits of exclusivity of the dealer's sales territory to minimize conflicts between differ—ent dealers handling the same artist's work.

This section might read:

a)   The Dealer shall represent the Artist exclusively in the (state/counties)* of . . . ., ..., and . . . ., but shall make no sales presentations elsewhere. The Dealer shall divide earned (commissions/discounts)* equally with the designated Dealer in any other sales territory in the event that a sale is made to a visiting resident of said territory. However, the Dealer shall receive full credit for earned (commissions/discounts)* where any sale is made to a resi—dent of the Dealer's sales territory or to a resident of an unassigned territory.

alternate a)   The Dealer shall exclusively represent the Artist in the United States and elsewhere and shall, from time to time, appoint secondary dealers to operate in various sales territories to further promote the sale of the Artist's works. No such subsidiary dealers shall be appointed without the prior approval of the Artist, and each shall represent the Artist only within established sales territories.

*Select one term or substitute another.

6. Who Sets Prices?

The dealer and the artist should set prices jointly and should decide, in advance, precisely how they plan to deal with the demand for discounts. Prices should be reviewed periodically.

This section might read:

a) Schedule "A," attached hereto and dated and initialed by the parties herein, lists the initial works turned over to the care of the Dealer, and sets forth the retail selling prices to be quoted by the Dealer to collectors and institutions, as well as any appropriate trade discounts to be offered to other dealers. (No other trade discounts will be permitted/traded discounts of no more than . . . . % will be permitted to bona fide art institutions and schools).* In the event a trade discount is authorized by both parties, the Dealer shall share the cost of said discount with the Artist on a pro rata basis. A volume discount of . . . . . % shall be made available to any collector who purchases on any single occasion, works with a total value, at retail, in excess of $ . . . .

b) Prices of all works in the Dealer's possession shall be reviewed twice each year, early in July and early in January. At these times, they shall be adjusted by mutual written agreement between Artist and Dealer. No interim price changes are authorized except by mutual written agreement.

c) Prices on works delivered to the Dealer after the com—mencement of this Agreement shall be subject to the same terms and conditions described herein.

*Select one term or substitute another.

7. *Who Pays for Returns?*

Occasionally a work is returned by a collector to a dealer for credit. Provision should be made to adjust the artist's earned income against the dealer's prior or current year's sales commitment and commission or discount structure, bearing in mind the effect of this adjustment on any guarantees or minimums cited earlier.

This section might read:

> *The Dealer shall include copies of credit memos covering returns and adjustments with regular periodic financial reports to the Artist. Previously earned (discounts/commissions)* and previously reported debits against advances or credits due will also be adjusted at this time.*

8. *Inventory Maintenance*

Since the dealer needs a fairly steady supply of works, a clause might be included of this nature.

> *As the Artist's sales agent, the Dealer will have access to (substantially all/all, excepting certain/a specific number, as detailed in Exhibit "A," attached hereto)* of the Artist's existing inventory of works and further replenishment up to . . . . % of the Artist's future output, during the term of this Agreement at times which shall be mutually acceptable, but not less than once every six months. It is agreed that the Artist will endeavor to keep the total retail value of works available for sale by the Dealer above $ . . . . . . at all times.*

*Select one term or substitute another.

9. Insurance

Since the artist's insurance is almost certainly ineffective when works are consigned to the dealer's care, the dealer should maintain insurance coverage, as follows:

> *The Dealer agrees to take out and keep in force a policy or policies of all—risk insurance for the benefit of the Artist covering the full wholesale value of all of the Artist's works while they are in the Dealer's custody, and to pay all the expenses associated with such insurance against damage or loss by fire or theft, with extended coverage.*

10. How Long Does the Agreement Last?

A contract without a termination date may be ruled invalid. A clause might be provided indicating that the agreement runs for a specific term, such as five years, subject to cancellation at the end of each calendar year by either party, on a minimum ninety days' prior written notice.

This section might read:

> *This Agreement shall commence with the present date and continue in force for a period of five years, except that either party may cancel this Agreement by giving written notice at least ninety days prior to the end of any calendar year beginning prior to the close of 19. . . . The Agreement shall then be void as of the close of said calendar year.*

11. How Can Court Fights be Avoided?

In order to minimize costly and time consuming litigation, the agreement should provide for arbitration under the rules of the American Arbitration Association, in the event that contractual disagreements arise between the dealer and the artist. This provision cannot eliminate the possibility of a misunderstanding or a serious disagreement, but it can reduce the cost of a legal dispute, often to a fraction of the cost of a civil court case. It can also expedite the time required to obtain a decision, which can otherwise be inordinately long.

This section might read:

> *Any controversy or claim arising out of this Agreement or the breach thereof in excess of the jurisdiction of the small claims court shall be settled by arbitration in the County of . . . . and the State of . . . . by and in accordance with the rules of the American Arbitration Association and in accordance with the laws of said state. Judgment on the award rendered by the arbitrator may be entered in the court of jurisdiction thereof.*

12. Verbal Understanding.

The agreement should include a representation to the effect that no other written or verbal agreements exist outside the actual contract.

It might be stated thus:

> *The Agreement herein represents the entire understanding between the Artist and the Dealer. There are no other understandings, verbal or written, except as provided speci—fically herein.*

140. Agreements for Special Projects (Commissions)*

Artists and art dealers are apt to find themselves involved not only with agreements characterizing their own inter—relationship but also with others such as those of clients. These agreements generally cover a short time period or a special art project. Sometimes, they are three—party affairs with artist and dealer performing specific tasks for a collector or with an artist and workshop accomplishing specific tasks for a dealer.

As with the agreements already discussed, the identities of the participants, the scope of their obligations and options, the timing and location of their agreement should be clearly set forth in writing, together with the pertinent stipulations regarding schedules, terms of payment, etc. Here, too, the services of qualified attorneys should be retained to draft the agreement and to counsel each participant regarding those special interests which are unique to the artist's or dealer's problems. A few comments on the main elements of several kinds of agreements are given below.

1. The Scope of the Work to be Done

As indicated earlier, art which is designed to fill a special need is best created after a certain degree of preliminary dis—cussion and preparation. Sketches may be appropriate and models may be prepared. When a special art project is com—missioned by a client, the approximate dimensions of the art work should be indicated in the agreement, together with a discussion of the materials to be employed, the effect to be sought, the kind of image which is intended, and the approx—imate location of the finished work. As much relevant information as is available should be indicated and, where latitude is given to the artist, this should be stated as well.

*Two useful Commission Agreement forms are reproduced in Diane Cochrane's excellent work, *This Business of Art*, (Watson—Guptill 1978).

So, too, when a limited edition is to be prepared by an artist for a publisher or dealer, or for the artist's own inven— tory, the first task is one of defining the scope of the project. This is true whether a limited edition is to consist of original prints or bronze castings. The approximate dimensions of the work, the intermediate and final materials to be employed, the size of the edition, and the intended ownership and dis— tribution of the impressions or castings should be set down.

In the United States, original graphics *ateliers* regularly keep the standard work against which other impressions are compared, called the *bon a tirer,* for the master printer. Sometimes they retain other impressions as well. How these works shall be designated, whether they shall be excluded from the edition and kept off the market *(hors commerce)* is a matter worthy of consideration. So, too, the proof that the edition has been completed is an important issue. *Ateliers* regularly furnish the artist with a cancellation proof, and foundries furnish a signed certificate that the mold has been destroyed once the edition is completed.

Quite often, the artist accepts a commission for a special art project without finalizing the specifications of the work to be done. Occasionally it is possible to reference sketches, photographs of models, or cartoons in an agreement covering work which is still to be created. As an alternative, reference can be made to sketches which shall be forthcoming at a future date. In this case, a mechanism may be needed for obtaining the approval of the client or publisher before actual work proceeds.

This raises a potentially controversial issue. Artists and dealers seem to be perennially making proposals, offering designs and sketches, submitting significant creative ideas under the assumption that a commission of substantial proportions will follow. I feel that, before any significant work is accomplished, the client should agree to pay a development fee of modest proportions which will be applied to the overall agreement if one is consummated, but forfeited otherwise. When an agreement is prepared to undertake a special art project subject to approval of sketches or designs, the agreement should also provide a cancellation penalty payable if the client rejects the sketches or otherwise wishes to withdraw. Of course, such a fee or penalty is unwarranted where the cost of preparing the proposal is really trivial. And such a fee is unwarranted where the artist is so anxious to obtain the assignment that he or she is willing to gamble the required time and materials.

Still another important issue to be treated in a contractual discussion of the scope of the project covers those significant factors which are to be intentionally omitted from the agreement. Thus, a major work may be executed by an artist but will be installed by others on footings or bracings to be designed and executed by others. Also, the responsibility for crating, freight, and insurance may be omitted from the scope of the agreement.

Finally, many agreements should include a mechanism for modifying the original scope of work. Occasionally, an edition of original prints must be curtailed or even turns out to be larger than expected. Or a unique work may for one reason or another turn out to be considerably smaller or larger than provided in the original plans. If such modifications are practical, they are generally subject to written mutual consent. The burden of additional or lower costs and the issue of increased or decreased prices should be discussed in advance. Where it is possible, a formula or a schedule of charges should be provided covering the price of modifications.

2. Distribution of Responsibilities

Special art projects almost always require the assignment of responsibilities and duties to various agents. The artist may be the primary active party, but the client or publisher may be required to furnish a suitable place for the artist to work, together with certain implements. The dealer, too, may have certain duties such as the acquisition, allocation, and control of working capital, or the locating and expediting of certain materials, equipment, and supplies.

Projects differ vastly in their complexity, but an effort should be made to identify specific tasks and assign them to the participants of the agreement. One task which is often troublesome concerns the artist's assistants. If the artist selects them and supervises their work, shall they be paid out of a limited, specially—provided fund or shall their cost be absorbed out of the artist's fee? Either approach has its advantages and disadvantages.

3. Completion Schedules and Terms of Payment

Clients, publishers, and distributors usually plan their work far in advance. While an artist may find it difficult to perform "on command," certain dates can be very critical, especially when they are tied to openings, promotional pro—grams, and building completion dates.

A well written agreement should include a few fairly firm dates for starting and completing the project and may well relate payment to the successful completion of certain tasks. It is not unusual for architects and building owners to with—hold 10% of the price until thirty days after a project is completed.

4. Ownership of Work–in–Progress, Sketches, etc.

The agreement should generally indicate that the work does not become the client's property until it is completed and has been fully paid for. At this time, it should be formally "released" to the client. Failure to specify interim ownership can cause great hardship in the event of difficulties such as the client's bankruptcy or disaffection.

Working sketches, models, plans, etc., should remain the property of the artist and should be so indicated. These materials can prove to have considerable worth in the future for their esthetic and historical interest. Occasionally, how— ever, where the client has paid a fee for a certain preparatory work, the sketches or maquette may properly become the client's property.

5. Termination

A well written special project agreement should provide for its termination as well as its operation. In the normal course of operations, the agreement will run its course and terminate itself. But if certain technical problems arise or if the artist is somehow incapacitated, it may be necessary to terminate a project prior to its completion. The contingent financial obligations of all parties should be determined in advance of this event.

6. *Options — Exclusivity*

When a publisher or dealer has undertaken a special project which is speculative or developmental in its nature, it may be useful to include an option in the agreement providing the terms and conditions of future comparable projects. This can be a valuable secondary benefit to all parties and can encourage everyone to try even harder to make the first venture succeed. As an added incentive, the publisher may wish to obtain exclusive rights from the artist for future special projects. Thus, a publisher may avoid encouraging others to publish a particular artist's work in competition with the original effort over a given period of years.

7. *Warranty*

The Artist and the *atelier* or foundry should indicate the precise degree and the time limits of their warranty regarding the quality and durability of their workmanship and materials. An omission of this question can lead the client to the assumption that the work is warranted indefinitely and without exception. On the other hand, the artist will probably wish to withhold the application of a warranty where the client exposes the work to harmful sunlight, weather, etc.

8. *Prepayments & Royalties*

When an artist creates an edition for a publisher, payment can be made in advance of the sales of the works or after the individual events. As in the case of "readymade" art, the share of the artist in the proceeds of the sales will properly vary. An artist who gets all or most of the fee before any work has been sold should expect to receive less than an artist who receives a royalty payment of some sort after sales have taken place. In either case, the fee paid may be a specific sum for the edition or for the individual work, or it may be a percentage of the sales volume, anticipated or actual. Some of the most spectacularly successful publishing ventures in recent art history have earned a great deal more for the publishers than for the artist simply because the artist was willing to accept a fixed fee rather than a percentage of the gross price.

141. A Sample Publishing Agreement

While many artists publish their own original print editions and make their own castings, working sometimes in their own facility and sometimes with others, a host of technical and economic factors have encouraged others to become publishers of the multiple originals of artists. The publisher may be a retail dealer or a wholesaler or even an interested collector. Since the funds required are not insignificant and the risk is relatively high, I do generally not recommend that novices should become publishers. A useful artist–publisher agree–ment follows. A separate agreement will be needed between the workshop or foundry and the publisher.

> *This Agreement is made this . . . . day of . . . . , 19 . . . . by and between . . . . , hereinafter called the Artist, and . . . . , hereinafter called the Publisher, at . . . . , ... , to wit:*
>
> *The Publisher undertakes to publish . . . . . . editions of original (litographs/intaglio prints/serigraphs/bronze castings/ other)* at the (workshop/foundry)* owned and operated under the name of . . . . These edition(s) shall be created by the Artist with the tech– nical advice and assistance of . . . . under terms and conditions described herein. The Artist warrants that the(se) edition(s) and all rights and privileges pertaining to them are and shall remain (his/her)* own original work and that they are not encumbered by prior obligations.*

*Select one term or substitute another.

It is contemplated that the(se) edition(s) will be (printed by hand/cast in bronze)* in a total of approximately . . . . . . (impressions/castings)* each, including Artist's Proofs, (Printer's/Foundry)* Proofs, and Publisher's Proofs as well as . . . . numbered works within each edition.

1. *All of the (impressions/castings)* produced by the (workshop/foundry)* shall become the sole property of the Publisher, except that . . . . (impressions/castings)* from each edition shall be designated Artist's Proofs and shall become the property of the Artist in partial payment for (his/her)* services and creative efforts. Also . . . . (impres— sions/castings)* shall be designated (Printer's Proofs/ Foundry Proofs)* and shall become the property of the (workshop/ foundry)* in partial payment for their technical services.*

2. *The retail selling price of all (impressions/castings)* produced herein shall be established by the Publisher in consultation with the Artist. Any and all (impressions/ castings)* offered for sale to collectors or through art dealers shall be sold exclusively by and through the Publisher except that the Artist and the (Workshop/Printer)* may otherwise sell their own works in any manner they choose after two years have elapsed from the date of this Agreement. The Publisher shall establish and maintain a trade discount schedule for sales made through bona fide art dealers.*

3. *The Artist shall (pay all personal housing and other expenses while working at the workshop/foundry/ be paid a sum not to exceed $. . . . . covering transportation, housing, and incidental expenses while engaged at the work— shop/foundry on behalf of this venture).* The Publisher shall pay all (workshop/foundry)* costs associated with preparing, proofing, printing, finishing, etc., in connection with this project in addition to crating and shipping costs.*

*Select one term or substitute another.

4.   *The proceeds of sale shall be divided as follows:*

   a) As each work is sold, the Artist shall receive a royalty payment in the amount of $ . . . .

   alternate a) As each work is sold, the Artist shall receive . . . . . .% of the net proceeds received by the Publisher.

5.   *Time is of the essence of this Agreement. The Artist and the Publisher agree to lend their best efforts to the early and successful completion of the publishing project described herein. The Artist will cooperate with the Publisher and with the (Workshop/Foundry)* toward this end and will examine works as they are completed, signing, numbering satisfactory (impressions/castings)* and completing appropriate docu— mentary material.*

6.   *The Artist agrees that the images related to this project are for the sole use thereof and that they are herby assigned to the publisher. The Artist and Publisher agree that at no time will these images be reproduced in any manner except for normal promotional and educational purposes.*

The remainder of this agreement includes a clause which provides for arbitration and one which states that this is the whole of the agreement as indicated above.

*Select one term or substitute another.

142. A Sample Reproduction Royalty Agreement

I am not too fond of the business of art reproduction because it is often employed by unprincipled promoters as an art substitute, which it is not. The fact remains that many excellent and ethical firms such as the New York Graphics Society print and distribute reproductions of art works to frame shops and other institutions where they do not compete with real art in any way.

The following form is based on one which was developed for a businessman who entered the art reproduction field recently.

> *This Agreement, between . . . .,*
> *hereinafter referred to as the Artist and . . . . ,*
> *hereinafter referred to as the Buyer this . . . . day of . . . .*
> *19. . . . at . . . . , ... , to wit:*
>
> *1. The Artist agrees herewith to sell all rights, title, and interest to those original art works itemized in exhibit "A," attached hereto, at a price described thereon, and under terms described, herein.*
>
> *alternate 1. The Artist agrees herewith to permit the use of his/her original art works itemized in Exhibit "A," attached hereto, for reproduction purposes, however these works shall remain the property of the Artist.*
>
> *2. The Artist warrants that these works are his/her own original designs and execution, that they are free of inherent vice, and that they are the unencumbered property of the Artist.*
>
> *3. The Artist has claimed any and all copyrights appropriate to these works, having made the necessary public declarations and having properly filed related registration documents. The Artist assigns, herewith, all rights to the faithful repro— duction of these works to the Buyer so long as these rights exist, subject only to the terms described herein.*

4. The Buyer may, at his/her option, elect to reproduce any or all of the art works described herein for distribution in this country and abroad. In this event, the Buyer will report quarterly to the Artist the total financial proceeds of this venture received by the Buyer and will pay the Artist a royalty equal to ten percent of the sums actually received as a result of such distribution.

5. In no case will the works so reproduced and distributed be substantially altered esthetically during the reproduction process. For example, colors will not be appreciably modified and subject matter will not be appreciably changed. Towards this end, the Artist will be asked to participate in reviewing and correcting color proofs of the works, when and if they are prepared for reproduction. As partial compensation for such services, the Artist will receive an advance payment of $ . . . . against future royalties for each work on satisfactory completion of color proofing.

6. Both parties agree that this is the sole agreement governing this transaction and that there are no other under— takings, oral or written outside of this agreement.

7. In the event that a dispute arises under this agreement which cannot be resolved by the parties, and which exceeds the jurisdiction of Small Claims Court, they will submit this dispute to an arbitrator appointed by the American Arbitra— tion Association, who shall decide the issue and render judgment in accordance with the terms of this agreement and the laws of the State of . . . . Costs shall be borne equally by both parties.

Financial Planning
Accounting & Budgeting

143. The Purposes of Accounting

The financial records of an artist or an art dealer, like those of any other business person, work in three different ways. They furnish the basis of the reports which must accompany tax returns to federal and state authorities. They may also be employed to prepare statements which are of interest to bankers and others who are concerned with the financial condition of the artist or the dealer. Finally, perhaps most important, they are a source of vital financial information which can be employed by the artist or the dealer to review recent performance and to plan and budget future programs and projects. Good planning and budgeting are not absolutely necessary adjuncts of every business, but they can be the difference between success and failure.

Anyone who engages in marketing art needs a set of "books" and a system of documents, policies, and routines which will assure that financial transactions are recorded in a regular, orderly fashion. Also needed is a system of reports, statements, and planning methods which will permit income, expenses, profits, and taxes to be properly categorized and summarized while assets, liabilities, and reserves are also recorded and reported uniformly and correctly.

Unfortunately, many otherwise excellent entrepreneurs are convinced that financial records and reports may be re— quired for tax purposes or to help get a loan but have no real use in running a business. Others, including a surprising number of artists and art dealers are so antagonistic to the whole idea of "bookkeeping" that they systematically hide and obscure information which is often essential to their own survival as artists and dealers. This section of the *Handbook* is designed not to turn artists into accountants, but rather to introduce some of the basic financial tools of business and to show how they can be intelligently and practically used in the art market. It is not necessary to become an expert accountant in order to understand the key issues, nor is it necessary to keep voluminous records in order to develop useful financial reports.

144. Bookkeeping in the Art Market:
Simple Accounting Systems

Financial records are quite impossible without good "source" documents. Every artist or art dealer should pay bills only by bank check, since a cancelled check and the check register against which the checks are drawn provides an almost fool proof method of recording information re— garding business expenditures.

If you have any significant number of purchases to make for your business, you will probably need a special business banking account. When an entrepreneur is engaged in more than one business, it is often wise to have different accounts for each activity. Thus, an art dealer might have one account for handling income and expense connected with art acquisi— tions and sales, another for the framing business, and yet another for wholesaling.

While check records can provide an excellent record of expenditures, bank deposits are not a very good source for detailed information regarding business income. I have found that the most reliable information of this kind can be accumulated through a "closed" system of sales invoices. A closed system is one in which consecutive, pre–numbered invoices are employed. No art work moves in or out of the seller's possession, whether at the time of sale or consignment, without being recorded on a sales invoice. One set of invoices, called the "audit" set, is kept in strict numerical order and is used for preparing sales tax records, recording cost data, etc.

To assist non– accountants in operating their businesses, a number of firms have designed and packaged standardized bookkeeping systems which are adaptable to the needs of the artist or art dealer. For instance, Litton Business Systems offer a so–called "write–it–once system" which is more appropriate to a small business than an elaborate accounting system and does not require the services of an experienced bookkeeper. Similar systems are available from other sources.

These "write–it–once" systems are designed to permit the simultaneous recording and distribution of certain classes of transactions. For example, the art dealer may employ it to record and accumulate payroll information and to segre–gate and collect withholding tax, insurance, and other data at the same time. The same system, organized a little differently, may be used to record sales transactions and to collect and classify artist–dealer income reports, sales commissions, accounts payables records, property accounting records, etc. In any case, it would be wise to retain the services of an out–side accounting firm to help design and install such a system and to periodically prepare key reports of income and expense as well as reports of financial condition.

If your business is currently in an embryonic state, such a program may still be premature. In this case, you may wish to buy a simple bookkeeping volume from a good stationery store which provides bound pages on which to record and segregate the main elements of your business. On the other hand, once your annual business volume has exceeded a hundred thousand dollars per year, you very probably would benefit from retaining an accounting firm which is capable of computerizing the elements of your general ledger and pro—ducing periodic reports with the aid of a computer program.

145. Establishing a Chart of Accounts

If you employ a professional accounting firm to help you start your business, the accountants will usually begin by developing an appropriate Chart of Accounts. These are the numbered categories into which business transactions are divided before they are collected and recorded. A simplified chart suitable for an artist or an art dealer may well include the following entry headings:

1. Assets

... Cash in Bank Accounts
... Petty Cash
... Trade Accounts Receivable
... Allowance for Uncollectable and Doubtful Accounts
... Inventory — Art Works at (Standard) Costs
... Inventory — Materials and Supplies
... Pre—paid Items
... Land
... Buildings and Building Improvements
... Allowance for Depreciation on Buildings
    and Improvements
... Machinery & Equipment
... Allowance for Depreciation on Machinery & Equipment

2. *Liabilities and Capital*

... Notes Payable
... Trade Accounts Payable
... Taxes Withheld
... Accrued Wages and Benefits, Including Paid Vacation
    Allowances
... Accrued Taxes
... Contributed Capital
... Retained Earnings

3. *Operating Income*

... Sales, Value of Shipments — Art Works
... Sales, Value of Shipments — Frames and Other
    Non Art Items
... Sales, Returns and Allowances
... Earned Commissions — Special Projects
... Income from Publishing Projects

4. *Cost of Goods & Operating Expenses*

... Purchases, Works
... Purchases, Framing
... Purchases, Materials, and Supplies
... Labor — Wages, & Bonuses
... Maintenance and Janitorial
... Utilities
... Rent
... Taxes, Real Estate
... Taxes, Personal Property
... Depreciation on Building
... Depreciation on Building Improvements
... Depreciation on Machinery & Equipment
... Insurance, Art Works

5. *Marketing Expenses*

... Sales Commissions, Advances, and Wages
... Taxes, Sales
... Crating
... Freight, Inbound
... Freight, Outbound
... Travel and Entertainment
... Advertising, General Media
... Advertising, Direct Mail
... Advertising, Postage
... Publicity
... Photography

6. *General and Administrative Expense*

... Executive Salaries or Draws
... Office Salaries and Wages
... Telephone and Telegraph
... Depreciation, Office Equipment
... Books, Subscriptions, Tuition, Dues
... General Postage
... Stationery and Non—Advertising Printing
... Professional Fees and Expenses
... Group Insurance
... Insurance, Liability
... Office Supplies
... Contributions
... Taxes, Wages
... Taxes, Income
... Miscellaneous Expenses

This Chart of Accounts may well provide more categories than are actually needed to collect financial data for a small, new art business, but it will be quite adequate for most artists and art dealers. It can, of course, be easily subdivided, ex— panded, or otherwise modified to accommodate many special accounting problems such as the need to study the activities of separate business branches or the need to record tax obligations in more than one tax collecting jurisdiction.

146. Maintaining Journals, Ledgers, & Inventories

All financial transactions involving operating income should be recorded in a sales journal which lists each sales invoice in numerical order and carries data regarding date and value of sales, discounts allowed, sales tax, etc. Original cost data, framing cost, freight cost, etc., may also be recorded in the sales journal or on the back of the audit copy of the sales invoice. This information should also be distributed to specific ledgers. For example, a sales tax ledger should collect the invoice numbers and the sales taxes payable on all transactions in any tax period. Another ledger might be used to collect commissions due to salespeople.

A payables journal should be used to record expenses associated with buying art works, frames or with costs of operating your business. These entries should always be based on some sort of source document such as a purchase order, a requisition, or a paid supplier invoice. Your bank checks may be designed with a special stub or inset audit box for recording and distributing various cost elements into their proper categories. For example, an artist's payment to a supply house may provide for recording and subsequent distribution of the cost of art materials separately from the cost of framing materials. If a check is issued for supplies to be used on two separate projects, it is often possible to differentiate specific payments by a system of project numbers at the time the check is prepared.

The design of the payables journal should include provisions which periodically remind the artist or the art dealer that specific obligations are about to fall due. Rental payments, time—purchase payments, and commission payments are seldom triggered by an invoice. Therefore, they should be planned in advance so that they can be paid promptly.

Ledgers for recording specific assests and liabilities such as reconciled bank balances, outstanding long term obligations, accounts receivable, etc., should be "closed" at least once every three months. In a particularly active business, it may be wise to close the financial books each month. These procedures are necessary in preparation for the statement of financial condition which is discussed below.

Physical inventories, a necessary adjunct to the conduct of any business dealing in valuable tangibles, should be taken at least every six months. A physical inventory generally is conducted outside of regular business hours and requires the careful recording, counting, and evaluating of each item in the possession of the artist or dealer at the time the count is taken. In interim periods, the value of inventory on hand may be determined through the maintenance of perpetual inventory accounts. New works should be recorded in the inventory ledger, and the value of works which have been sold should be transferred out of the perpetual inventory and into accounts receivable as the transactions occur. Errors and losses can be identified and corrected when the next physical inventory is taken.

To determine the value of inventory on hand, the artist or dealer may employ the actual cost of individual works or a "standard" cost, which represents an average of the actual costs of works of a particular category over a certain period of time. Standard costs should be revised periodically. I particularly like to use standard costs in identifying the value of an artist's inventory or the value of a workshop's inventory.

147. Controlling the Accounting of Sales

Like others in business, art dealers and artists sometimes find the term "sale" rather confusing. A sale may seem to occur when an order is received, when a contract is signed, or when a payment has been received. But these transactions are not sales. The first is properly called a "booking." The second might be called a closing, and the third is a cash receipt. The United States Department of Commerce states that a sale has been made when goods are shipped to a customer, regardless of when the customer orders, receives, or pays for those goods. Monies paid in advance of actual shipment are called "deposits on future sales," and monies paid after the shipment has left the studio are called "payments on out—standing accounts receivable." A sale should be recorded at the time the work is shipped to a collector or, in the case of a special project, at the time it is released to the client. At this time, the receipt or transfer of the work should be acknow—ledged by the client on the sales invoice. The client generally receives the executed first copy of the invoice.

In some cases, a client may agree to accept a partial ship—ment of works, thus leaving a sales back order. When this occurs, only that portion of the order which has become payable is called a sale. The remainder should be recorded only when the shipment is completed. Then, a revised sales invoice should be issued, indicating the additional obligation.

As suggested above, sales invoices may be used to record non—sales transactions such as loans or consignment of works. It is unwise to permit any works to ever leave the custody of the artist or art dealer without generating a controlled docu—ment which fully describes the nature of the activity, the responsibility, and the values involved.

Trade discounts and sales tax should be figured on the face of the invoice itself. When a retail dealer or wholesaler buys a work from an artist or another dealer for subsequent resale, the original seller is not obliged to collect sales tax. In this case, the invoice may be issued tax free, but only if the customer has deposited some sort of "resale declaration" giving the buyer's own retail sales tax number. There are, of course, many abuses of this procedure. I do not like to encourage collectors to avoid paying sales taxes by claiming that an acquisition is intended for subsequent resale. The penalites and embarassment whenever such transactions are uncovered can be significant.

The seller may offer a cash discount if the invoice is paid within a given period of time, such as 1% of the net amount if the sum is paid within ten days. The sale is usually recorded at full price and then the discount is recorded when and if it is actually earned. The reverse side of the invoice should also carry a warranty and a statement of the terms and con-ditions of sale. One such statement is shown earlier in this *Handbook.*

Occasionally, a statement must be issued at the end of the month to remind a client of unpaid invoices. The outstanding invoice numbers should be recorded on this statement. The form of the monthly statement may be very simple. A letterhead indicating the outstanding invoice number(s) and the total amount due is sufficient.

The second copy of the sales invoice should be filed away under the customer's last name or business name. By reviewing these files, the artist or dealer may evaluate a client's tastes and enumerate the volume of business which has been trans-acted.

The third copy of the invoice is the previously mentioned audit copy. It should be filed in numerical sequence. This copy assures that all invoices are accounted for. It also aids in sales analysis for a particular period of time and may be used for auditing and for determining outstanding sales tax, payable sales commissions, and other costs.

Some dealers use a fourth invoice copy as a "packing slip," including it in their shipment. This copy, with prices and terms blocked out, enables employees uncrating works to check a shipment without knowing the actual price of the works. A fifth invoice copy may be used to notify the artist or a salesperson that a shipment has been made to a particular client.

148. Cash versus Accrual Accounting

An artist's or dealer's accounting records may be kept on an accrual or a cash basis. In a cash system, all expenditures actually made within a particular time period and associated with producing either current or future income are recorded in Statement of Income and Expense for that period.

On the other hand, in the accrual system, these expenditures may be accumulated or "accrued" on the books and "charged off" when the appropriate works are actually sold. Unsold works are carried in inventory at standard or actual cost or at market value, whichever is lower. In this system, the cost of the work is charged directly against the income produced by the sale of that particular work. So, too, the cost of the frame is not expensed until the sale actually occurs.

If an artist is engaged primarily in the sale of services, or if a gallery sells only consigned works, the difference between the cash and accrual systems is rather trivial because income and related expenditures almost always occur within the same accounting period. If one has a stable business, where income and direct expenses are relatively constant from one period to the next, then the choice between cash or accrual cost systems is also academic. But when volume is growing or shifting significantly from year to year, then the cash system of handling direct costs can be quite misleading. It confuses costs of one work with income obtained from the sale of others, and it creates tax liabilities and business deductions which are not in consonance with income from sales. That is, it permits expenses to be recorded without considering any associated income, and it permits income reporting indepen—dent of related expense. Clearly the accrual system is more appropriate to the needs of most artists and art dealers.

Tax collecting organizations, such as the Internal Revenue Service, will generally accept either system as long as the tax—payer does not capriciously shift from one approach to another, but many accounting firms seem to prefer the cash system on the grounds that it is easier for them to deal with the expenses of their clients by writing them off as they occur.

I generally disagree with this view and insist on the accrual system despite the fact that it requires regular physical inven—tories and it prevents artists from writing off certain expenses until the work is actually sold. The benefit of having a more realistic statement of Income and Expense far exceeds the difficulties, in my view.

149. Deriving Gross Margin (Gross Profit)

The difference between income produced by sales (net of discounts given to clients and credits for returned works) and the direct cost of works sold and services provided is the gross margin. This is the figure from which all other operating expenses must be deducted.

The gross margin, being a portion of the sales income, must always be less than 100% of operating income. However, some businesspersons mistakenly confuse margin with "mark—up." A dealer or an artist may mark up a work by almost any percentage the client is willing to absorb. For example, a work costing the dealer $100 may be marked up 200% to sell for $300.00. The margin in this case would be 66 2/3% since $200 is two—thirds of $300.00. To achieve a gross margin of 50%, a dealer must mark up all works by an average of 100% over costs. If a work costs $2,000, and the dealer sells it for $4,000, the mark up is 100% and the margin is 50%.

In an effort to simplify the possibility of numerological confusion, many retailers have adopted the old practice of "keystoning" their costs. Thus, the operator of a furniture store will often price so that retail more or less equals twice the cost of the item offered for sale. The term derives from the fact that a keystone (employed in building arches) has a base which is one half the size of its topmost dimension. So, too, a wholesaler will often arrange prices to produce a double keystone. This involves setting a retail price by doubling the cost twice. In the costume jewelry trade, a triple keystone pricing policy is common. Here, if the fabricating cost is two dollars the retail price may be set at sixteen dollars.

In my own experience in the art market, a retailer can expect very little profit in a business where the gross margin is much smaller than fifty percent. Whenever a dealer is able to safely predict the salablility of the work, it should always be bought outright at half the selling price or less. So, too, when an artist or dealer has made an investment in framing, the selling price should at least double the framing cost.

150. Operating Expenses in the Art Market

As with most retail businesses, many expenses necessary to the artist's or art dealer's business cannot be attributed directly to the cost of making or acquiring art works for subsequent sale. These indirect costs, collected and listed as "operating expenses" include management salaries, rent, light, general advertising, office salaries, insurance, and professional fees. Certain of these expenses are relatively consistent from month to month. But others, such as advertising expenditures, may be increased or decreased with regard to specific marketing programs. Business operating expenses usually involve payments for services rendered by employees, for incidental materials used, and for the other necessities of a business including telephone, utilities, and insurance.

As indicated earlier, I generally recommend that a mature art gallery devote approximately ten percent of its anticipated sales volume to promotional costs, including media advertising, direct mail, printing, promotional postage, and publicity materials. Artists, too, should find ways of devoting about ten percent of their expected income to useful promotion. A larger portion may be needed during the years of early growth of an artist's or dealer's business.

Depreciation of fixed assets is treated as an operating expense, although it doesn't represent an actual cash expen—diture. Accountants assume that equipment or property (other than land) has an objectively determinable life expec—tancy. Instead of recording the cost of equipment or building improvements in the year they are acquired, each item is assigned a life expectancy based on government furnished guidelines, and a specific portion of the original cost is annually depreciated. This depreciation is recorded in accord with one of several available formulae.

The sum of money actually paid by an artist for a welding outfit or for improvements by a dealer to a gallery building is stretched out over a "reasonable" time period, rather than being deducted as an expense at the time of purchase. Less expensive items, such as easels or lamps, need not be capital—ized and depreciated, unless they are purchased in quanity, as when a gallery or studio first opens.

Depreciation practices may seem arbitrary, since the "book" or "depreciated" value of the item may, at some point in time, be less or more than the actual market value at that same moment. Depreciation is a tax—related concept and plays a role in taxes and in financial analysis only. Thus, the depreciated value of fixed assets seldom approximates the true market value of buildings or equipment or objective usefulness of these assets.

Although certain operating expenses, such as property and payroll taxes, insurance, and vacation expenses, must be paid annually or semi—annually at specific points in time, their cost should be distributed uniformly through the year. Then, the "Statement of Income and Expense" for any given month will not represent these costs as too high or too low for that period.

Patents, franchises, and licenses, like tangible depreciable assets, have a limited life expectancy. Accountants write off the cost of such intangible assets over a period of years by reporting their value at cost less a depreciated amount which increases and accumulates each year until the asset is fully depreciated.

151. "The Bottom Line" — Net Income

Net income is the sum remaining over a period of time, after the cost of goods, services, and operating costs have been provided for. If the dealer or artist is incorporated, this sum is subject to federal and state income taxes at corporate rates. If the business is a proprietorship or partnership, the income generated during any year must be included in the personal income tax calculations of either the proprietors or partners. Although all or part of the net income after taxes may be distributed to the owners of a business, most of it is generally needed for business operations and this portion of net income is, therefore, also called "retained earnings." When earnings are retained in a business, the worth of that business increases.

Since many artists and art dealers need to expect more than one or two years of hard work and significant investment before they can produce a positive net income from their business activities, it is often unwise to incorporate too early. As proprietors or partners, the participants in art marketing enterprises may conveniently "write off" their early losses against otherwise taxable income from different sources.

152. Using the "P & L"

All the elements discussed above must be considered in preparing the Statement of Income and Expense, often called a "Profit and Loss Report." This statement, listing the actual income and expense of a business, indicates whether the artist or dealer showed a profit or a loss for a specified time period. By comparing actual performance over a period of time with budgeted or expected performance or with prior performance, you can see where your plans failed or succeeded. This examination may suggest where improvements are needed — where costs should be curtailed or increased.

New forecasts and budgets are likely to be much more realistic when they are based on the records of earlier performance. Omissions and unrealistic estimates are less likely to occur. Relationships are more likely to be useful.

Two different slightly disguised statements of art gallery income and expenses are illustrated. These forms compare the current with the prior year. They might also have compared actual with budgeted performance for the current year. Note that both sample institutions indicate that, in each year, the works sold brought in approximately twice what they cost. Even so, only when operating expenses were well below 40% of net sales was any significant profit possible.

I have come to the conclusion, after many years of studying operating statements, that an art dealer has great difficulty earning much more than modest wages until the annual sales exceed one hundred and twenty five thousand. The more modest sized institutions do not generate enough gross margin to leave any significant net income after operating expenses have been accounted for.

In the case of artists, of course, the applicable figures vary widely depending on life style, other income sources, etc. Where making and selling of art is the artist's primary economic activity, I like to see a minimum target of fifty thousand dollars in annual sales. The cost of goods and services sold seldom run much higher for artists than one—third of this sum, on an accrued basis.

Thus, an artist who receives sixty thousand annually in sales income might spend no more than twenty in making the work. Of the remaining forty, another twenty might be spent on such operating expenses as studio rent and promotion, while the remainder will become pre—tax net income.

Typical Annual
Statement of Income and Expenses
for a Moderate–Sized Gallery
($000's)

	Prior Year	%	Current Year	%
1. *Gross Receipts from Sales*	124.5	—	206.0	—
2. Less Returns and Allowances	6.0		7.0	
3. *Net Sales*	118.5	100	119.0	100
4. Inventory at start of year*	95.0		118.0	
5. Works purchased*	82.0		105.2	
6. Total (4 plus 5)	177.0		223.2	
7. Year–end Inventory*	118.0		127.0	
8. *Cost of Works Sold*				
(6 minus 7)	59.0		96.2	
9. *Gross Profit (Margin)*				
(3 minus 8)	59.5	49.8	102.8	51.6
Operating Expenses				
10. Salaries	20.0		24.0	
11. Rent	9.0		15.8	
12. Taxes, Payroll	3.2		2.0	
13. Advertising	6.5		16.8	
14. Publicity	1.0		1.1	
15. Travel and Entertainment	3.5		2.4	
16. Insurance	1.5		2.4	
17. Professional Fees	1.0		5.9	
18. Dues & Subscriptions	.5		.7	
19. Security	.9		.9	
20. Accrued Vacations and Bonuses	—		—	
21. Supplemental Benefits & Comp.	—		1.9	
22. Repairs and Maintenance	—		.4	
23. Utilities	0.6		0.6	
24. Office Supplies	1.0		1.6	
25. Telephone and Telegraph	2.0		4.9	
26. Crating and Freight	1.2		3.4	
27. Licenses & Property Taxes	.7		.7	
28. Depreciation	.6		.6	
29. *Total Operating Expenses*	51.8	43.7	84.5	42.5
30. *Net Income Before Taxes*	7.7		18.3	
31. *Reserve for Income Taxes*	—		—	
32. Net Income after Provision				
for Taxes (30 minus 31)	—		—	

At lower of cost or market values.

Typical Annual
Statement of Income and Expenses
for a Major Gallery
($000's)

	Prior Year	%	Current Year	%
1. *Gross Receipts from Sales*	362.0	—	419.0	—
2. Less Returns and Allowances	12.0		14.0	
3. *Net Sales*	350.0	100	405.0	100
4. Inventory at start of year*	242.0		159.0	
5. Works purchased*	95.0		176.0	
6. Total (4 plus 5)	337.0		335.0	
7. Less Year–end Inventory*	159.0		136.0	
8. *Cost of Works Sold*				
(6 minus 7)	178.0		199.0	
9. *Gross Profit (Margin)*				
(3 minus 8)	172.0	49.0	206.0	51.0
Operating Expenses				
10. Salaries and Commissions	54.0		64.0	
11. Rent	20.0		20.0	
12. Taxes, Payroll	12.1		13.0	
13. Advertising	16.5		18.3	
14. Publicity	6.5		6.5	
15. Travel and Entertainment	6.0		7.0	
16. Insurance	3.8		4.4	
17. Professional Fees	6.0		6.0	
18. Dues & Subscriptions	1.0		1.5	
19. Security	1.0		1.0	
20. Accrued Vacations and Bonuses	—		—	
21. Supplemental Benefits & Comp.	2.0		2.5	
22. Repairs and Maintenance	.5		.5	
23. Utilities	1.3		1.8	
24. Office Supplies	2.3		2.3	
25. Telephone and Telegraph	2.4		2.4	
26. Crating and Freight	2.8		3.0	
27. Licenses & Property Taxes	3.0		3.0	
28. Depreciation	2.0		2.0	
29. Interest	2.2		3.0	
30. *Total Operating Expenses*	143.4	41.0	159.7	39.0
31. *Net Income Before Taxes*	28.6		46.3	
32. *Reserve for Income Taxes*	—		—	
33. Net Income after Provision				
for Taxes (30 minus 31)	—		—	

At lower of cost or market values.

153. Balance Sheets

The Statement of Financial Condition, often called a "Balance Sheet," shows the balance between the sum of things the artist owns (assets) and the sum of those things owed (liabilities) plus the book value (net worth) of the art dealer's or artist's business. Putting it another way, the artist or dealer has a net worth equal to the difference between the sum owned and the sum owed. The balance sheet describes the financial position at some specific point in time, usually at the end of a month or year, rather than over a period of time, as is the case with a Statement of Income and Expense.

Balance Sheets are particularly important to bankers and others who might wish to lend money to a business person for the purpose of helping a business to get better established or to expand its operations in some way. Prudent lenders generally wish to assure themselves that the business in which their funds are to be employed is substantial enough to warrant a loan. In this respect, they may want to see not only a good net worth but also several other measures of business strength which are discussed below.

154. Assets

Art dealers and artists, like others with property, have two classes of assets — current and fixed. Current assets consist of cash on hand or in bank accounts, inventory, (that is: materials and supplies destined to become salable works or finished works plus framing materials and frames) and accounts receivable. Fixed assets include land, buildings, building improvements, equipment, patents, and licenses, all net of depreciation. Both current and fixed assets change in value, but current assets change more readily.

The Balance Sheet shows inventory as the total value of materials and supplies, work—in—process, plus finished work listed at the actual or standard cost or at the current market value, whichever is lower. The value of the labor which an artist has invested in a work of art cannot be retained in an artist's inventory unless the artist is a wage earning employee of some corporation which owns the inventory. In that case, wages might be included in calculating inventory values. An art dealer's inventory consists of those art works and frames which the dealer owns plus framing materials which are intended for eventual sale.

As suggested earlier, a well managed gallery or studio will need a physical inventory at least biannually, once at the midpoint of the operating year and once at the end of the year. During intervening periods, the inventory value may be estimated by consulting the perpetual inventory. This documentary record is regularly updated on the basis of office records of receipts, sales, and usage.

Accounts receivable, representing the total outstanding and receivable sales invoices, is shown on the balance sheet, less an appropriate reserve for bad debts. If a sales invoice system is conscientiously employed, your receivables may be easily determined at any time. Gallery or studio records will indicate when your specific receivables are due and overdue. Artists who leave work with dealers on consignment are often at a loss to know when a work which they own has been sold. Such artists are well advised to canvass their dealers regularly to determine whether sales have recently been made and monies are due. I have a client who systematically exchanges all works on consignment for more than three months as a simple device for checking her inventory and determining her receivables.

The reserve for bad debts carried on the balance sheet estimates that portion of overdue accounts which may be uncollectable. Generally, any account that has not been paid for ninety days is, indeed, overdue. Some portion of such accounts may remain unpaid.

Among the "fixed" assets, only the cost of land is not treated as depreciable since, with time, it generally increases in value. A Balance Sheet may list the aggregate original cost of all buildings, building improvements, machinery or equipment, together with depreciation previously claimed on these items to date. The remaining or undepreciated net book value of such fixed assets is a critical factor, however, and is always recorded on the balance sheet. Behind these figures, the art dealer or artist will need a property ledger which shows the date of acquisition of each individual asset, together with the original cost, the method of depreciation, and the amount depreciated to date.

155. Liabilities

Your liabilities, representing obligations on which the dealer or artist must make payments, like your assets, are divided into two classes: current and long term liabilities. Current liabilities include accounts payable, accrued expenses, and the current portion of long term obligations. Long term liabilities include all obligations extending beyond the current operating year, including loans due to investors. For tax purposes, some owners of a business may wish to lend money to their gallery or studio rather than increase their original investment. Sometimes, such stockholder's or partner's loans may be classified not as liablilities but as part of the institution's working capital, which, indeed, they usually are.

A single piece of equipment belonging to an artist may be represented in more than one place on the balance sheet. For example, a station wagon purchased on three years' time payments, may have been in an artist's possession for one year. The full original cost will be listed as a part of fixed assets. The allowance claimed to date for the depreciation on this item of equipment and its current book value, net of depre— ciation, will also be indicated. That portion of the wagon's cost which is due and payable in the current operating year will be included as part of the current portion of long term obligations. Any sum still expected to be due at the end of the current operating year will be included in contracts payable under long term liabilities. The difference between the net depreciated value of the car and any sum still payable against the original price constitutes the equity or net invest— ment that the artist has in that car. This equity varies with time. It will be expressed as part of the artist's net worth.

Values and obligations involved in creating and marketing art may also be distributed to different sections of the balance sheet. A portion of the value of the works may be carried at original cost in inventory. If works have been purchased, but are not yet fully paid for, portions of their cost and margin will be listed under accounts receivable. Accounts payable may include bills for framing which are still unpaid and for outstanding financial obligations to the artist. The net dif— ference between the inventory's asset value and liability value constitutes a source of retained earnings which will be shown on the balance sheet as part of the artist's or dealer's net investment in the gallery or studio or as part of the retained earnings of the business.

156. Net Worth

A gallery's net worth includes that portion of the original investment and after—tax earnings which is retained in the business. Net worth may be improved only through additional investments or through new retained earnings. When the new indebtedness incurred with business expansion is lower than the net profit which that expansion provides, the net worth improves.

Financial stability is needed to weather unexpected busi— ness reverses and slower—than—expected project development. If a gallery's business is healthy, its net worth should improve regularly as profits from operations are retained and put to work acquiring and marketing new works. A sample State— ment of Financial Condition is shown here for the major art gallery which was illustrated earlier in this section of the *Handbook*.

A vexing problem regularly arises from the way art is carried on the Balance Sheet of artists. Art can only be carried at market value when this happens to be less than the cost of materials of which it is constructed. This seldom happens. Instead, an artist suddenly becomes aware, often rather late in life, that the art to which a good portion of a lifetime has been devoted has a vast unrealized market value. I have met a number of artists of modest means who possess inventories which have a market value far beyond their heirs' tax paying capability. It seems very incongruous, but the same taxing agencies which deny any benefits to an artist who donates a work to a tax free institution will insist that the artist's heirs must pay inheritance taxes on the full market value of the artist's inventory. Since the book net worth tends to conceal or vastly understate such values, they should be employed cautiously.

Typical Year—End
Statement of Financial Condition
for a Major Art Gallery
($000's)

ASSETS	Prior Year	Current Year
Current Assets		
Cash on Hand or in Bank	19.5	26.0
Accounts Receivable, Trade	90.0	106.0
Less Reserve for Bad Debts	(2.5)	(3.0)
Inventories	159.0	136.0
Deposits	3.0	3.5
Total Current Assets	269.0	278.5
Fixed Assets		
Land	—	—
Buildings and Improvements	35.0	35.0
Furniture and Fixtures	18.0	18.0
Less Reserves for Depreciation	(5.0)	(7.0)
Other Assets	—	—
Total Fixed Assets	48.0	46.0
Pre—paid Expenses	—	—
Total Assets	317.0	324.5
LIABILITIES		
Current Liabilities		
Accounts Payable	61.0	88.0
Accrued Expenses	—	—
Current Portion, Long Term Liabilities	15.0	15.0
Total, Current Liabilities	76.0	103.0
Long Term Liabilities		
Bank Loan	35.0	45.0
Stockholders' Loan	100.0	50.0
Total Long Term Liabilities	125.0	95.0
Total Liabilities	201.0	198.0
STOCKHOLDERS' EQUITY		
Capital Stock Issued & Outstanding	50.0	50.0
Retained Earnings	56.0	75.5
Net Worth	116.0	126.5
TOTAL LIABILITIES AND EQUITY	317.0	324.5

157. Evaluating Financial Performance

Both private investors and lending institutions employ several standard measures or "ratios" to evaluate the perform— ance of a business. A few such ratios, their sources, and their interdependence are discussed here. The artist or art dealer should derive these ratios regularly and learn to interpret the significance of their fluctuations.

Return on Sales

This ratio is used to evaluate most commercial enterprises. To compute the return on sales, one must first establish the operating profit for a particular period of time. This consists of the difference between net sales income and all expenses for operations and for works sold occurring during that period. This, divided by the sales, yields the return on sales ratio or operating profit as a percentage of sales. Federal taxes and income or expense from sources other than gallery operation are omitted from these calculations. To convert the resulting ratio into a percentage, multiply by 100%.

Using the data for the illustrated major gallery's current year, return on sales for the year is determined as follows:

$$\text{Return on Sales equals } \frac{\text{Net Income Before Taxes}}{\text{Net Sales}} \times 100$$

$$\text{equals } \frac{\$ 46,300}{\$405,000} \times 100\%$$

$$\text{equals } 11.4\%$$

This pre—tax operating profit, as a percent of sales, is compar—able to the 10% to 20% return on sales of other well established business organizations. It is possible only because of the high rate of gallery sales shown in the example and the satisfactory relationship between costs and prices. Note that the illustrated moderate sized gallery's performance is not as encouraging and amounts to less than 10%.

Investment Turnover

Not all gallery investments are free from encumbrances. For example, in the typical Statement of Financial Condition illustrated here, liabilities at the end of the current year totaled $198 thousand. They were $201 thousand at the end of the previous year. Fortunately, the total assets in both years exceeded the total liabilities by $126.5 thousand at the end of the most recent year and by $116 thousand at the end of the previous year. Although the assets were not wholly gallery property, they were all used in the gallery's behalf. Therefore, their full value should be included when caluclating "invest—ment turnover."

To determine investment turnover, divide net sales by total assets. These assets are generally carried net of reserves for doubtful accounts and depreciation. With the data shown earlier, the investment turnover is determined as follows :

$$\text{Investment Turnover equals} \quad \frac{\text{Net Sales}}{\text{Total Assets}}$$

$$\text{equals} \quad \frac{\$405,000}{\$324,500}$$

$$\text{equals} \quad 1.25 \text{ times per year}$$

Thus, the entire investment in the illustrated gallery turns over at a rate of 1.25 times per year. Many retail institutions turn their assets more quickly, but this is a fairly satisfactory rate for an art gallery. Some galleries turn their assets over much more slowly which is generally an indication of a serious business problem. I know an investment banker who will not advise his clients to invest in any business where the investment does not turn over at least one and one half times each year. This illustrated gallery would qualify for his interest, at least on this score.

Return on Investment

The most widely used measure of financial performance is "return on investment," often called ROI. This ratio, usually represented as a percentage, provides a handy comparison for the relative merits of different kinds of investments. An investor or banker often speaks of the rate of return available to a savings and loan depositor, comparing this return with that available to a buyer of stocks or bonds. Since an investor receives approximately 6% on federally insured savings, for business investments to be attractive, they should produce higher return rates. Of course, a business investment also involves a higher rate of risk, and it can seldom be withdrawn or liquidated at will, as it can from a savings institution.

To determine return on investment, divide the operating pre—tax profit by total assets :

Return on Investment equals $\dfrac{\text{Operating Profit}}{\text{Total Assets}} \times 100$

equals $\dfrac{\$ 46,300}{\$324,500} \times 100$

equals 14.3%

Notice that the return on investment rate is calculated before deducting taxes, thus making the ratio comparable with prior and subsequent years, even when tax rates may differ. For corporate income, about half of the rate of return on invest— ment must be absorbed by federal income taxes. A little more must be devoted to state taxes. The return rate shown here is quite satisfactory as compared with rates of return in other businesses. Of course, for many smaller, less profitable galleries, it is not this attractive.

Nor can this rate be expected in the first years of a gal— lery's operation. For example, in the illustrated Statement of Financial Condition, total retained earnings at the end of the prior year totaled only $56 thousand on an investment of $317 thousand. The implication is clear, that in prior years, the gallery under discussion did not produce a very high rate of return on investment. In fact, it is not unusual for a gallery's early years to be quite unprofitable. I have many clients who hold that a gallery cannot be expected to reach break—even before three years of operation.

Inventory Turnover

One of the most significant ratios in a gallery or artist's studio is the ratio of inventory turnover. This is a measure of how fast the investment in art works is revolving. Many artists and dealers fail to calculate this ratio carefully and, thereby, delude themselves regarding their own situation. An inventory turnover rate which is slower than 18 months suggests that the art works are not being marketed actively. A really healthy gallery will try to turn its inventory over annually. Never— theless, I have seen some gallery records which showed an inventory turnover of only once in seven years. This is a sign of impending calamity.

To find the turnover rate:

(1) Average Inventory Level

        equals   most recent year—end inventory

        plus   prior year—end inventory

        divided by two

        equals $\dfrac{\$159{,}000 + \$136{,}000}{2}$

        equals $147,500

(2) Average Net Sales

        equals $\dfrac{\text{Current Annual Net Sales}}{365 \text{ days}}$

        equals $\dfrac{\$405{,}000}{365 \text{ days}}$

        equals $1,110 per day

(3) Average Net Sales, at Cost

        equals $1,110/day x (100% less Gross Margin Rate)

        equals $1,110 x 0.49

        equals $544/day, at Cost

(4) Inventory Turnover

        equals $\dfrac{\text{Average Inventory Level}}{\text{Average Sales/Day, at Cost}}$

        equals $\dfrac{\$147{,}500}{\$544}$

        equals   271 days to turn over inventory

The inventory of the illustrated gallery turns over once every 271 days or once every 9 months. Although this turn—over rate may seem slow in comparison with many other retail businesses, it is excellent for an artist's studio or for a gallery. If it were to slow down significantly, however, the operating funds of the business would then quickly become frozen in inventory.

158. Break—Even Analysis

Contrary to popular opinion, preparing a break—even analysis requires only a little knowledge of accounting and arithmetic. Every operator of a small business should learn how to assemble the necessary information in graphic or tabular form. Essentially, the break—even point for any business is that point at which income for a particular period precisely equals all expenses during that period, including those needed to cover the cost of operations, as well.

To identify the basic elements of a break—even analysis, first accumulate all sales during a fairly extensive time period, such as a year. Next, divide by the number of works sold during that period. Using the data for the illustrated major gallery, if four hundred art works of all kinds were sold, pro—ducing $405 thousand in income, clearly the average income per work sold was $1,012,50.

In the same manner, we may accumulate the cost of the works sold and divide by the number of works to get an average cost per work. In the case of the illustrated major gallery, this would be $199 thousand divided by 400 or $497.50. The remaining costs of operating the gallery came to $159.7 thousand during the current year. If we assume that all of these costs would have been incurred whether this sales volume was achieved or not, we may consider this sum the "fixed" costs of this period. In practice, of course, certain of these costs, such as sales commissions, fluctuate with sales and could indeed be considered part of the cost per work sold. Note that, in the illustrated prior year, oper–ating costs were only $143.4 thousand.

At any rate, we now have three figures — all that is necessary to construct a break–even analysis chart. We know the average income per work, the average cost per work, and the operating cost per year. To plot the chart, take a piece of graph paper and mark off works along the horizontal axis and dollars on the vertical axis. These axes intersect at zero.

Now construct a table. If no works are sold during the year, no costs per work will be reported. But, of course, operating expenses will be incurred. If a hundred works were sold, with an average income of $1012.50 each, an income of $101.3 thousand could be expected and a cost of approxi–mately $49.6 thousand would be reported for these works. Adding operating costs of $159.7 thousand would produce a loss of about $108 thousand for the year.

It is fairly easy to see, through constructing a simple table or through the use of high school algebra, that if 309 works are sold during the year, the income from sales will total about $312.9 thousand, and the total cost will be $313.0 thousand, including the cost of the works sold and the cost of operations for the year. Thus, no losses would have been incurred in this gallery even if sales for the year were 23% lower than actually achieved.

In determining break–even for the year by the algebraic method, we may use the following formula:

$$ax = bx + c$$

where x is the number of works which must be sold to break–even, a is the average income per work, b is the average cost per work, and c is the operating cost per year.

In this case:

$$1012.5 \, x \;=\; 496.1 \, x \;+\; 159.700$$

$$x \;=\; \frac{159,700}{516.4}$$

$$x \;=\; 309 \text{ art works}$$

159. Profit Planning

To be sure, for most artists and even for most art dealers, profits are not the primary motive of their business operations. The ability to communicate effectively in non—verbal terms with a particular audience is the touchstone of success in the art world. But the failure to operate profitably can prevent any artist or art dealer from achieving such noteworthy ends. Unless one has virtually unlimited access to funds, the pres— sures of operating an unprofitable business can quickly become intolerable. I think this may explain why so many very wealthy people grow tired of their galleries and close them down after years of sustained losses. I believe that most artists who have talent and are willing to work and most dealers with taste and energy can operate profitable businesses. But this requires a good plan.

A good profit plan proceeds from a carefully wrought and clearly conceived understanding of the business mission of the artist or dealer. If the plan can be founded on actual prior experiences, new ventures and modifications of old approaches will be likely to reflect possible achievements more truly than a plan which is more conjectural. In many cases, I have found that mature artists and dealers need only to add one or two new kinds of sales activities and then systematically organize their efforts to achieve dramatic improvements in their financial condition.

Your marketing plan should give rise to a budget which sets forth expenditures needed to assure its accomplishment. Budgets which are not based on practical marketing plans usually prove meaningless and more often prove misleading as well. There is little sense in spending limited funds on bro—chures, advertising, sales efforts, etc. unless a particular sales objective is to be achieved with these expenditures.

Whenever prior efforts have been made, they should be studied carefully. Where a new activity is being launched, the efforts and methods of others should be studied critically, in the light of the discussion of this text. The artist and the dealer must know precisely how much effort and expense are required to produce a given sales result. They must also know how they plan to improve on current performance.

A few other key questions to which answers must be found:

1. What is the current ratio of initial to repeat sales? How can the relative number of repeat clients be improved?

Not long ago, a client of mine decided that he was not properly following up his old clients. By improving his efforts at selling more works to these clients and their friends, he managed to triple his annual volume.

2. Which works and which artists produce the most significant margins? Why? What can be done to improve this picture?

I have often managed to open significant new markets for artists whose sales seemed relatively unchanged from year to year by urging them to make original prints, where the ratio of costs to income was better than it was in their other media.

To be sure, the process of making editions of original prints or multiple bronzes requires a greater financial investment and, unless the artist or the art dealer has a firmly established market, a rather significant risk as well; but it can also be a source of more financial strength.

3. What is your current total operating cost per thousand dollars' worth of sales? What can be done to spread these fixed operating costs over a broader range of income?

In many cases, my artist and art dealer clients had not been spending enough on operating their businesses when I first began working with them to achieve their own ends. A badly located, low–rent studio or gallery, inadequate publicity, and poorly produced brochures can reduce the effectiveness of an art marketing effort quite as much as poor works or improper framing.

4. Which key non–recurring events contributed most signi–ficently to last year's profits or losses? How can these key events be imitated, improved upon, or avoided this year?

We must have a clearer understanding of where we have been most effective or most ineffective or our plans tend to be disconnected and lacking in continuity. Every artist and art dealer should be able to quantify the results of specific marketing activities and to appreciate their related costs. Thus, an expensive party for an exhibition opening which produced no appreciable sales should not be confused with a marketing program in support of "visiting fireman" sales activities which resulted in excellent sales.

5. What are the minimum sales and profit to be expected this year? For next year? What is the maximum for each year?

In an artist's or art dealer's business, once the appropriate sales activities have been selected and tested, minimum and maximum sales results can be predicted quite accurately. Simply schedule these activities and then follow the schedule closely. If you have learned that private sales presentations are a major factor in your business and if you have discovered that you can readily sell five art works for every ten sales presentations, then you need only to decide how many such presentations you are going to make, and you can predict your minimum sales readily. Thus, in fifty weeks, if you make an average of three sales presentations each week, you would (in this example) expect to sell at least seventy—five works. If your average sale is five hundred dollars, then this particu—lar activity will yield at least thirty—five thousand. Now, if you can increase your prices by an average of ten percent without any loss in sales and if you can increase the effec—tiveness of your sales presentations by ten percent as well, then your sales volume might rise for private sales presentations to a maximum of about forty—two thousand.

Once you have combined these projected figures with the projections arising from other kinds of anticipated sales acti—vities, you can go on to predicting your profit. If you have kept good financial records, you should be able to predict your costs for works and your operating costs, as well, based on past experience.

6. Which of the following steps should be undertaken?
    o Increase sales of existing works by increasing the level at which you engage in certain sales activities.
    o Engage in new sales activities. These might include: institutional sales or "visiting fireman" efforts. Should you give private sales parties?
    o Increase attention to certain artists now in your gallery, to certain works now in your collection.
    o Find new artists or work in new media.

o Create different images, different styles of work. Are your works communicating effectively with your target clientele?
o Offer more non—art items : frames, books, services, etc.
o Expand your selling staff.
o Improve the selling skills of the existing staff.
o Revise your sales policies : discounts, prices, etc.
o Increase or reduce your exhibition costs and your advertising costs.

7. What effects can these changes be expected to have on costs, on sales, on profits?

8. How can operating results be regularly reviewed and used to revise and improve your profit plan? I like to develop or revise a profit plan at least twice each year.

160. Cash Flow Forecasting

Every business person should produce a new Cash Flow Forecast at least twice a year. This forecast should be based on the planning discussed in this section of the *Handbook,* coupled with anticipated capital investments. If you are starting a new gallery or moving to a new studio, a Cash Flow Forecast can be indispensable. The forecast is designed to show, on a calendarized basis, what your expenditures will be and how you expect to provide the needed cash to deal with these expenditures.

Determining the level of your expenditures is, of course, a function of the quantified sales activities we have been discussing. We must add to this the value of your planned cash outlay for building improvements, fixtures, tools, etc. Your total planned expenditure for any given period of time is the sum of your anticipated cost of works and cost of operations plus the cost of capital investment during that period. I like to prepare a Cash Flow Forecast for a new business for a three year period divided into three month quarters.

Once the anticipated expenditure for each quarter has been established, you should estimate your income from sales for each quarter, as well. With a new business, you may be wise to project quarters where little or no sales income is expected while you are getting a facility ready. After you open you business, you can expect that a number of quarters will occur in which costs will exceed sales income. For these quarters, you must project a negative cash flow. That is, you will have to put enough money into your business to cover the difference between sales income and expenditures.

It is not unusual for an artist or art dealer to invest funds and energy for eight to twelve quarters before a positive cash flow is achieved. Without adequate planning, you may never obtain this desirable level. At any rate, a carefully designed forecast of cash flow will tell you how much you need.

In preparing it, remember that not all seasons are alike. Some of my clients find that they can do forty percent of their annual volume in the last three months of the year. Others find that their summer months are very slow. In either case, the anticipated income and expenditure level must be adjusted appropriately.

I am often asked to predict how much it will cost to start up a gallery or to establish an artist's studio. This is a difficult question since every artist and art dealer has individually different aspirations and interests, and since some are much more willing to contribute valuable labor than others. In one case, I had an art dealer client who, over a three year period, invested only twelve thousand dollars in outside funds, to— gether with a great deal of his own and his spouse's energy. His business volume at the end of this time was averaging better than one hundred thousand a year, and he was just beginning to withdraw a few dollars from the business for his own needs. Until then he was living on a small income which came to him from outside of the business. The twelve thousand which he invested was from a savings account. Another client, operating on a broader scale, achieved an annual sales volume of close to two hundred thousand in only two years, but his investment exceeded one hundred thousand dollars. Part of this went into the development of a facility, and the rest went for inventory, framing, and early operating costs. The money came from a family trust fund.

Some funds for investment can be obtained from banks, but bankers seem wary of new businesses unless the borrower can provide good collateral. Most studio and gallery funds come from savings, family contributions, and internal opera— tions. Of course, once you know what your cash needs will be, it is necessary to identify the available sources to meet those needs.

Finding
&
Training
Salespersons

161. Locating a Qualified Salesperson

To begin, artists and dealers must do their own selling. But to function effectively, they will need to proliferate their own talents by finding and employing sales representatives. Unlike the artist, whose primary tasks are generally conceptual and functionally creative or the dealer who must attend to many management, financial, and promotional functions, a salesperson can specialize almost exclusively in locating and cultivating clients and in showing and selling art works.

Sales representatives are not usually concerned with selecting artists or art works. They seldom participate in establishing prices or in developing the strategic business objectives of the artist or art dealer. Their primary emphasis is on selling. This can be a rewarding, full—time job for a hard working, talented individual with taste and an interest in art.

Art Marketing Handbook

I know many artists who are willing to employ assistants to prepare canvasses and to do other clerical and manual tasks. Only a few have been intelligent enough to engage salespeople. Thus, the sculptor Harry Jackson has developed several ex— cellent representatives who work closely with his dealers and who can also find and develop collectors.

Lacking any significant prior experience in hiring, art dealers and artists often place heavy reliance on the judgment of earlier employers. They look for "experienced" help in the hope that their experience elsewhere will somehow transfer appropriately to the new job situation. But a sales representative who has experience, even within the art world, might possess exactly the wrong personality for a different type of sales activity. So, too, the esthetic values employed at the earlier situation may be in sharp variance with those of the new employer. Further, the qualifications required of a sales person in a small organization are much more varied than those required in a larger institution. Only rarely has prior experience proven useful to a salesperson hired by my clients.

It is more appropriate for the prospective employer to establish job specifications which are peculiar to the gallery or studio in question. Then such an employer should patiently seek a person who understands the proposed sales role and is willing to learn to fill it successfully, even if that candidate does not already possess all of the specifications which such a role requires. For example, if the proposed job requires a knowledge of architects and architecture, it might be more useful to find a motivated and flexible salesperson and develop the necessary esthetic and sales knowledge rather than seek someone who has this information, but who displays other deficiencies.

Even large, well organized business institutions have experienced great difficulty in successfully selecting candidates for their sales jobs who will, over the long run, produce enough sales to justify their investment. During the sixties, the Sales Executive Club of New York conducted a nation—wide survey of 500 different companies which employ sales personnel. They had hired a total of 16,000 employees in a single year and had spent an average of $8,700 each on recruiting, train— ing, and supervising these candidates. By the beginning of the following year, one—third of these employees were no longer on their jobs. It was expected that only one—half would survive through that year. Thus, tens of thousands of dollars had been wasted on unsuccessful salespeople.

The employers surveyed believed that many of their fail— ures were due to the fact that they had not hired salespeople with the proper qualifications in the first place. Inadequate training practices were also blamed. In short, even these relatively sophisticated employers failed more than half the time in their selection of salespeople.

A prospective employer should always begin by clearly defining the terms and conditions of employment which are to be offered. Job titles, job objectives, responsibilities, and duties, limits of authority, terms and amounts of payment, periodic performance review and evaluation procedures should all be carefully outlined. A systematic training program should be established even where only one sales employee is to be added to the organization and even where the employee has valid prior experience. These formal procedures will not eliminate the chance of failure, but they will certainly improve the prospects for success.

The salesperson's proposed job title should be carefully considered. In some art organizations, the word "salesman" or "saleswoman" may be considered unattractive or overly commercial. Some art dealers may prefer to avoid the use of the word "sales." Sales representatives and sales agents are somtimes called "fine art consultants." Others are called "fine art specialists." I find that this fear of the very word masks a distaste for selling which can be quite contagious.

The once popular designation "Assistant manager" has, in recent years, fallen into disuse because it is not really descriptive of the sales representative's job and because of its menial implications. "Assistants" of any kind seldom sound qualified to accomplish significant business tasks. Once a job title has been decided upon, it should be exhibited in corres— pondence, on the salesperson's business cards, and on a desk plate.

Next, the issue of the sales representative's territory should be resolved. If the owner of the art gallery, the artist's spouse, or some other member of the organization is already engaged in selling art works to prospective collectors, a definition of sales territories is needed. For example, new customers who arrive at the gallery without an appointment might be the sole responsibility of the new salesperson or, if more than one seller is actively engaged in handling gallery floor traffic, a system of orderly rotation could be used to divide these customers. I call this the "up" system because, if salesperson "A" is up next, then the next available prospective collector belongs to that seller and then salesperson "B" is up.

Existing clients and identifiable prospects should be divided even more precisely. Here, some attention should be given to the need of the newcomer for a starting point in building up a personal clientele. Some art dealers and artists have designated certain fields as the primary responsibility of their new sales representatives. For example, they may assign certain designers, architects, and builders to the new employee's territory, or they may assign certain prospective institutional accounts and clients who live in certain neigh—borhoods to this territory. If the art gallery owner or the artist wishes to reserve certain clients and certain institutions as "house" accounts, these limitations should be clearly outlined to the new saleperson at the beginning of the term of employment. Misunderstandings and confusion arising from a failure to anticipate this problem can be costly and very demoralizing.

162. Earnings

The basic function of any salesperson in an art marketing organization should be the development of a consistent sales pattern at satisfactory price levels. While it may not be possible to establish a sales quota for a new employee, a target should be established and agreed upon. It should be known and acceptable to both the salesperson and the employer. Thus, a sales representative who is employed by an art dealer at a cost of seventy—two hundred dollars per year, plus certain supporting expenses, might be expected to produce sales which encompass a gross margin well in excess of ten thousand. It may not always be practical for the salesperson to achieve this volume during the first year's activity. But it should be possible to show definite progress towards this goal by the end of the first year, and it should certainly be exceeded during the second year of employment.

An established salesperson who earns $600 a month in wages or in guarantees against commission should be advised that sales must exceed twenty thousand per year if the insti—tution retains an average of 50% gross margin on all sales. Where the salesperson needs a larger annual income, the margin which must be produced will have to be proportionately higher.

A first rate seller should be able to generate between fifty and one hundred thousand in margin annually, given appro—priate support. Out of this sum, earnings of ten to twenty thousand would be appropriate. These earnings might be paid in the form of a fixed salary or a commission. I agree with most marketing authorities that a sales representative needs some sort of financial incentive which compensates effective performance.

Generally, when a salesperson is employed on a com—mission basis, some effort must be made to support that person at the beginning with a regular advance (sometimes called a draw) against future earnings or with a guarantee. In either case, the funds advanced seldom equal the value of the fixed salary, but the possible commissions can greatly exceed such a salary. When a salesperson works exclusively on a fixed salary, it cannot be expected that the same moti—vation will be generated as is found in a more typical incentive payment system.

163. Duties & Personal Qualities

The duties of a salesperson in an art gallery or in an artist's studio begin with locating and qualifying sales prospects. The salesperson's employer may be able to offer some assis—tance in this task through an advertising and promotional program and through referrals. Sometimes the location of the gallery or studio will generate prospects. On other occa—sions, the salesperson must learn to use the many methods discussed earlier in this *Handbook.* In any case, a salesperson usually needs to be involved in establishing and operating promotional programs at some level. While a salesperson may spend a certain amount of time on the gallery floor, serving casual drop—in visitors, the main emphasis of prospecting efforts should be pointed towards seeking private sales pre—sentation opportunities.

Toward this end, every salesperson should prepare a Daily Call Report listing the name, address, and phone number of each prospect contacted, together with other pertinent in—formation including comments on the advisability of further follow—up. This report can be very useful in establishing the salesperson's commission claims regarding a client. It will also help to determine that employee's success ratio, mea—sured by the number of private sales presentations which are actually made, compared with the number of calls made in any given month.

When a sale is made, the salesperson should be responsible for preparing the invoice, collecting payment or arranging credit if this is indicated, and supervising the proper delivery of the work. In addition, the salesperson may be asked to offer advice and assistance in framing and in other corollary functions of the artist's or art dealer's business activities.

In some cases, the salesperson may be authorized to grant certain discount terms or credit considerations to a particular class of client. In some organizations, these prerogatives are often held by the gallery owner or the artist exclusively. The salesperson should only be assigned such rights if maturity and sound judgment have been demonstrated and firm guide—lines have been established. In no case, however, should a salesperson ever be in doubt regarding the limits of these privileges.

In a small organization, the employer may wish to add certain supplementary assignments to the normal tasks of the salesperson. These may include work on the preparaton and maintenance of mailing lists, the mailings themselves, and various other non—sales activities. Where such tasks are assigned, everyone involved should clearly appreciate the economic values which are implied. If a salesperson can earn the equivalent of six dollars an hour for the dealer or artist, after subtracting all costs, should such an employee be in—volved in doing work which can be performed by others at a cost of three dollars per hour? I find that many dealers and artists are rather short sighted on this issue. I have often found art sellers who are literally prevented from doing their real work because they are bogged down by a host of petty, non—sales activities.

In the art world, a good salesperson generally exhibits a personality which can be associated with sophistication, individuality, dignity, and attractive appearance. The novice collector as well as many intermediate and advanced collectors need the services of an art salesperson who knows a good deal about art. Therefore, the specialist ought to be conversant with many aspects of the contemporary art world and should be able to discuss current trends and esthetic problems with some degree of authority. This person should also know something about the leading national and international figures of the art world as well as the major regional artists.

While no individual can be expected to deny personal preferences and esthetic prejudices, a good salesperson should be able to discuss the fine points and positive values of an artist whose style and interest are not too attractive to the seller. It also may be useful if the salesperson is active in various art and cultural organizations, preferably those in which collectors congregate. While extensive verbal capabilities are not absolutely critical, the salesperson should be enough of a conversationalist and should be verbally personable enough to operate credibly in a wide variety of social and business situations.

In addition, such a person needs an earned reputation for honesty, reliability, and emotional stability. If the salesperson also has a gregarious personality and is capable of influencing, advising, and assisting the artist's or dealer's clientele, there is an even greater chance for success. It is not necessary for a salesperson to be aggressive or demanding with relation to others, but there should be well founded self—respect and self—confidence especially regarding matters of taste, since such attitudes tend to encourage collectors. I always advise against employing individuals who are too opinionated, too cocky, or too willing to stretch the truth. High pressure selling types have no place in the art market.

At the outset, every salesperson should be assured that performance on the job will be systematically and regularly evaluated by the employer. It should be understood that a persistent salesperson who conscientiously seeks sales pre—sentation opportunities and steadily shows art works, generally will do a better selling job than a more flamboyant sales specialist who concentrates a great deal of time and energy lining up a few affluent clients or developing large scale projects. Presuming that the policies under which the dealer or artist operates are legitimate, and the work is of good quality, the only significant measures of a salesperson's value are the annual volume which that person achieves and the margin which is generated by that volume.

It should be possible to measure this volume and the rate at which it is improving from the beginning of the sales—person's career. In addition to actual sales performance, the sales representative should be evaluated in terms of the number of contacts made each month, the success which has been achieved in turning these contacts into firm sales presentations, and the backlog of prospects for sales over the near future.

164. Sources of Employment Candidates

First, the artist or the dealer should set down, fully and satisfactorily, the tasks to be undertaken by the salesperson. Next, applicants can be sought, screened, and evaluated. Curiously, the best potential candidates may already be employed and, therefore, ordinary help—wanted ads, which are read primarily by the unemployed, may not be the most suitable source of applicants. A small display ad on the art page of a metropolitan newspaper or in one of the many regional periodical art jounals will reach more individuals who are already involved in the art world than a conventional help—wanted ad. An appropriate ad might read as follows

ART SALES REPRESENTATIVE WANTED

Man or woman over 25, with strong background in contemporary art for selling career with established art dealer/artist. Good income opportunity for per— sonable, hard working, talented individual. Some training will be furnished. Integrity essential. Send resume of education and experience to Box . . . .

In addition to such advertising, inquiries might be made at the offices of local art organizations for possible applicants. However, young, aspiring artists seldom make the best can— didates. An applicant who seeks this type of employment as a transitional activity, useful "for keeping body and soul together" until something more desirable comes along, should be avoided since the cost of finding and training a salesperson is too high to be wasted on temporary help. In some cases, friends and relatives can make good candidates for employ— ment. I have seen several instances where collectors who are clients of the artist or art dealer have become excellent salespersons and even one instance where a former volunteer museum docent worked out well.

165. Processing Your Candidates

When applications have been obtained, the prospective employer should be sure to obtain information in writing on the following items :
Applicant's name
Date of Application
Home Address
Telephone Number
Length of Residence
Dependents
Education
Vocational activities during school years
Hobbies
Current health
Serious Illnesses in past five years
Working time lost due to illness during past five years
Sports activities
Cultural activities
Clubs and associations
Prior employment, including name of company and type of business, type of work done, salary, start and finish dates, and reason for leaving.
Sales experience
Advertising and promotional experience
Business and personal references
Credit references
Bank references
Make and year of car

Every applicant who has supplied the necessary informa— tion and who seems even superficially qualified should be given at least one interview by the prospective employer. This first screening is designed to eliminate those who clearly lack the minimum qualifications for the job. Seldom can this be discovered entirely through the use of written applications. While the interview may be informal, it should be aimed at two related issues.

First, the dealer or artist should explain to the applicant a little more fully what kind of job is available. The applicant should be told or shown what kind of art works are to be sold, what type of clients are to be contacted, how clients are to be handled, what training and assistance will be given, and what level of compensation may be expected after the sales—person has mastered the job.

Once the applicant knows what is being offered, a series of questions should be posed regarding the values, interests, hobbies, experience, esthetic priorities, and plans for the future of the applicant. A good interviewer will also encourage the applicant to pose questions since this will indicate something regarding the applicant's verbal ability, level of interest, and understanding of the employer's needs.

At the conclusion of this preliminary interview, the artist or art dealer should privately grade the applicant, on a scale of 1 to 5, in terms of general appearance, ability to reason, ability to respond, conversational initiative in a formal situa—tion, aggressiveness, neatness, etc. The applicant's outside interests, prior experience, apparent attitudes regarding the art to be sold and regarding selling should also be noted.

166. Testing Candidates

The artist or art dealer should plan to interview between ten and twenty applicants for every available sales job. Those who seem worth processing, beyond the screening interview level, might next be given a series of objective tests by an agency which specializes in professional personnel testing. Such testing programs are not without their shortcomings, but properly selected and administered, they can very often indicate traits, tendencies, capabilities, failings, and interests which are otherwise not discernible. Such information can be a useful supplement to the subjective reactions of the prospective employer.

Personnel tests commonly used by professional testing agencies fall into a number of distinct categories. Some seek to measure the applicant's ability to learn, to resolve problems, and to handle unusual situations. Others are designed to evaluate the applicant's tact, diplomacy, and social capabilities. A third group of tests, such as the Kuder Performance Record, will indicate the applicant's professional interests. Still ano— ther group is designed to measure sales aptitude. One such test is the Baker and Voelker Detroit Selling Inventory.

Most metropolitan communities have a number of person— nel testing centers which can furnish, administer, and assist in evaluating these or comparable tests. The fees will generally amount to one hundred dollars or more for each applicant. While such a program may appear expensive, it can help considerably in the separating of protentially successful from potentially unsuccessful salespersons.

Once the screened applicants have been tested and eval— uated, a further winnowing should take place, designed to eliminate the less suitable candidates. Survivors should then receive another interview after their personal and credit references have been checked. This interview should be designed to give the applicant a better opportunity to display personality, interests, and capabilities. If this seems to be an inordinately time—consuming and expensive process, consider the even greater loss of time and money associated with hiring and training an unsuitable candidate. Consider also the cost associated with lost sales opportunities.

167. Hiring Your Salesperson

The artist or gallery owner should, at this time, further reinforce the applicant's interest in the job since the best applicants very probably have a fair choice of other jobs. The employer should be prepared to show not only the fin—ancial potentialities of the job, but also the benefits in terms of social and cultural opportunities and any other factors which might interest the applicant. Some employees are attracted by a special discount policy on buying art, others by travel opportunities or vacation benefits etc.

The interviewer should prepare a series of questions and comments relating directly to the job. Once again, the appli—cants should be rated for education, appearance, mannerisms, social adjustment, mental alertness, energy level, and a variety of other traits. An effort should also be made to evaluate the applicant's motivation, capability for regular work, and prior work history. These factors should be summarized and care—fully compared to the reports of the other surviving candidates so that the outstanding applicant may be selected. Hiring a salesperson works best when it utilizes the principle of in—formed camparison shopping.

Once a decision has been reached, a final communication should be sent first to the successful candidate and, subse—quently, after this person's formal acceptance, to those who are no longer under consideration. Your written employment offer should restate briefly the main features of the job, the terms of compensation, and any special requirements for training or for sales performance which are conditions of employment. Such a letter is designed to minimize future misunderstandings and to set a professional tone to the relationship. A particularly well organized client of mine even prepared a set of written personnel policies for inclusion with his job offer letters. These policies covered such subjects as sick leave and vacation, non—compensatory absence, non—sales duties, expected dress code, and a number of other issues.

168. The Salesperson's First Month

Once a new salesperson has started to work, a calendar should be established with certain performance, training, and review dates clearly indicated. At two or three points during the first eighteen months of employment, a decision should be made regarding the wisdom of continuing the relationship. It should be recalled that any program which succeeds in re—taining more than half of its initial sales employees for more than two years is exceeding the estimated national average. It is, therefore, a wise art dealer who hires two salepeople because there is a definite need for one.

No art salesperson can be expected to know everything one needs to know about the new job. Nor can this person be expected to be an outstanding public speaker or to have fully defined esthetic tastes in every case. The primary requirements for success in sales work are persistance, courage, courtesy, honesty, and self—confidence. Expertise, verbal capacity, and refinement are also important and valuable, but they are not as critical as the more homely virtues which should be given greater weight in any performance evaluation. The training program outlined below should afford plenty of opportunities to underline the importance of these virtues in addition to helping to develop certain working skills and habits.

169. Evaluation and Self Evaluation

To evaluate the new employee at the end of the first ninety days, the art dealer or artist should consider the following issues:

1. Are the gallery's/studio's sales programs and plans understood and supported?
2. Does the salesperson plan short term and long term acti—vities well and perform these plans systematically?
3. Is the employee enthusiastic about the art and the job, and is the salesperson self—assured?
4. What is the salesperson's level of interest in clients? with others?
5. Are initiative and leadership exhibited?
6. Is the salesperson industrious, reliable, and persistent?
7. Is this employee tactful and patient?
8. What is the quality of judgment exercised in client rela—tionships?
9. How much knowledge does the salesperson have of the works now in the collection?
10. What level of understanding of artists and others is dis—played?
11. Is the employee's personality pleasant and friendly?
12. Are the health and personal appearance of the sales re—presentative acceptable?
13. How many private sales presentations does the salesperson make monthly?
14. What is the average volume of sales per sale presentation? Is this volume improving? At what rate per month?

The employer's evaluation should be discussed with the employee. It can easily be substantiated through a self–evaluating analysis which the salesperson may be asked to prepare during the first six months of employment. Typical questions which might be included in such an analysis are:

1. Do you make short and long range sales plans regularly?
2. Do you follow them up carefully?
3. What division of your time do you make between con–tacting prospects, making sales presentations, and other work activities?
4. Do you prepare sales activity reports regularly?
5. How well do you relate to clients? to others?
6. How well do you know the works represented in the collection? What do you think about these works?
7. Are you making enough contacts? enough appointments? How many per month?
8. What kinds of sales resistance do you encounter? How do you handle this resistance?
9. When and how do you ask for a client's business?
10. How well do you feel you cooperate with others in the gallery/studio? Do you receive cooperation?
11. How do you visualize your future in the gallery/studio?
12. Approximately how many sales presenation opportuni–ties do you currently achieve per hundred personal contacts?
13. What is your current average sales volume per sales pre–sentation?
14. Are you thoroughly pleased with the present condition of your health and with your personal appearance?
15. Can you make suggestions regarding the potentialities for improving your performance as a salesperson?

170. Planning a Training Program

In some merchandising fields, professional salespersons are regularly trained through a specialized training program which is available at a school or college. Thus, many adult evening schools offer programs where one might learn the elements of real estate selling. A few community colleges and even two or three universities offer programs in hotel and restaurant management which include courses in catering and convention sales. Mass merchandising is a readily available class topic.

Nevertheless, sales personnel are more often trained at the expense of their employers, since this approach makes it possible to develop a specialized, custom—tailored program suited to the needs of a particular business institution. Admittedly, these programs can be time consuming and expensive, but they are generally the only alternative to a hit—or—miss sales program in which the novice learns only by a series of unfortunate, even more costly experiences. Further, since a formal training program is planned and positive, it has a better chance of succeeding than an unplanned approach which sometimes manages only to reinforce bad work habits.

Where the art dealer or artist is not too experienced in successful selling or in sales training, it might be useful to design a program of cooperative study in which the novice salesperson joins with the dealer or artist in the individual steps of the training program. This will insure that everyone has a common fund of information and an opportunity to exchange views and ideas on approaches, work methods, disposition of resources, etc. It will also give the artist or art dealer a valuable opportunity to review and reexamine certain gallery and studio methods and policies which may need reconsideration.

Your training program should be conducted at regular hours each week over a period of at least eight weeks. If a three or four hour period is dedicated to this purpose at each session, it should be possible to assemble a program consisting of twenty—four to thirty—two hours of study. The best time for these class periods is outside of regular business hours, but sometimes the work can be done during slack periods. If the time is planned carefully, it can be most useful to all participants.

171. The First Session — Mission & Methods of the Gallery/Studio

The first session of your training program should be devoted exclusively to a discussion of the mission of the gallery or studio. A few of the key questions which need careful analysis and exploration are listed below. The artist or art dealer will undoubtedly wish to expand and modify this list.

1. What is the esthetic bias of the art in the gallery or studio collection? What kinds of artists or art works are and are not present? Why? What media are available? What price ranges are represented?

2. Who are the actual and potential clients of this studio or gallery? What interests and needs do they fulfill when acquiring these? What else can be said to describe these collectors and their motivations?

3. Are there other prospective clients who are not now clients of the gallery or studio but who should become significant collectors in the near future? What inhibits their action? What kinds of people are they? How can they be reached?

4. Who are the most important competitors of this gallery or studio? How do they function? What are their main operating advantages and disadvantages? Who are their artists? What kind of works do they offer? What media do they employ? What price ranges do they encompass?

5. What are the artist's or dealer's primary sales goals for the current year? What is the monthly sales target for each salesperson? Are these goals realistic?

6. What promotional programs and campaigns have recently been conducted by the artist or dealer? What is planned? How are these materials utilized?

7. What are the primary sales activities used in the gallery or studio? Who supervises these activities? What reports are needed?

172. Next Steps

The next few training sessions should review the actual works in the collection and the operating and marketing plans for the year ahead.

1. How much does the art sales representative know about the individual works now in the collection and the artists represented?

2. How much is known about the media, the works, and artists not now represented but expected in the course of the coming year? How can more expertise be gained?

3. What exhibitions are planned? How are they to be promoted?

4. Are commissions for special projects to be sought? How?

5. Are publishing projects to be sought? How?

6. Are institutional sales to be sought? How?

Another important subject for these early sessions con— cerns documentation, provenance, and conservation.

7. How are the works to be handled, stored, and exhibited?

8. What documentary evidence does the dealer or artist have of the sources and authenticity of these works?

9. What are the technical qualities of the works?

10. Are all the works signed, dated originals? Have any been exhibited elsewhere? Have any been critically recognized or received special awards? Have they been illustrated in publications?
11. Are these works significantly related to other works by the same artist or to those of a particular school of art?
12. Are works of this artist in important collections?

173. Pre—Selling and Support

In the subsequent training sessions, the problems and methods of pre—selling should be examined. Promotional materials currently in preparation or previously employed and materials utilized by other artists and dealers should be studied and examined critically. Not all of the elements of a valid promotional program can be considered fully in a classroom situation, but they should be identified and dis—cussed. Assignments can then be made to assist the new salesperson in learning more about these subjects.

The topics for consideration at this time include the following:

Advertising

1. What are the primary elements of an exhibition invitation?
2. How can the preparation of special—purpose brochures be divided — e.g., copywriting, information, exhortation, testimonials, illustrations, etc.?
3. What are the most appropriate design factors e.g., layout, logotype, type specification, paper specification, the use of illustrations and colors?

Publicity

1. What are the elements of a valid press release?
2. How can one prepare feature articles or assist commis—sioned feature writers?
3. How do we stimulate feature articles?
4. How can the gallery or studio employ other media — radio, television, documentary films, feature films?
5. Should we engage in certain cooperative promotions — e.g., charity, fashion, show window, loan exhibitions? What are the pitfalls of such programs?

Developing and Using Sales Aids

1. Making reprints and clip sheets.
2. Preparation of and use of presentation portfolios.
3. Using color slides.
4. Using film cassettes.
5. Preparation of brochures, invitations, and monographs.

Working Out a Campaign

1. How can we develop a campaign? — Setting tactical and strategic goals, methods, critical approaches, duration, budgets.
2. How can we control the campaign? — Clarity versus am—biguity, systematic healthy image, growth versus notoriety, sales versus cultural amusement.

The Use of Direct Mail

1. How do we build and operate a valid mailing list?
2. How are lists maintained? — Additions, deletions.
3. What are the primary varieties of mail campaigns — exhibitions, prestige, initial contacts?
4. How is telephone follow—up used with direct mail pro— grams? Can you prepare a telephone campaign?

Each salesperson should prepare a personal collection of sales assistance materials. At the least, this will consist of a portfolio, brochures, clippings, photographs, and slides. It may also include a number of interesting and unique items such as monographs, sketches, sample materials, feature stories, mementos, and even letters. The items should be informative and supportive. They are not intended to function in the place of the salesperson and should almost never be left with a client to show to others. They should be employed instead as a useful supplement to illustrate and underline the virtues of a gallery's collection or an artist's work in order to help the salesperson make a sale.

174. Mastering the Selling Process

When the salesperson has begun to master the elements of pre—selling, the training program may move on to the next and most significant consideration, the selling process itself. First, the formal steps of the process should be examined, in terms discussed elsewhere in this *Handbook:* finding and qualifying prospects, arranging appointment, showing works, stimulating interest, identifying needs, uncovering and hand—ling collector problems, closing sales, and follow—up. This *Handbook* should be employed in this phase of the work.

But successful selling also involves the acquisition of certain verbal skills — questioning, answering, evaluating, stimulating — which can only be learned through experience. The most significant variety of activity which a training pro—gram can employ is the simulated sales situation in which the trainee is made to confront a variety of recurrent problems under conditions which imitate real sales situations. The salesperson and the art dealer can make no better use of their training time than in simulated role—playing in which a variety of sales situations may be considered and analyzed.

With these game—like situations, the trainee may learn to verbalize the appropriate approach to a client of a particular kind, the best language for showing and discussing an artist's work, the use of sales aids, the appropriate way of learning more about a collector's interests, prejudices, and needs. Here, too, a variety of trial close questions may be practiced; objections can be analyzed, evaluated, and handled in a number of ways; pricing and credit questions can be anwered; and alternative closing techniques can be refined.

To begin, the dealer may wish to prepare a few prototypi—cal case studies, featuring undeveloped novices, intermediate collectors who are learning more about contemporary art, professional buyers, and advanced collectors. Some "clients" may represent institutions while other will portray indivi—duals. These simulated clients may be assigned a variety of needs and problems. Real clients always have one or more needs and concerns. They may not know how to "read" a work, they may be insecure, or they may be simply indecisive. Such difficulties are discussed in detail in the section on selling.

In each case, the salesperson should be encouraged to learn how to recognize the real nature of the problems with which the client is struggling. The key to the success of this aspect of the training programs may be measured by the degree to which the simulated clients and their problems are realistically portrayed and the extent to which the approaches and solutions taken in the role—playing situations are trans—ferable to reality.

One way to insure that this occurs is to dramatize actual situations from the recent history of the gallery. Starting with a recent prospect and a recent sales problem, the sales—person can try a different approach from the one which was taken in reality. What works should be shown? How should a certain comment be handled? When is it appropriate to move on to other works? When should prices be discussed? How can interest be heightened? Which trial close question is most appropriate? Was the client's objection legitimate or was it a cover for a more profound problem? How should the objection be handled? Does the salesperson understand the client's needs? Can the collection satisfy these needs? What is an appropriate closing technique?

Several sessions should be devoted to simulated sales situations. Even after the formal training program has been completed, it will be useful to schedule additional role–playing sessions from time to time to freshen the approach and sharpen the skills of all sales personnel. The art dealer or artist should also take a turn at "selling." A tape recorder might be used to assist in critical analysis. Novice sellers are often rather nervous about role–playing, but they almost always sell more effectively as a result of the practice.

175. The End of Formal Training

The final sessions should be devoted to marketing planning. Every salesperson should be asked to produce a quantified marketing plan showing the variety and level of new customer contacts which are anticipated during any given period, and the expected level of old customer contacts as well. The anticipated number of salespersons and the average volume per presentation should also be estimated. These efforts will be unreliable at the start, but they will improve with time. Again, the art dealer should participate in coordinating these exercises.

Every salesperson should learn to calculate success ratios and should also master the arithmetic and the logic for deter– mining individual contributions to gross margin as compared with distributed costs of operation. This *Handbook* contains a good deal of information on such marketing planning and costing matters.

When the formal training program has been completed, it should be replaced with weekly staff meetings in which new plans can be discussed, artists and their works can be evaluated, sources of prospective clients can be considered, and proposals can be examined. Such meetings should have an agenda and should be the scene of a free exchange of ideas and critical evaluations.

Staff meetings should not consist only of "pep" talks or destructive criticism. Such sessions can become boring or even harmful. Employees should always be critically evaluated in private. A staff meeting should be a place where important information is available, where plans can be discussed, where suggestions can be made, and where results can be reported. An hour's time is generally quite adequate for a weekly session.

Index

Art Marketing Handbook

Selected
Bibliography

These directories list many established artists and art dealers, plus a number of advanced collectors. They are published once every two or three years and generally accept brief biographies of legitimate artists and dealers without charge or other obligation.

Rhodes, Anne, ed. *Who's Who in American Art 1978* (New York: 1978) Jaques Cattell Press. R. R. Bowker: Xerox

Rauschenbusch, Dr. Helmut, ed. *International Directory of Arts* (Berlin: 1975, 1976 2 Volumes) Deutsche Zentral—druckerei AG

Kay, Ernest, ed. *International Who's Who in Art and Antiques* (Cambridge, England :1976) Melrose Press

These directories list museums, art schools, major competitions, etc. In addition, they list established galleries. *Fine Arts Market Place* also lists wholesalers and publishers of original prints, fine arts craters and shippers and sources for fine arts insurance. The 1979 edition of *Artist's Market* carries useful essays on the market, including two by the author of this **Handbook.**

Rhodes, Anne, ed. *American Art Directory 1978* (New York: 1978) Jaques Cattell Press: R. R. Bowker: Xerox

L. Lapin and E.A. Wones, eds. *1978 Arts & Crafts Market* (Cincinnatti, 1978) Writer's Digest Books

Cummings, Paul, ed. *Fine Arts Market Place* (New York: 1977) R.R. Bowker: Xerox

This free publication provides a membership application and opportunities to subscribe to all the major arts magazines at discounts or in some cases at no charge to new members.

American Federation of Arts Savings Kit 1978 (New York: 1978) American Federation of Arts

These are the best available sources for technical data on making art, useful information on pigments, papers, canvas, preparation, etc. Mayer writes regularly for *American Artist.* The Wehlte work is translated from the German.

Mayer, Ralph. *The Artist's Handbook of Materials and Techniques* (New York : 1970) Viking Press
Wehlte, Kurt. *The Materials and Techniques of Painting* (New York, 1975) Van Nostrand ; Reinhold

The following newsletters vary in their focus. *The American Artist Business Letter* is directed primarily at artists but is also useful to art dealers. The *Art Letter* and the *Art Newsletter* focus on the art market while the *Print Collector's Newsletter* reports on developments in the field of original prints.

Cochrane, Diane, ed. *American Artist Business Letter,* published monthly by *American Artist* in New York.
Rosenbaum, Lee, ed. *Art Letter,* published biweekly by *Art in America* in New York.
Esterow, Milton, ed. *The ART Newsletter,* published biweekly by *ARTnews* in New York.
Brody, Jacqueline, ed. *The Print Collector's Newsletter,* published bimonthly by PCN, Inc. in New York.

This is an excellent classic treatment of the nature of original prints with a fine glossary appended.

Zigrosser, Carl. *A Guide to the Collection and Care of Original Prints* (New York: 1965) Crown Publishers

Useful material on artists and the law will be found in these two books.

Epstein, Paul H., ed. *The Visual Artist and the Law* Rev.
(New York: 1974) Praeger
Hodes, Scott. *What Every Artist & Collector Should Know
About the Law* (New York: 1974) E.P. Dutton.

Several fine works which in one way or another treat certain materials also covered by this **Handbook** are listed below. Ms. Cochrane's book is particularly interesting in that it con— tains a good deal of important material refined from the pages of the *American Artist Business Letter,* which Cochrane edits. Ms. Chamberlain's book is based on her extensive experience as director of the Art Information Center in New York. She also writes an important column regularly for *American Artist.*

Chamberlain, Betty, *The Artist's Guide to His Market* (New
York: 1975) Watson Guptill
Cochrane, Diane, *This Business of Art,* (New York : 1978)
Watson Guptill
Katchen, Carole. *Promoting & Selling Your Art,* (New York:
1978) Watson Guptill

There are only a few useful texts in print on the important subject of Framing. The most practical of these is listed below.

Frederick, Paul, *The Framer's Answer Book* (St. Louis :
1976) *Decor* Magazine